MW00799344

William Howard Russell's Civil War

William Howard Russell's
CIVIL WAR

Private Diary and Letters, 1861–1862

EDITED BY

Martin Crawford

The University of Georgia Press

Athens and London

© 1992 by the University of Georgia Press
Athens, Georgia 30602
All rights reserved
Designed by Kathi L. Dailey
Set in Mergenthaler Century Schoolbook by
Tseng Information Systems, Inc.
Printed and bound by Braun-Brumfield
The paper in this book meets the guidelines for
permanence and durability of the Committee on
Production Guidelines for Book Longevity of the
Council on Library Resources.

Printed in the United States of America

96   95   94   93   92   C   5   4   3   2   1

Library of Congress Cataloging in Publication Data

Russell, William Howard, Sir, 1820–1907.
   William Howard Russell's Civil War : private diary and
letters, 1861–1862 / edited by Martin Crawford.
      p.   cm.
   Includes bibliographical references and index.
   ISBN 0-8203-1369-6 (alk. paper)
   1. United States—Description and travel—1848–1865. 2.
United States—History—Civil War, 1861–1865.   3. Confeder-
ate States of America—Description and travel.   4. Russell,
William Howard, Sir, 1820–1907—Journeys—United States.
I. Crawford, Martin, 1948–   . II. Title.
E167.R9636 1992
973.7'82—dc20   91-14194
                                                    CIP

British Library Cataloging in Publication Data available

Frontispiece: Photograph of William Howard Russell by
Mathew Brady, Washington, D.C., 1861. Russell is dressed in
the uniform of a Deputy Lord Lieutenant of Ireland.
(News International Record Office)

Contents

Preface

ISTORIANS HAVE LONG RECOGNIZED THE VALUE OF William Howard Russell's commentaries on the American Civil War. In his reports to *The Times* and in his *My Diary North and South*, first published in 1863, the celebrated British reporter offered unique insight into the early stages of the American crisis, including a fascinating account of a visit to the southern states. As his modern biographer observes, Russell was not a great literary stylist, but he was an effective writer with a range of descriptive and analytic talents well suited to the demands of foreign correspondence. "What his eye sees his hand can describe. That is his particular excellence," conceded one American critic in 1861.[1]

My Diary North and South remains one of the indispensable Civil War volumes. Published more than a year after Russell's return from the United States, the book's attraction in great part derives from its vivid and seemingly spontaneous observations upon the sectional struggle. But how faithfully does it reflect Russell's experiences in America during 1861–62? In the strict sense, it is not a "diary" at all but a narrative reconstruction based upon the correspondent's notebooks and reports. An early return to the United States had not been ruled out as Russell completed his work, and this possibly accounts for the book's moderate language and generally sympathetic characterization. More fundamentally, the book also reveals Russell's acute awareness of American sensitivity to foreign criticism. Despite its often severe judgments on American society and conduct, *My Diary*

North and South provides a broadly reassuring account of the war's early development and of the political and military leaders responsible for directing it.

No such inhibitions inform Russell's private diary and letters, published here for the first time.[2] Despite obvious parallels, there are unmistakable differences in both style and substance between the public and private accounts of Russell's visit to the United States. In some cases, the portraits of William H. Seward and Mary Lincoln, for example, the contrast is exceptionally marked and, incidentally, highly unflattering to the subject; in others, minor changes in language effect small but significant amendments to the final sketch. One example will suffice. In *My Diary North and South*, Pres. Jefferson Davis's slate-colored suit is described as "rustic"; in the private diary, on the other hand, the chosen adjective, "drab," more effectively conveys Russell's initial perception of the Confederate leader, whom he regarded as less impressive than his northern counterpart. The published portrait of Davis, in fact, seems almost self-consciously retrospective when compared to the brief, dismissive characterization of the private diary.[3]

On occasions the private diary and letters seem to confirm what George Templeton Strong discerned as Russell's "quiet unconscious Anglican deprecation of everything outside England,"[4] including, it should be added, his anti-Semitism. On other occasions we glimpse a far more charitable observer of the American condition. But above all, the private diary and letters reveal for the first time the anxieties of the correspondent himself as he sought to come to terms with his American mission. From the outset, apprehensions about his wife's health provoke immediate concern, but as the months pass Russell's disillusionment with his treatment in the United States elicits a more fundamental self-examination that culminates in the decision to return home in the spring of 1862.

This edition includes all of William Howard Russell's existing diary and a selection from his private correspondence for the period of his visit to the United States. Unfortunately, the diary itself ends on 31 December 1861. Although Russell clearly continued making daily notebook entries throughout early 1862, two of which are quoted by his first biographer, John Black Atkins, all efforts to trace these and other notebooks have failed. It has not been felt appropriate to include those brief unverified extracts in this edition. In selecting let-

Lat 43° 31′ Lon. 54° 55′. Run 242

[...] Wind light but right in teeth.

Mr. Mitchell informs me that Woods was not at Richmond at all when the Prince visited it & seems to think the acct. was a lie. To write enquire —

Wind slightly on the beam — sea blue & tho' they wind very cold. Little Bowen tells me ample tales of 250 ships which sailed from Liverpool men never [...] all in one year — We jog along very pleasantly — toward evening there is scarcely any wind & the sea is so smooth as to excite one's admiration. But ye captain says it is not unusual to have fine weather in the middle of March — Cameron tells stories of good shooting in Canada — cutting off heads of wild turkeys with bullets at 180 yards right — left which except from a man of position wd be incredible — See the force of character [...] no one would dream of doubting him & Grande negotieur.

I bought a tarpaulin hat — went up on deck off went the hat to sea — a porpoise is now wearing it.   Little know the merry dolphins what my chapeau cost

Manuscript page from the diary kept by Russell during his trip to America in 1861–1862 as a special correspondent for *The Times*
(News International Record Office)

ters, I have tried as far as possible to maintain a consistent narrative voice and to include material that both supplements and enhances the private diary. The majority of letters are to Russell's fellow correspondents and editors on *The Times*, but also included are several letters that provide valuable insight into his wider associations in the United States.

In editing Russell's private diary and letters, I have been greatly concerned to maintain the integrity of the original text. Indeed, much of the interest in the material lies in the spontaneity of expression contained therein, which aggressive editorial intervention would only destroy. However, for the sake of clarity, a number of limited textual alterations have been found necessary, including the regularization of several proper names. The main problems arising from the original text derive almost entirely from Russell's highly personal punctuation. William Howard Russell's private diaries and, to a lesser extent, his letters, reveal a chaotic landscape of dashes, full stops, commas, and other less distinguishable marks that I have attempted to rationalize without undermining the stylistic and substantive integrity of the material. It was important, for example, to separate out individual names by the addition of a comma; at the same time I have resisted all temptation to employ punctuation as a means of "modernizing" Russell's text. Only on a very few occasions has punctuation been added to permit basic understanding of sentences that, without such intervention, would have remained virtually incomprehensible. On all these occasions it has not been thought appropriate to provide textual indication. Numerous illegible or incomplete words and phrases have been omitted from this edition, as well as one or two other peripheral items, including one concerning the ordering of clothes attached to a letter to Bancroft Davis; such omissions are denoted by the conventional suspension points. None of the omissions contain material of significant interest. Except for one or two cases where Russell's meaning is unclear, translations of the more unfamiliar Latin and other foreign phrases are provided in the notes. It has unfortunately not been possible to decipher Russell's few lapses into private shorthand, denoted here by the use of suspension points in square brackets.

Finally, a note about Russell's persistent and irregular use of abbreviations. In order to provide an accessible text for a late twentieth century readership, the majority of abbreviated words have been expanded, indicated here by the use of square brackets. However, a small number have been left unaltered to preserve the textual immediacy that distinguishes Russell's private writings from his published narratives. These are "cd." (could); "drs." (dollars); "shd." (should); "wd." (would); and "wh." (which).

Notes

1. *Harper's Weekly*, 27 July 1861.

2. Brief extracts from Russell's private writings have appeared in various biographies and other works. These include the somewhat misleadingly titled essay by Louis M. Sears, "The London *Times'* American Correspondence in 1861: Unpublished Letters of William Howard Russell in the First Year of the Civil War," *Historical Outlook* 16 (October 1925): 251–57, which incorporates several of Russell's letters to Bancroft Davis in a narrative account of the correspondent's visit.

3. William Howard Russell, *My Diary North and South*, 2 vols. (London, 1863), 1:249–51.

4. Allan Nevins and Milton Halsey Thomas, eds., *The Diary of George Templeton Strong*, 4 vols. (New York, 1952), 3:166.

Acknowledgments

WILLIAM HOWARD RUSSELL'S PRIVATE DIARIES RUN from 1854 until 1907. They were deposited in the archives of *The Times* at Printing House Square in 1973 by Russell's great-grandson, the late Col. R. J. Longfield. Since then they, together with Russell's other papers, have moved with the newspaper to Gray's Inn Road and finally to the News International archives in Wapping, East London.

William Howard Russell's letters printed in this edition derive from the following collections:

News International Record Office, London
William Howard Russell Papers (letters to John T. Delane, 16 July, 13 September, 14 October, 13, 22 December 1861; to Mowbray Morris, 7, 11, 26 January, 16, 19 February, 15, 21 March, 4 April 1862).
John T. Delane Papers (letters to John T. Delane, 26 March, 20 December 1861, 16, 27 January, 11 February 1862; to George W. Dasent, 15 September 1861).

West Sussex County Record Office, Chichester
Lord Lyons Papers (letters to Lord Lyons, 19 April, 21 May 1861).
By courtesy of Arundel Castle Trustees Limited and with acknowledgments to the West Sussex Record Office and the County Archivist.

Library of Congress, Washington
J. C. Bancroft Davis Papers (letters to J. C. Bancroft Davis, 2, 7, 12,
   14, 20, 24 April; 1, 2, 7, 20 May, 22, 25, 29 June, 4, 16 July, 3, 22,
   24 August, 14, 16, 25 September, 3, 19 October, 8 November, 10,
   16, 17, 25 December 1861).
Edwin M. Stanton Papers (letter to Edwin M. Stanton,
   2 April 1862).
George B. McClellan Papers (letter to Randolph B. Marcy,
   2 April 1862).

Rush Rhees Library, University of Rochester
William Henry Seward Papers, Department of Rare Books and
   Special Collections (letters to William H. Seward, 8 April, 10 July
   1861; to Frederick W. Seward, 6 July 1861).

*Henry Shelton Sanford Memorial Library and Museum,
Sanford, Florida*
Henry Shelton Sanford Papers, Box 105, Folder 6 (letter to J. C.
   Bancroft Davis, 22 July 1861).

Houghton Library, Harvard University
Charles Sumner Papers (letters to Charles Sumner, 5, 10,
   10 September, 2, 14 October, 25 December 1861, 28 March 1862).
   By permission of Houghton Library.

The Historical Society of Pennsylvania, Philadelphia
Gratz Collection, Case 11, Box 9 (letter to [unknown],
   14 September 1861).

The New-York Historical Society, New York
Misc. Mss. Russell, William Howard (letters to Edmund [last name
   unknown], 6, 29 March 1862). Courtesy of the New York State
   Historical Society.

I am grateful to all the above institutions for permission to reprint
the William Howard Russell letters contained in this edition.

IN UNDERTAKING THIS PROJECT, I little dreamed it would take so
long or place me in so many people's debt. Repayment, I fear, will be
much extended. It was Gordon Phillips, archivist at Printing House
Square, who first alerted me to the diary's existence. I am still not
sure whether to thank or to curse him. For permission to proceed
with editing of the diary, I am extremely grateful to the late Col.

R. J. Longfield, Russell's great-grandson, and to the then editor of *The Times*, William Rees-Mogg. I am indebted also to Mrs. Charlotte Longfield and to Russell's outstanding biographer, Alan Hankinson, for responding to my requests for family information. Thanks also to Melanie Aspey, the current group records manager at News International, for courteous assistance during the final stages of the project. A number of travel grants from the University of Keele Research Fund materially aided in its completion.

A full list of those archivists and librarians on both sides of the Atlantic who responded to my requests for information and advice, both in person and by mail, would necessitate a companion volume; I am particularly indebted, however, to the following individuals and institutions:

United States
Virginia H. Smith, Massachusetts Historical Society; Eleanor S. Darcy, Charles Carroll of Carrollton Papers, Maryland Historical Society; Mrs. I. W. Athey, Maryland Historical Society; Kathleen Howard, South Carolina Historical Society; George W. Schroeter, Mobile Public Library; Harriet H. Callahan, Virginia R. Smith, State Library of Louisiana; Frank J. Wetta, Galveston College; Mississippi Department of Archives and History; Michael P. Musick, National Archives; New York Public Library.

Canada
Susan Hart, British Columbia Archives and Record Service; Brian J. Young, McGill University; Ramsey Cook, York University; Allan Smith, University of British Columbia.

Great Britain
Ged Martin, Centre of Canadian Studies, University of Edinburgh; Fiona Scharlau, Angus District Council; Iain Flett, City of Dundee District Council; Janet Smith, Liverpool Records Office; Mrs. I. M. McCabe, Royal Institution.

France
Monique Constant, Ministère des Affaires Etrangères.

Without the daily companionship of friends and colleagues in the Department of American Studies at the University of Keele, William Howard Russell's diary and letters would still be buried beneath archival dust. I am particularly fortunate to occupy the office opposite

Charles Swann, whose unrivaled knowledge and fresh eye for the illegible have proved an invaluable resource. For help with translations, I am grateful to Oliver Goulden, Martin Harrison, David Laven, and Richard Wallace. Karen Harrison and Maureen Simkin foolishly undertook to type the manuscript; even with the advantage of word processors, it proved a "cruel and unusual" task. I should like to take the opportunity to thank Karen especially and to wish her well in her move from Keele. She will be greatly missed. Thanks are also due to Malcolm Call and the staff at the University of Georgia Press, and to Susan R. Korb for her sensitive and efficient copyediting.

My debt to Christine Turner can never be repaid. She has sustained me when it mattered, ignored me when it didn't, and generally kept everything in proper perspective. She also helped to decipher Russell's dreadful handwriting, a job far beyond the call of spousal duty. She, I know, will be delighted when Billy leaves home. This volume is inadequately dedicated to her.

Introduction

THE EVENING BEFORE WILLIAM HOWARD RUSSELL LEFT London on his way to report the disunion crisis in the United States, he dined at the famous Garrick Club, to which he had been elected a member in 1853. In many ways the Garrick was, and would remain, a second home to the celebrated war correspondent. Russell liked the company of men; he enjoyed the irreverent conviviality of the Garrick, which provided a haven from the private and professional storms that invariably engulfed him throughout his life. On this occasion his dining companion was his close friend, the novelist William Makepeace Thackeray, a leading light at the Garrick. Thackeray had been a source of great comfort during the recent and near fatal illness of Russell's wife, Mary, and was therefore an obvious choice for the correspondent's eve of departure celebration. During the dinner Thackeray cut off a lock of his snowy white hair and, placing it in an envelope, gave it to Russell for transmission to a friend in New York. The envelope, which the "wretch" failed to deliver, bore the inscription: "Be kind to the bearer of this." It was an appropriate sentiment. Throughout the next twelve months, as the American conflict deepened, *The Times*'s correspondent became the focus for intense hostility in the United States, and by April 1862 Russell was back in London, his mission, by his own standards at least, a failure.[1]

William Howard Russell was forty years old when he set sail for the United States in the spring of 1861. Born in Ireland, the son of a Catholic mother and a Protestant father, Russell's early life was characterized by a high degree of family insecurity from which, as his modern biographer notes, he appears to have emerged remarkably unscathed. In 1838 he entered Trinity College, Dublin, but failed to take a degree or to make any immediate impact on that institution. The turning point of his life came three years later when his cousin Robert, a journalist on Britain's leading daily newspaper, *The Times*, asked for help in reporting the 1841 general election in Ireland. The experience was a transforming, as well as an exciting, one. Up to this moment the younger Russell had shown no interest in journalism or indeed writing of any form, but when the election was over, he moved to London in search of permanent employment with *The Times*.[2]

Such career opportunities were not immediately forthcoming, however, and throughout the 1840s Russell struggled unsuccessfully to establish himself as a regular member of the Printing House Square staff. During the winter of 1843–44 he was back in Dublin covering the trial of the Irish nationalist leader Daniel O'Connell; but for the majority of the decade it was as a parliamentary reporter that he was most frequently employed, notably on the subcommittee investigations into railway corruption. Despite his apparent lack of progress, this was a vital period in Russell's career, when he first refined the skills that he would later employ to such good effect in the Crimea and elsewhere. In the meantime Russell kept his professional options open by pursuing his legal studies, and in June 1850 he was admitted to the Bar.

For a short period in the mid-1840s Russell abandoned *The Times* in favor of a regular position with the rival *Morning Chronicle*. The move, which proved unsatisfactory, reflected the young reporter's disenchantment with his lack of status at Printing House Square and was prompted above all by the need to achieve some degree of financial security. As Alan Hankinson has wryly observed, the only fixed thing about Russell's income during these early years "was that he constantly lived beyond it."[3] Moreover, in Dublin, Russell had met and courted a nineteen-year-old Catholic girl, Mary Burrowes. After overcoming the considerable hostility of her family, the two were married on 16 September 1846, and in May of the following year their first child, Alice, was born. Three more children, two boys and a girl, followed in quick succession, increasing the responsibilities that Russell was bound to feel as he carved out a career in the precarious world of newspaper journalism.

William Howard Russell returned to Printing House Square in the autumn of 1848. This time, however, it was by invitation and, more importantly, as a permanent member of the paper's staff. To begin with, Russell was used primarily as a legal and parliamentary reporter; but in July 1850 he was dispatched to observe the conflict that had developed between Denmark and the duchies of Schleswig and Holstein. By all accounts it was an undistinguished debut, although sufficiently promising to persuade *The Times* of Russell's aptitude for descriptive writing. Among the prestigious events that he covered in the next few years were the Cherbourg naval review, the tour of the Hungarian radical, Louis Kossuth, and in November 1852 the funeral of the Duke of Wellington at which, according to his own report, a million and a half people stood in reverential attendance.[4]

Russell's growth to prominence as a descriptive reporter coincided with *The Times*'s own ascendancy within British society. First established in 1785, the paper's early history was scarcely distinguishable from that of its leading metropolitan rivals. In 1803, however, John Walter, the son of the paper's founder, assumed full control. Under his astute direction *The Times* gradually acquired the commercial and political independence upon which its editorial authority would subsequently depend. However, it was not until after the appointment of Thomas Barnes as editor in 1817 that the paper's role as the guide and interpreter of British opinion began fully to emerge. On a variety of issues, including Peterloo, the trial of Queen Caroline, Catholic emancipation, and reform, Barnes deliberately associated his newspaper with the aspirations of a burgeoning middle-class public. It was a highly successful and, needless to say, commercially profitable policy. When Barnes died in 1841, Printing House Square's prestige had never been greater, and by the end of the decade the paper was selling four times as many copies as its three leading rivals combined.[5]

Under John Thadeus Delane, Barnes's successor, *The Times* further consolidated its powerful position in the vanguard of the British daily press. It was Delane who was responsible for Russell's return to Printing House Square in 1848, initiating a close personal as well as professional relationship that would last until the editor's death in 1879.[6] If anything, Delane's achievement as editor was even greater than that of his illustrious predecessor. During the 1850s the successful campaign for the repeal of the compulsory stamp duty was in

Portrait of John Thadeus Delane, editor of *The Times*
(National Portrait Gallery, London)

great part a movement against Printing House Square and the monopoly of public expression that, it was claimed, *The Times* exercised. Although the paper's circulation suffered badly as a result of post-repeal competition, it was not until after Delane's retirement in 1877 that there was any observable diminution in *The Times*'s influence.[7]

William Howard Russell's first expedition as a war correspondent had lasted only a few weeks; his second, to the Crimea, would keep him away from his family for twenty-two months. When he arrived back in England at the end of 1855, having exposed the bungling civilian and military conduct of the war, he was a national hero with an established reputation as one of the leading journalists of his generation. Russell's vivid, critical, and, above all, compassionate dispatches transformed both the art and function of war reporting, which, before the Crimean campaign, had hardly existed in any recognizably modern form. It was, as Philip Knightly has written, "an immense leap in the history of journalism."[8]

The much feted correspondent returned to the Crimea in February 1856 in order to observe the conclusion of the war, remaining there until the last British soldier had departed on 12 July. After a brief sojourn in London, however, he was soon on the move again, this time reporting the coronation of Czar Alexander II in Moscow. By now, Russell's status at Printing House Square was guaranteed, and when the Sepoy mutiny broke out in northern India the following spring, he was a logical choice to represent *The Times* in what would turn out to be a dangerous and demanding mission. In many respects, the Indian assignment would provide a sterner test of Russell's abilities than had the Crimean, since the paper charged him not only with reporting on military operations, should any arise, but also with investigating the underlying political and racial tensions from which the Sepoy outbreak originated.[9]

Russell's willingness to undertake such lengthy and hazardous tours was bound to have a deleterious effect upon his family life. Just a few weeks before his departure for India at the end of 1857 his fifth child, a son, was born: it was to live for only a year. When he heard of the death and of his wife's accompanying illness, *The Times*'s correspondent was in Lucknow, his mission almost complete. In his diaries and letters home Russell invariably betrayed deep anxiety over the condition of his abandoned family, and he repeatedly urged his employers to compensate him or to make special provision so that

Sketch of Russell in his Crimean War garb
(News International Record Office)

his wife and children could be adequately protected. This they frequently did, but such appeals could not disguise the lack of personal fulfillment that marriage and fatherhood had brought. Even when he was at home in London, Russell much preferred the company of his friends at the Garrick, and as the years advanced and Mary's health continued to deteriorate, he found it increasingly difficult to accommodate himself to the claustrophobic confines of domestic life. In the summer of 1859, Russell took his family to Switzerland on a restorative holiday, but the trip proved largely unsuccessful, with Mary miscarrying only a few days after their arrival back in England.[10]

Financial difficulties also continued to plague him. On his return from Switzerland, Russell was employed by Delane in the unfamiliar guise of leader writer, but it was not a job he particularly enjoyed nor, more importantly, did it provide him with sufficient income to meet his ever spiraling expenses. The solution to the problem came in the shape of an offer to edit a new military magazine, the *Army and Navy Gazette*. After some complicated bargaining, the offer was accepted, and on 7 January 1860 the first issue appeared. Russell remained in charge of the *Gazette* for well over forty years. As a consequence of the new venture, he ceased to draw a permanent salary from *The Times* but on the clear understanding that he would be available for any new foreign assignment, should his services be required.[11]

As part of his agreement with Bradbury and Evans, the publishers of the *Army and Navy Gazette*, Russell had been commissioned to write a book on the imminent American presidential election; but in the end circumstances conspired to prevent him from crossing the Atlantic in 1860. While in Switzerland, however, he met and befriended the New York journalist John Bigelow, who greatly stimulated his already keen interest in the United States.[12] In February 1860 Bigelow arrived with his family in London. During the next few months the two friends were to be found in frequent discussion over the deteriorating American crisis. A prominent Republican, Bigelow predictably opposed the political ambitions of the slave South, and in William Howard Russell he appears to have found a like-minded companion. Dining at the Garrick on 7 May, the two men were both "shocked" by the proslavery pronouncements of the Democratic editor John L. O'Sullivan.[13] Earlier, in March, Bigelow had helped Russell compose a highly favorable editorial on a speech by the leading

Republican contender for the presidency, William H. Seward. "All who are interested in the deliverance of the Western Republic from the curse of Negro slavery," the article concluded, "will see with pleasure the cause of freedom transferred to the guardianship of a great and responsible party, the policy of which will supersede the impotent and irritating devices of agitators."[14]

Any thoughts of an early visit to the United States were soon abandoned. On 26 October, after a protracted labor, Mary Russell was delivered of their sixth child, a boy. For several weeks after the birth Mary remained in critical condition, and it was not until the New Year that Russell was able to return to full-time work, let alone consider any new foreign commission. In many ways, it was a similar situation to that of three years earlier, when the couple's previous child was born: on both occasions Russell was anticipating a lengthy assignment abroad, and on both occasions, sadly, the child was to die before the correspondent's return to England.

In the meantime, the disunionist tide across the Atlantic was rapidly advancing. By February 1861 the secession of the deep South and the formation of a new Confederacy had persuaded *The Times* that an increase in its American correspondence was urgently required. Printing House Square's permanent representative in the United States was J. C. Bancroft Davis, a thirty-eight-year-old New York lawyer who had provided excellent weekly service since his appointment in 1854.[15] Davis was very much a part-time correspondent, however, confined to New York through family and professional commitments. He was also a committed Republican, whose letters since secession had barely disguised the hostility with which he regarded the southern cause. As the magnitude of the transatlantic crisis became more apparent, therefore, it was vital that *The Times*'s editorial authority should not be compromised by an exclusively American news correspondence. Writing to Davis on 22 February, the paper's manager, Mowbray Morris, explained the desirability of receiving the impressions of somebody "who has not been mixed up with your domestic politics, and whose sympathies are not engaged in the struggle now going on."[16]

Not unexpectedly, it was to William Howard Russell that Delane and Morris turned for such an important assignment. As an inducement, they offered Russell the substantial salary of £1,200 per an-

Sketch based on a photograph by
Mathew Brady of J.C. Bancroft Davis,
New York correspondent for *The Times*
(*Harper's Weekly*, 3 February 1872)

num, plus expenses, and an understanding that he could return home should the situation in the United States become too dangerous. The correspondent also negotiated an advance of £750 from Bradbury and Evans for a book on America, after reassuring them that the *Army and Navy Gazette* would not suffer as a result of his absence. All that remained was to make provision for his wife and new baby. Mary had still not fully recovered from her recent ordeal, and it was finally decided that they would stay in Bath with the family of Russell's friend, John Connellan Deane. By the end of February the arrangements had been completed. After a brief, reassuring visit to Bath, the correspondent made his way, via Liverpool and Dublin, to Queenstown in the south of Ireland, from where, on the evening of 3 March 1861, he took passage for New York on the Cunard steamship *Arabia*.[17]

AS SPECIAL CORRESPONDENT of *The Times*, William Howard Russell was uniquely situated to influence the attitudes of the British middle and upper classes toward the American crisis. By 1861 the

Portrait of Mowbray Morris, manager of *The Times*
(News International Record Office)

declining prestige of church and aristocracy had paved the way for the daily press as the principal source of public knowledge within British society, and in the face of new and vigorous competition *The Times* was determined that its authority in foreign news should not be superseded. Interest in the United States had been steadily growing throughout the late antebellum period. In 1854 the appointment of Bancroft Davis as New York correspondent brought much-needed improvement to the paper's American coverage, and two years later the editor himself made a brief transatlantic visit, during which he witnessed the election of James Buchanan as president. The same year one of Printing House Square's most experienced reporters, Louis Filmore, undertook an extended assignment as special correspondent. The dispatches Filmore sent back from places as far apart as Niagara and New Orleans were well designed to compensate for the British public's lack of familiarity with American society, particularly in its expanding regional character.[18]

By the end of the 1850s Anglo-American relations had visibly improved after the turbulence of the previous decade. In part, this accommodation demonstrated the new maturity of Anglo-American diplomacy; but it also reflected the changing balance of power in the western hemisphere and the recognition by Great Britain, with its paramount European commitments, that outright opposition to the United States in Central America and elsewhere could no longer be sustained. The one exception, of course, was Canada. In 1854, however, the signing of the Reciprocity Treaty marked an important turning point in stabilizing relations along the northern border.[19] Underwriting the diplomatic accommodation was the continuing economic interdependence of the two societies. During the 1850s economic collaboration between Great Britain and the United States reached its peak, with the common pool of land, labor, technology, and capital reinforcing the exchange of primary and manufactured goods, including, most notably, cotton. Although many of the conditions that sustained the North Atlantic economy had already begun to change, such changes were little in evidence on the eve of the Civil War. In fact, it was not until after Appomattox and the explosive development of American industrialization that the economic relationship between the two nations would fundamentally alter.[20]

Inevitably, tensions between Great Britain and the United States were bound to recur. The time-honored rituals of rivalry and suspicion upon which the Anglo-American relationship had for so long relied were not easily abandoned. Nor can it be claimed that there was complete harmony of interests across the North Atlantic divide; diplomatic rapprochement had been achieved through an adjustment, not an abandonment, of vital national interests, while in the economic sphere America's continued adherence to protectionism aroused regular condemnation in free trade Britain. Despite such legacies, however, it is likely that by the end of the 1850s the prospects for continuing friendship between the two countries had never been greater. In October 1860 the visit to the United States of the young Prince of Wales revealed an enormous reservoir of affection across the North Atlantic divide. For nearly all those who commented upon it, the tour was a highly significant event, a symbol of the revived association between the kindred societies, based upon their historic commitment to Anglo-Saxon liberty and progress.[21]

As the leading organ of governing-class opinion, *The Times* strived conscientiously to reflect the maturing rapprochement between the two countries. In the paper's view, the rapid economic and political progress of the western republic was both inevitable and desirable, "of essential advantage to ourselves, as Englishmen, and to the general interests of mankind."[22] Despite its reservations about many aspects of American society and conduct, including slavery and protectionism, there are few signs from the paper's editorial commentaries during the 1850s of any intrinsic hostility toward the United States. Yet this did not mean any softening of critical judgment, and *The Times* was particularly severe on those elements in the American experience that, it felt, posed a serious threat to relations between the two countries.

High on the paper's list of grievances was the irredeemable character of the American press, whose splenetic energies were all too often directed across the Atlantic. It is "too corrupt," reported Delane after his visit in 1856.[23] Equally serious, however, was the structural weakness of government in the United States. This weakness, which the paper attributed to an exaggerated dependence upon the popular will, was invariably deployed to explain the often dangerously erratic path of American foreign relations. As an editorial noted in 1855 at the height of the filibustering controversy, the American people were so free "that they will not be controlled by a Government of their own choosing."[24] As the disunion clouds darkened at the end of the decade, the British belief in American governmental inadequacy would achieve much greater urgency. After all, the first duty of governments was to govern and, in Printing House Square's view, the United States's inability to prevent its own dismemberment provided a sad commentary upon a political system of which the Americans appeared so inordinately proud. It was also a system that certain political groups were intent on reproducing in Great Britain, an idea that *The Times* ridiculed to the full.[25]

Even as it was attacking the inadequacies of transatlantic democracy, however, *The Times* remained sensitive to the political and moral dilemmas posed by slavery and the sectional conflict. Despite the declining authority of organized abolitionism in Great Britain, antislavery sentiment remained pervasive among the British middle and upper classes.[26] Throughout the 1850s the paper consistently condemned the illiberal ambitions of the South's planter class and the labor and caste system upon which its authority rested. In Printing House Square's opinion, slavery was both economically inefficient and morally unsupportable, and it left few opportunities of reminding southerners that they would find little sympathy across the Atlantic for their reactionary views. Radical abolitionism, on the other hand, was also to be condemned since it too encouraged violent solutions to the sectional impasse. For governing-class opinion in Great Britain, slavery could only be extinguished and the stability of the republic maintained through the cautious if persistent application of liberal principles.[27]

On the other hand, Britain depended on slave-grown cotton, and, as the sectional crisis intensified, it was possible that fears for the continuing supply would play a major role in the calculation of British interest. As *The Times* commented in 1857, "Our eggs are all in one basket, and those eggs are very precious indeed."[28] Surprisingly, however, the cotton supply issue would have little or no impact on the paper's responses to the United States before 1861. Throughout the antebellum decade *The Times*'s editorial advice was invariably directed toward reducing British dependence on southern cotton by encouraging the development of alternative sources, notably from India.[29]

Slavery was only one of the numerous dilemmas posed by the transatlantic crisis. Despite Printing House Square's revulsion at the South's conduct, particularly in the passage of the Fugitive Slave

Act and later in "Bleeding Kansas," it could not fail to notice that the same region had consistently supported free-trade legislation in the United States. In February 1861 the protectionist Morrill Tariff was passed by the Republican-dominated Congress in Washington. The act, which even such a committed supporter of American democracy as John Bright believed to be one of extreme folly, posed a serious challenge to Anglo-American economic cooperation and, by extension, to the wider relationship between the two countries.[30] It also demonstrated how potentially complex the problem of British responses to the sectional crisis had become, notwithstanding the broad antislavery sympathies to which the majority of educated opinion undoubtedly subscribed.

In the presidential election of 1856, Britain's leading newspaper had unequivocally endorsed the Republican candidacy of Col. John Fremont. Four years later, with the fabric of the Union rapidly crumbling, *The Times*'s antislavery convictions were confirmed as it greeted with pleasure the victory of Abraham Lincoln. His success, an editorial commented, "is the natural reaction against the outrages and excesses of 1855 and 1856, the protest of the freest and best educated part of the American people against the acts of high-handed violence and oppression which preceded the advent of Mr. BUCHANAN to power."[31] Although privately the paper's directors remained uncertain as to the significance of Lincoln's election, publicly at least there could be few doubts as to where its editorial sympathies lay. "Let there be no mistake on this subject," an article concluded in November. "If we have paid a sincere homage to the rising greatness of America, it has not been to that which the Southerners are so anxious to conserve, but to that which they are striving to destroy."[32]

By early 1861, however, *The Times*'s attitude had already begun to change. The failure of the Federal government to contain the secession movement held out little prospect that civil war would in the end be averted. Despite its "natural sympathies," Printing House Square was now forced to review the American crisis in the light of its potential impact upon British interests, the guardianship of which remained the paper's overriding concern.[33] In fact, within a few weeks of William Howard Russell's arrival in the United States, *The Times* had become seriously disillusioned with the conflict across the Atlantic. With the passage of the Morrill Tariff on 20 February and the enactment of an export duty on raw cotton by the Confederate Congress a few days later, it was clear that British economic interests were bound to suffer as a result of what the paper now called this "inglorious and unnatural combat."[34] If civil war did occur, moreover, what further consequences would ensue, particularly in respect of Anglo-American commerce and, most vitally, the cotton supply?

As a former leader writer at Printing House Square and the paper's principal foreign correspondent, William Howard Russell undoubtedly shared his employer's general attitude toward the United States. In his published account, Russell claimed to have approached his American assignment with a completely open mind, devoid of any prejudices or preconceptions about what he would discover across the Atlantic: "I was a free agent, bound to communicate to the powerful organ of public opinion I represented, my own daily impressions of the men, scenes and actions around me, without fear or favour, or affection of or for anything, but that which seemed to me to be the truth."[35] As we have already seen, however, Russell's views on essential aspects of the American conflict had already been formed prior to his arrival in the United States. Despite his innate conservatism, the special correspondent evidently found little to applaud in the South's conduct or in the system of black slavery it sought so unreasonably to defend. One fellow passenger on the *Arabia,* in fact, a South Carolinian, while admitting that Russell was "fair & candid" in his expressions, reported him as possessing "strong abolitionist opinions."[36]

Whatever his precise views, there could be no escaping the significance with which *The Times*'s correspondent regarded events in the United States. Writing to John Bigelow a few weeks before his departure, Russell confirmed that the crisis now unfolding across the Atlantic posed a serious challenge to the "march of constitutional liberty" in the Western world. "Every friend of despotism rejoices at your misfortune," he observed. Finally, Russell left his American friend in little doubt as to the attitude of his own country. No good Englishman, he concluded with obvious conviction, "feels any sentiment but one of intense respect and great sympathy."[37]

RUSSELL ARRIVED in New York on 16 March 1861 armed with an outstanding reputation. He is, John Bigelow advised the Federal secretary of state in an introductory note, "one of the witnesses which

posterity will call to testify to the great deeds done in his generation."[38] While in New York Russell gained instant notoriety with an
impromptu St. Patrick's Day speech at the Astor House. The occasion
failed to impress his employers in London, however, who, perhaps
mindful of the traditional American sensitivity to British advice,
warned him against such public appearances in the future.[39] Significantly, it also failed to impress one of the leading Republican
newspapers, Horace Greeley's *New York Tribune*, which claimed the
speech afforded clear evidence "of the mistaken idea prevailing in
England concerning the nature of the present American difficulties."
The paper particularly objected to Russell's characterization of the
crisis as a test of republican institutions, whereas, it argued, it was
merely a conflict between freedom and slavery, the latter being the
aggressor.[40]

After a brief stay in New York, during which he met Bancroft
Davis, Russell moved to Washington, putting up at Willard's Hotel
at the corner of Fourteenth Street and Pennsylvania Avenue. Since
so much of the capital's business was undertaken from that celebrated establishment, it was the obvious choice for the newly arrived correspondent, although its size and unique lack of intimacy
clearly distressed him.[41] During the next two weeks Russell entered
smoothly into Washington's leading political, diplomatic, and military circles. Among the prominent people he dined with were the
army commander, Gen. Winfield Scott, the recently defeated Democratic candidate, Sen. Stephen A. Douglas of Illinois, and the British
minister, Lord Lyons, as well as several members of the cabinet. It
was on 27 March at a White House reception that Russell was first
introduced to the new president. The meeting has long since been
remembered for Lincoln's comment comparing the power of *The
Times* to that of the mighty Mississippi River. Unlike his predecessor, Abraham Lincoln was not widely known across the Atlantic, and
his emergence as a national leader at such a critical moment seemed
in some respects to confirm the widely held belief in Great Britain
about the capricious and unrepresentative character of the American
democratic system. On the other hand, after his election victory, *The
Times* had recognized some of the essential qualities upon which the
president's authority would subsequently rest. "Mr. LINCOLN can do
anything he sets his mind to, partly from natural pliability, partly

by an impressive power of fixing his attention on whatever is before him," it observed on 28 November. At their first meeting Russell
was entranced by Lincoln's extraordinary physical appearance; but
he also acknowledged the resolution and "natural sagacity" that the
president's elongated frame concealed.[42]

Washington during the last week in March was a city with one
subject on its mind: what attitude would the new Republican administration adopt toward the departed states and, more specifically,
how would it deal with the contentious issue of the southern forts?
With the new president preferring to keep his own counsel, much
of the attention focused on the enigmatic figure of William Henry
Seward. Russell first met the secretary of state at the home of Bancroft Davis's friend, Henry Sanford. "He talks a great deal and is very
much given to raconter and badiner," was his first apt impression, "a
subtle quick man, not quite indifferent to kudos."[43] On the following
evening Russell dined at the secretary's house and for the next two
weeks, prior to the correspondent's departure for the South, the two
men were to be found frequently in each other's company. Despite his
failure to win the presidential nomination, Seward was still regarded
by many as the principal architect of Republican strategy toward the
South, an impression that he himself did little to dispel. For his part
Seward also saw obvious advantages in patronizing Russell. In the
weeks following Lincoln's inauguration the secretary of state was
anxious to counter any support that the European powers might afford the rebel cause, and in *The Times*'s correspondent he recognized
an important avenue of communication through which his intentions
could be made known.[44]

Despite his expectations, however, Russell soon discovered how
difficult it was to gain any real information about the government's
plans. By the second week in April, in fact, the correspondent's lack of
progress had convinced him to abandon Washington and to turn his
attention to the South. The decision was undoubtedly precipitated
by fears that reinforcement of the southern forts would produce an
imminent outbreak of hostilities between the sections. On 12 April
Russell took the train to Baltimore, from where he embarked by
steamer for Norfolk, Virginia. Here he learned of the Federal surrender at Fort Sumter. "I hear I'm late for the fair," he informed Bancroft
Davis in a brief note.[45] Two days later, after a fatiguing rail jour-

ney through the Carolinas, the correspondent arrived in Charleston, where he met up with his traveling companion, the inimitable Sam Ward, who was on a private reconnaissance mission to the South.[46]

As the storm center of secession and the scene of the first hostilities in the American conflict, Charleston was a natural attraction for *The Times*'s reporter, and within a few hours of his arrival Russell had plunged headlong into a society about which he was almost entirely ignorant. Predictably, one of the first objects of his curiosity was Fort Sumter itself, which he toured on the 17th accompanied by Maj. William Whiting, the engineer in charge of Confederate emplacements. In the event, Russell was not over impressed by the physical remains he examined, finding little evidence to justify the enormous excitement that the bombardment had aroused. "A very small affair, indeed, that shelling of Sumter," was the correspondent's overly dismissive conclusion.[47]

Russell's two-week stay in Charleston and surrounding districts set the pattern for his subsequent experiences in the rest of the South. Military matters aside, the correspondent's main ambition was to examine the social and political institutions that the southern rebellion was attempting to conserve. As his diary confirms, Russell's personal reputation combined with his position as *The Times*'s ambassador guaranteed his immediate acceptance into the upper echelons of Confederate society. On his first evening in Charleston, for example, he dined with leading members of South Carolina's political elite, and in the weeks that followed he profited handsomely from a host of private invitations, including visits to several local plantations. Planters, politicians, editors, bankers, and soldiers were all anxious, it seems, that the British correspondent should scrutinize Confederate society through their eyes, even as they must have been aware of the critical independence upon which his reputation as a journalist rested. "People here care a great deal for what Russell says," noted Mary Chesnut on 4 July, "because he represents the *Times*, and the London *Times* reflects the sentiments of the English people."[48] Later, Russell's letters would arouse considerable hostility in the new republic, with southerners reacting sharply against what they regarded as the dishonorable betrayal of their hospitality.

Russell's next port of call was Savannah, Georgia, but by 4 May he had reached the capital, Montgomery, where he made contact with many of the principal characters in the Confederate drama, including the president, Jefferson Davis. Accompanied by his self-appointed guide, Louis Wigfall, Russell was also introduced on the floor of the Confederate Congress. Regrettably, the occasion was marred by the degrading spectacle of a slave auction that the correspondent was forced to witness as he made his way to the capitol building. Nevertheless, the assembled legislators appeared to have made a considerable impression on the British visitor: "I fancy that, in all but garments, they were like the men who first conceived the great rebellion which led to the independence of this wonderful country— so earnest, so grave, so sober, and so vindictive."[49] Jefferson Davis, on the other hand, seemed at first glance a less imposing figure, particularly when compared to his counterpart in Washington. Russell would soon detect clear qualities of determination and resilience in the Confederate leader, however, who in turn made every effort to reassure the correspondent that he would "receive every facility it is in our power to afford you" while he remained within the South. "You are among civilized, intelligent people who understand your position, and appreciate your character," Davis told him.[50]

The capital itself, "a dull, lifeless place,"[51] held few attractions, however, and, anxious to penetrate deeper into the Confederate heartland, Russell was soon on the move again. On 9 May he took the river steamer to Mobile, from where he participated in an adventurous excursion to the Federal outpost at Fort Pickens, the defenses of which he evaluated in a report to the British minister, Lord Lyons.[52] His next and most important destination was New Orleans. *The Times*'s correspondent arrived in the Crescent City on the night of 20 May, and once again he was overwhelmed with invitations from the region's leading political and commercial figures. He also took the opportunity to inspect the New Orleans city gaol, including its condemned cell, the wretchedness of which obviously appalled him. The highlight of Russell's stay in the delta region, however, was undoubtedly his visits to several large sugar plantations, including that of the former governor of Louisiana, André Roman, where he was once again able to give close attention to the workings of the slave system.

Everywhere he traveled in the South, Russell was warmly received by his planter hosts, thereby laying him open to the charge that his independence as a journalist was being compromised. As a writer in *Harper's Weekly* would suggest in July 1861, Russell's breeding had left him with "a taste for the flavour of aristocracy. He found it also at the South; he enjoyed it, and he reported it. The tone of admiration and confidence in his first letters undoubtedly helped the rebellion in the public opinion of England."[53] Clearly, the special correspondent was not immune to the South's charms; a confirmed bon vivant, Russell patently enjoyed the hospitality that was lavished upon him and, despite his reservations about the secessionist cause, could not fail to be impressed by both the courage and conviction of its leading proponents. At the same time, he was not about to be seduced by southern civilization. Traveling by rail from Savannah to Macon, he glimpsed barefoot children and "miserable" ill-kept villages, in striking contrast to the "trim, snug settlements" he had encountered in New Jersey and other communities to the north.[54]

Whatever affinity Russell may have felt for upper-class society in the South, moreover, there could be no disguising his repugnance at its peculiar labor system, as his reaction to the Montgomery slave auction testifies. "I am neither sentimentalist nor Black Republican, nor negro worshipper, but I confess the sight caused a strange thrill through my heart," he reported to *The Times*.[55] In his diary, Russell's casual use of the epithet "nigger" betrayed the characteristic racism of the mid-Victorian period; but in his visits to plantations in South Carolina and Louisiana he also revealed a sensitive awareness of the dehumanizing condition in which the Confederacy's slave population was condemned to live. "It was not that I expected to come upon anything dreadful," he wrote, explaining his reluctance to enter a slave cabin, "but I could not divest myself of some regard for the feelings of the poor creatures, slaves though they were, who stood by, shy, curtseying, and silent, as I broke in upon their family circle, felt their beds, and turned over their clothing. What right had I to do so?"[56] Nor was Russell willing to accept the repeated assurances of his planter hosts that the system was secure from internal revolt. "There is something suspicious in the constant neverending statement that 'we are not afraid of our slaves,'" he reported from Montgomery.[57]

Slavery was only one aspect of the Confederacy's condition, however. Dominating all Russell's impressions was that of the southerners' determination not to reenter the Union. In fact, the extent of popular commitment to the Confederate cause was something for which *The Times*'s correspondent, despite earlier intimations, was plainly unprepared. As he wrote to Lord Lyons from New Orleans, the southern people were "resolute and unanimous to a most extraordinary degree."[58] Almost as impressive, however, was southerners' belief in the irresistible power of cotton to effect European assistance. Although Russell was the first to acknowledge that interruption in the cotton supply would produce serious economic distress across the Atlantic, he was obviously irritated by the argument, repeatedly put to him, that material considerations alone would dictate British policy toward the American struggle.[59]

The special correspondent left New Orleans at the end of the first week in June. As he moved up the Mississippi valley, the pace of his journey quickened. On his way north Russell paused at Baton Rouge, Natchez, Vicksburg, Jackson, and Memphis, Tennessee, where he was invited to accompany the Confederate general Gideon Pillow on a short inspection tour of river defenses. While in Memphis, however, he learned from northern newspapers of the mounting pressures for a Federal advance into Virginia, and this resolved him to curtail his tour and return to the East. Although the Confederate states still offered enormous scope for his journalistic talents, the developing military situation had made the transmission of his letters increasingly difficult. On 3 July 1861, after brief stops at Chicago and Niagara Falls, Russell arrived back in Washington. He had been away from the capital for more than two and a half months.[60]

DURING RUSSELL'S ABSENCE in the South, relations between Great Britain and the Federal states had visibly deteriorated. The focal point of the new animosity was the Queen's neutrality proclamation of 13 May 1861. The proclamation, which was issued in response to the recent maritime declarations from Washington and Montgomery, granted belligerent status to the Confederacy and prohibited British participation of any sort in the American conflict.[61] The growth in Anglo-American tension, however, evidenced a more profound breakdown in communication between the two countries. As northerners viewed it, the British lack of enthusiasm for the Federal cause masked a serious betrayal of the nation's antislavery tradition. "I say we are disappointed," the Massachusetts orator and former diplomat Edward Everett told the British foreign secretary in May, "because up to the commencement of this great struggle, all the organs of opinion in England, official and unofficial, had ever leaned the other way. The Anti-Slavery sentiment of the North was stimulated in season and out of season in England."[62]

For their part, British middle- and upper-class observers soon became disillusioned with the virulent transatlantic reaction against neutrality. The passage in June of the protectionist Morrill Tariff had already angered many in free-trade Britain, and the new outburst, which was based, they believed, upon a blatant misrepresentation of British motives, posed a serious challenge to Anglo-American co-operation. As *The Times* complained on 11 June, "England must not presume to move a finger in America, but, on the other hand, she must not presume to say she will not." Suspicion over the conduct and motives of William H. Seward had also increased during Russell's absence, with even those British observers highly sympathetic to the North's cause expressing their anxiety lest the secretary of state's diplomatic excesses should lead to a violent confrontation between the two countries.[63]

How much the changed climate in Anglo-American relations affected Russell personally at this stage is difficult to assess. After two and a half months away from the capital, *The Times*'s correspondent was eager to resume the associations he had begun to foster before his departure, notably with the Federal secretary of state. Accepting an invitation to dinner on 10 July, Russell apologized to Seward for having "neglected somewhat the observances of civilized life" since his return to Washington.[64] The two men had already met the previous week at the State Department. After receiving Seward's congratulations on his safe return, the correspondent reminded him of the battles that would need to be fought if the resolute southerners were to be overcome. The secretary was in no mood to compromise, however, and forcefully reemphasized his government's determination to use every necessary means to restore the Union and uphold the Constitution. On relations with Great Britain, Seward was equally forthright: although denying any intention of provoking a war over the issue of neutrality, he told Russell that America had less reason to fear a foreign war than any other nation in the world. "A contest between Great Britain and the United States would wrap the world in flames, and at the end it would not be the United States which would have to lament the results of the conflict," the secretary of state confidently predicted.[65]

If William Howard Russell was impressed by Seward's display, he was also astonished that such sentiments were forthcoming when the security of the capital was under serious threat. A little over two weeks after the interview, the first major battle of the war was fought at Bull Run, less than thirty miles from the State Department. The result, a catastrophic defeat for northern arms, ended any hope for an early reconstruction of the Union and, incidentally, dealt a serious blow to the Federal image overseas. As the secretary to the American Legation in London observed on 5 August, the news from Virginia would "have a bad effect for the North in Europe."[66]

Bull Run was also a turning point for the special correspondent. Indeed, for many people Russell's portrait of Federal demoralization became the single compelling image of the engagement. Published in *The Times* on 6 August, the dispatch was widely reprinted on both sides of the Atlantic.[67] Russell himself, however, as American critics were quick to point out, did not arrive at the Bull Run battlefield until midafternoon on the 21st when hostilities were already far advanced, and in his report he concentrated entirely on the Federal retreat, during which, as he wrote to Bancroft Davis the following day, he was "nearly murdered" by northern troops as they streamed back into the capital.[68] Unfortunately, Printing House Square failed to heed Russell's instruction to preface his account of the retreat with descriptions of the battle itself, an error for which the correspondent would subsequently pay dearly.[69]

It would be at least a month, however, before the Bull Run letter arrived back to the United States. In the meantime, Russell settled back into the domestic routines of Washington life. Anxious to curb his ever-rising expenses, the special correspondent had moved into cheaper lodgings over a Swiss "wine merchant" on Pennsylvania Avenue, but his new landlords, the Josts, proved less than accommodating, and in November he was forced to move again. Despite these tribulations, however, and the bouts of "Potomac fever" to which he regularly succumbed, Russell seems generally to have thrived on the daily regime of army visits, dinner parties, and late night carousing. After his return from the South in July, he had quickly established himself as one of the leading members of the Anglo-American bachelor community that centered around the British legation. In fact, without the sustaining companionship of the attachés, army and naval officers, and other Washington transients with whom he spent most of the time, Russell would have found it difficult to survive the melancholia that progressively overtook him during the second half of his American visit, the signs of which are clearly visible in his private diary. In mid-August the special correspondent left Washington for a brief excursion into Maryland, where he spent a pleasurable albeit damp few days with the Carroll family of Doughoregan Manor. He also visited Harper's Ferry, the scene two years earlier of John Brown's historic intervention in the sectional debate.[70]

Among the many leading figures that William Howard Russell was able to observe closely during this crucial period, two stand out as significant emblems of the larger political and military experience. Neither the Federal secretary of state, William H. Seward, nor the commander of the Army of the Potomac, Gen. George B. McClellan, ever developed a close personal friendship with *The Times*'s correspondent, but both respected Russell's position and both sought occasionally to explain to him the problems that they confronted. In private Russell was frequently scathing about the two men, particularly "Shiny William," whose inconstancy and disingenuousness he regarded as all too typical of American democratic politics; but as a professional journalist he valued such important contacts and took every opportunity to exploit them to the full.

Initially, it was the secretary of state who invited the closest interest; but after his return from the South Russell's attention was more obviously focused on the North's growing military establishment. The Bull Run debacle had precipitated widespread changes in the Federal military, not the least of which was the replacement of Gen. Irvin McDowell, whom Russell personally liked, with the young McClellan. As an experienced observer of European warfare, the special correspondent was soon impressed with McClellan's energetic reorganization of the Army of the Potomac, and by the end of September he felt that the North's new military strength, "if properly handled," must ultimately prevail.[71] At the same time, he remained skeptical as to northern popular enthusiasm for the struggle. Within a few weeks, moreover, doubts about McClellan's own weaknesses had already begun to surface in Russell's mind, and by early November, with no Federal advance in sight, he was openly anticipating the "young Napoleon's" demise.[72]

In fact, the more Russell examined the North, its society, its political and military organization, the more persuaded he became of its lack of collective purpose, essential if the rebellion was to be crushed. Much of this perceived disunity was the result of the correspondent's exposure to the internecine politics of Washington and New York; however, it also reflected the already clear division between those who believed the conflict should evolve into a war to end slavery and those, including many in the military, who were determined it should not. Wherever he went in the North, Russell encountered a bewildering variety of opinions on this and other critical issues of wartime policy, opinions that, he feared, could not forever be contained by the republic's inherently weak governmental authority.[73] At the very least, the North's disunity was not conducive to a successful prosecution of the war against the slave South, a situation that Russell personally found cause to regret.

From the time his first reports arrived back in the United States several months earlier, William Howard Russell had been a popular target of such widely circulated papers as *Harper's Weekly* and the *New York Herald*. Like most British observers Russell was thoroughly disenchanted with the American press, but nothing hitherto had prepared him for the chorus of dissent that greeted the Bull Run dispatch. "I hear I'm the best abused man in America," he wrote to John Bigelow on 27 August.[74] Some northerners, including the Boston historian Francis Parkman, deeply lamented the attacks,[75] which Charles Sumner explained were the result of Russell's condescending tone. "They feel that this is not friendly, that it is *dehaut en bas,* that you write down upon us—and this you can imagine is not pleasant," the senator told the British reporter candidly in September.[76] Perhaps significantly, one of the few northern newspapers to take a moderate stance over Russell's Bull Run reports was the *Albany Evening Journal*, edited by the secretary of state's close confidant, Thurlow Weed. "He is a free man in a free country, and if one *will* prefer darkness to light he must be allowed to have it," a leading article noted.[77]

That same month disquiet arose in the North over Russell's letter of 10 August, published in England two weeks later, in which he cast doubt over the preparedness of the Federal troops around Washington. Although the correspondent himself was astonished over the furor, claiming that he could find nothing exceptional in the report, the result was a petition to the secretary of state from a group of Philadelphia citizens demanding his expulsion from the United States. Seward, to his credit, failed to act on the petition, although his statement of rejection was hardly reassuring.[78] Nonetheless, for the next two months Russell was on the defensive, forced to justify his conduct in what had become an increasingly hostile environment.

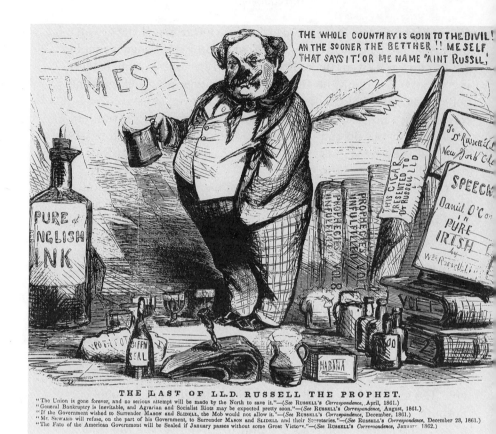

THE WHOLE COUNTH RY IS GOIN TO THE DIVIL! AN THE SOONER THE BETTHER !! ME SELF THAT SAYS IT! OR ME NAME "AINT RUSSLL,'

PURE ENGLISH INK

THE LAST OF LL.D. RUSSELL THE PROPHET.

"The Union is gone forever, and no serious attempt will be made by the North to save it."—(See RUSSELL's Correspondence, April, 1861.)
"General Bankruptcy is inevitable, and Agrarian and Socialist Riots may be expected pretty soon."—(See RUSSELL's Correspondence, August, 1861.)
"If the Government wished to Surrender MASON and SLIDELL, the Mob would not allow it."—(See RUSSELL's Correspondence, December, 1861.)
"Mr. SEWARD will refuse, on the part of his Government, to Surrender MASON and SLIDELL and their Secretaries."—(See RUSSELL's Correspondence, December 23, 1861.)
"The Fate of the American Government will be Sealed if January passes without some Great Victory."—(See RUSSELL's Correspondence, January 1862.)

Caricature of Russell at the height of his American unpopularity
(*Harper's Weekly*, 15 February 1862)

To the charges of Dr. Charles Ray, the editor of the *Chicago Tribune*, that he had not in fact witnessed a half of what he reported at Bull Run, Russell composed and had printed a detailed narrative of his movements on the day in question. Nor did Russell feel secure from personal attack. A visit to the western states in September resulted in the correspondent's arrest and fine on a fabricated charge of shooting on a Sunday, while back in London the paper's manager, Mowbray Morris, was convinced that "some enraged patriot" would shoot him through the head on account of the Bull Run report.[79]

Russell's difficulties during this period, however, did not stem solely from his own conduct. With northern sensitivity over the Bull Run defeat still strong, the special correspondent found himself the unwitting beneficiary of *The Times*'s hostility to the Federal cause. In letters home he complained bitterly about the effect his employer's attitude was having upon his personal situation in the United States. "They take me as the exponent of Englishmen England and The Times and would like to avenge themselves upon me," he told his editor in September.[80] Although Russell was always prone to exaggerate his condition during periods of stress, there could be no disguising the ostracism he was now suffering from those who, like Seward, had initially flattered and encouraged him. Beset by a host of personal and professional anxieties, not the least of which was the condition of his wife in England, the special correspondent seriously considered abandoning his commission and returning home but was dissuaded from doing so by his employers. However, from the late summer of 1861 onward, there can be little doubt that Russell's authority as a reporter of the American crisis was substantially diminished, prompting Alan Hankinson to identify the months that followed as "the most unhappy period of his professional life."[81]

Russell's diary and letters throughout this dismal period reveal both the strengths and frailties of the special correspondent's character. As his modern biographer notes, he was a man who needed constant reassurance in both the public and private sphere and, when failing to get it, could blame all around him for his peculiar condition. Yet, amid all the posturing and self-doubt, there was an essential toughness of spirit about William Howard Russell. A vain, pompous, even on occasions absurd figure, he was also an affectionate and generous companion, who abhorred the pretensions of others, whether individuals, classes, or nations. In calmer circumstances, perhaps, such independent qualities might have been regarded with some admiration; but in the turbulent atmosphere of civil war America, they were bound to arouse the deepest suspicion.[82]

Indeed, on the professional level, the critical objectivity that Russell so stubbornly deployed on his American visit was also his greatest burden; as attacks upon his conduct in both the northern and southern states intensified, Russell failed fully to comprehend the nationalistic forces that conspired against him. "I write for the English people, not for the American," he argued with evident frustration.[83] As Anglo-American understanding collapsed in the wake of the Queen's neutrality proclamation, Russell's sharp reporting of northern affairs, including the defeat at Bull Run, was bound to be resisted by a people confident in its patriotic virtue. Yet throughout his ordeal the special correspondent remained a highly sympathetic neutral, convinced in the long run that the North would and should prevail. Despite his acknowledgment, derived from firsthand observation, of the South's determination to sustain its independence at all costs, Russell never overcame his belief in the essential rectitude of the Federal cause.[84] At the same time, as he wrote to Charles Sumner in October, resentment at the American government's recent conduct, together with the failure to define the struggle as an antislavery crusade, was certain to undermine popular sympathy for the North in Great Britain.[85] For *The Times*'s correspondent, this was a deeply unsatisfactory condition, which the events of the next few months would only serve to aggravate.

The arrest of the Confederate envoys James M. Mason and John Slidell from the British steamship *Trent* on 8 November 1861 should have provided William Howard Russell with the perfect opportunity to revive his faltering mission: in the event, the *Trent* affair merely demonstrated how ineffectual the special correspondent had now become. Although the gradual easing of northern resentment had produced some improvement in Russell's personal circumstances, notably in his relationship with the secretary of state, throughout most of the diplomatic crisis he remained completely in the dark as to the Federal government's intentions and right up until the final announcement appeared convinced that the two prisoners would not be given up.[86]

The settlement of the *Trent* affair was a major victory for pragmatic diplomacy; for *The Times*'s correspondent, however, it was but

another milestone in his increasingly abortive career in the United
States. "I have now been a year in this country all but a few days &
I am I fear more & more unpopular each moment I stay here," he reported back in mid-February.[87] A brief trip to Canada provided some
respite but failed to mollify his employers at Printing House Square
who had become increasingly frustrated at the lack of progress. *"You
must either go to the front or come home,"* demanded Mowbray Morris
at the beginning of March.[88] To the harassed correspondent such
peremptory advice was far from welcome. Since the late summer
of 1861 Russell had made repeated requests for permission to accompany the Federal army on its projected advance in Virginia but
to little avail, and with the new campaign season approaching, he
was clearly unprepared to continue his mission under such adverse
circumstances. In late March the special correspondent came under
renewed attack in the North after accusations that he had used confidential knowledge about the release of Mason and Slidell for his own
advantage. The charge was almost entirely without foundation, but
it only served to confirm the impotence of Russell's situation in the
United States. After a final rebuff from the War Department, which
left him "hideously outraged" according to one American source, he
sailed for England on the Cunard steamship *China*, arriving home
at the end of April 1862.[89]

Although the possibility was discussed at Printing House Square,[90]
Russell did not return to the United States before the end of the
Civil War. Nor was he ever fully informed of the reasons behind the
Federal government's refusal to grant him an army pass. Despite
the *Trent* settlement, by the spring of 1862 hostility to *The Times*
was universal in the United States, and in a confidential letter to
John Bigelow at the end of June Secretary of State Seward confirmed
that it was this above all that was responsible for the action against
Russell. "The Secretary of War does not propose to have any discussion about it, and certainly I can afford to engage in none," Seward
admitted candidly.[91] It is also likely that Russell was the victim of
political skirmishing between the newly installed secretary of war,
Edwin M. Stanton, and the army commander, General McClellan,
although here again nothing was ever publicly revealed.[92]

On returning to England the special correspondent was soon pre-
occupied with reviving his ever-depleted finances. A small annuity
from *The Times* furnished some assistance, and in July 1862 he be-

came half owner and full-time editor of the *Army and Navy Gazette* at an annual salary of over £1,200. A few months later Russell also completed his two-volume account of his American visit, based on his private notebooks and dispatches, which was published the following year as *My Diary North and South.* His views on the transatlantic conflict, however, were now clearly at odds with the increasingly jaundiced editorial pronouncements of his employers, and as a result, he was given no opportunity to comment further on American affairs in *The Times.* Although obviously distressed by his treatment in the United States, his belief in both the moral and strategic superiority of the Federal cause never faltered. "Russell says everywhere that the North is ennobled by its devotion, and that its Army is the best in the world," confirmed Thurlow Weed from London in May 1862.[93] For the remainder of the war, in fact, the special correspondent remained convinced that British opinion in general, and Delane in particular, had seriously misjudged the American struggle and that this misjudgment would have lasting consequences for future relations between the two countries.[94]

The Civil War was not the last adventure of William Howard Russell's extraordinary career; but, Bull Run notwithstanding, a great opportunity had been missed in America, and in future campaigns—including the Franco-Prussian War of 1870–71 and the Zulu War of 1879–80—the special correspondent discovered how difficult it was to recapture the glories of Balaclava and Lucknow.[95] In January 1867 his wife, Mary, died after years of physical and mental deterioration. Though deeply saddening, her passing undoubtedly encouraged Russell to fulfill many of the private social and cultural ambitions that had hitherto eluded him. Foreign travel, in particular, remained an abiding passion, and over the next quarter of a century he revisited many of his old haunts, including India and, in 1881, the United States, where he was gratified to be received at the White House by the recently elected president, James A. Garfield. Three years later Russell remarried, his bride a thirty-six-year-old Italian countess, Antoinette Malvezzi. By all accounts it was a highly successful relationship, providing Russell with the care and companionship that he had always craved and that his advancing years increasingly demanded. Remarkably, Antoinette also managed to reorganize the family's finances so that by the beginning of 1885 Russell found himself in the unusual predicament of solvency. Toward the end of his life he also achieved belated recognition from the British establishment. A knighthood in 1895 was followed seven years later by investiture as a commander of the Royal Victorian Order. Sir William Howard Russell died at his home in London on 10 February 1907, a few weeks short of his eighty-eighth birthday.[96]

Notes

1. Thackeray to Mrs. Baxter, 24 May 1861, in Gordon N. Ray, ed., *The Letters and Private Papers of William Makepeace Thackeray*, 4 vols. (London, 1946), 4:235.

2. For Russell's pre–Civil War career, see Alan Hankinson, *Man of Wars: William Howard Russell of The Times* (London, 1982), 7–153, a first-rate study. There are two other biographies of the special correspondent: John Black Atkins, *The Life of Sir William Howard Russell, C.V.O., LL.D.*, 2 vols. (London, 1911); and Rupert Furneaux, *The First War Correspondent: William Howard Russell of The Times* (London, 1944).

3. Hankinson, *Man of Wars*, 28.

4. Hankinson, *Man of Wars*, 42–43.

5. For the early history of the newspaper, see *The History of The Times*, vol. 1, *"The Thunderer" in the Making* (London, 1935); and vol. 2, *The Tradition Established* (London, 1939).

6. See Hankinson, *Man of Wars*, 35. On Delane, see Arthur Irwin Dasent, *John Thadeus Delane, Editor of "The Times": His Life and Correspondence*, 2 vols. (London, 1908), and the briefer but more insightful biography by Sir Edward Cook, *Delane of The Times* (London, 1916).

7. See Brian Inglis, "The Influence of *The Times*," *Historical Studies* (Cork, 1961), 39–41.

8. Philip Knightly, *The First Casualty: The War Correspondent as Hero, Propagandist, and Myth Maker from the Crimea to Vietnam* (London, 1975), 4. For Russell's Crimean activities, see Hankinson, *Man of Wars*, 46–104; and *History of The Times* 2:166–92.

9. Hankinson, *Man of Wars*, 118–43.

10. Hankinson, *Man of Wars*, 146.

11. Hankinson, *Man of Wars*, 147–48.

12. Margaret Clapp, *Forgotten First Citizen: John Bigelow* (Boston, 1947), 125, describes how the two men first met.

13. See John Bigelow, *Retrospections of an Active Life*, 5 vols. (New York, 1909, 1913), 1:280–81.

14. *The Times*, 22 March 1860. See John Bigelow to William H. Seward, 22 March 1860, Seward Papers, Rush Rhees Library, University of Rochester.

15. Martin Crawford, "Anglo-American Perspectives: J. C. Bancroft Davis, New York Correspondent of *The Times*, 1854–1861," *New-York Historical Society Quarterly* 62 (July 1978): 191–217.

16. Mowbray Morris to J. C. Bancroft Davis, 22 February 1861, Manager's Letter Books, News International Record Office, London.

17. Hankinson, *Man of Wars*, 148–53.

18. Martin Crawford, *The Anglo-American Crisis of the Mid-Nineteenth Century: The Times and America, 1850–1862* (Athens, 1987), 15–35.

19. For the history of Anglo-American relations during the late antebellum period, see Wilbur Devereux Jones, *The American Problem in British Diplomacy, 1841–1861* (London, 1974); and Kenneth Bourne, *Britain and the Balance of Power in North America, 1815–1908* (London, 1967), 75–205.

20. The economic relationship is analyzed in detail in Jim Potter, "Atlantic Economy, 1815–1860: The U.S.A. and the Industrial Revolution," in L. S. Pressnell, ed., *Studies in the Industrial Revolution* (London, 1960), 236–80.

21. Crawford, *Anglo-American Crisis*, 9–11.

22. *The Times*, 17 March 1853.

23. John Thadeus Delane to Lord Clarendon, 2 December 1856, in Dasent, *John Thadeus Delane* 1:248.

24. *The Times*, 25 October 1855.

25. See, for example, *The Times*, 1 February 1850. The impact of American society and politics upon Great Britain is explored in two outstanding works: D. P. Crook, *American Democracy in English Politics, 1815–1850* (Oxford, 1965); and Frank Thistlethwaite, *The Anglo-American Connection in the Early Nineteenth Century* (Philadelphia, 1959). For *The Times*'s own responses, see Crawford, *Anglo-American Crisis*, 39–55.

26. Howard Temperley, *British Antislavery, 1833–1877* (London, 1972), 221–47.

27. Crawford, *Anglo-American Crisis*, 56–61.

28. *The Times*, 11 February 1857.

29. See, for example, *The Times*, 21 July, 22 September 1860. The search for an alternative cotton supply is thoroughly examined in Arthur W. Silver's *Manchester Men and Indian Cotton, 1847–1892* (Manchester, 1960).

30. See John Bright to Charles Sumner, 20 November 1861, Sumner Papers, Houghton Library, Harvard University.

31. *The Times*, 20 November 1860.

32. *The Times*, 29 November 1860.

33. See the important editorial statement in *The Times*, 12 March 1861. The evolution of the paper's policy during the secession period is explored in detail in Crawford, *Anglo-American Crisis*, 75–105.

34. *The Times*, 6 April 1861.

35. William Howard Russell, *My Diary North and South*, 2 vols. (London, 1863), 1:7–8.

36. J. Dillon to Mowbray Morris, 6 April 1861, Morris Papers, News International Record Office.

37. Russell to John Bigelow, 4 February 1861, in Bigelow, *Retrospections* 1:346–47.

38. John Bigelow to William H. Seward, 19 March 1861, Seward Papers.

39. Mowbray Morris to Russell, 4, 10 April 1861, Manager's Letter Books, News International Record Office.

40. *New York Daily Tribune*, 20 March 1861, in Howard Cecil Perkins, ed., *Northern Editorials on Secession*, 2 vols. (New York, 1942), 2:939.

41. See Russell, *Diary North and South* 1:47–49, for a memorable description.

42. Russell, *Diary North and South* 1:57.

43. Russell diary, 26 March 1861, News International Record Office.

44. Seward's diplomatic strategy is sympathetically reviewed in Norman B. Ferris, *Desperate Diplomacy: William H. Seward's Foreign Policy, 1861* (Knoxville, 1976). More critical is Brian Jenkins, *Britain and the War for the Union*, 2 vols. (Montreal, 1974, 1980), 1:25ff.

45. Russell to J. C. Bancroft Davis, 14 April 1861, Davis Papers, Library of Congress, Washington.

46. Ward's letters to George Ellis Baker, the secretary of state's friend and associate, written under a pseudonym, provide an important commentary on Russell's progress in the South. See Carlos or Charles Lopez to George E. Baker, 19 April, 18 June, 7 July 1861, Seward Papers.

47. Russell, *Diary North and South* 1:157.

48. C. Vann Woodward, ed., *Mary Chesnut's Civil War* (New Haven, 1981), 88.

49. Russell, *Diary North and South* 1:243.

50. Russell, *Diary North and South* 1:251.

51. Russell, *Diary North and South* 1:239.

52. Russell to Lord Lyons, 21 May 1861, Lyons Papers, West Sussex County Record Office, Chichester.

53. *Harper's Weekly*, 27 July 1861.

54. Russell, *Diary North and South* 1:232.

55. *The Times*, 30 May 1861.

56. Russell, *Diary North and South* 1:371–72.

57. *The Times*, 7 June 1861.

58. Russell to Lord Lyons, 21 May 1861, Lyons Papers.

59. See, for example, *The Times*, 30 May, 10 July 1861.

60. See Russell, *Diary North and South* 2:1–87, 96–119, for the final stages of the correspondent's tour.

61. See Jenkins, *Britain and the War for the Union* 1:91–128; Frank J. Merli, *Great Britain and the Confederate Navy, 1861–1865* (Bloomington, 1970), 19–47; and David P. Crook, *The North, the South, and the Powers,*

1861–1865 (New York, 1974), 71–81. Highly critical of the British government's action is Ferris, *Desperate Diplomacy*, 203–4.

62. Edward Everett to Lord John Russell, 28 May 1861, Everett Papers, Massachusetts Historical Society, Boston.

63. See, for example, Duke of Argyll to Charles Sumner, 4 June 1861, Sumner Papers.

64. Russell to William H. Seward, 10 July 1861, Seward Papers.

65. Russell, *Diary North and South* 2:124–26.

66. Sarah Agnes Wallace and Frances Elma Gillespie, eds., *The Journal of Benjamin Moran, 1857–1865*, 2 vols. (Chicago, 1948), 2:858, 5 August 1861.

67. Thomas J. Keiser, "The English Press and the American Civil War" (Unpublished Ph.D. diss., University of Reading, 1971), 164.

68. Russell to J. C. Bancroft Davis, 22 July 1861, Henry Sanford Papers, Sanford Memorial Library, Sanford, Florida.

69. See Russell to J. C. Bancroft Davis, 24 August 1861, Davis Papers.

70. Russell, *Diary North and South* 2:284–94.

71. Russell to J. C. Bancroft Davis, 25 September 1861, Davis Papers.

72. Russell, diary, 6 November 1861.

73. Russell, diary, 10 September 1861. See James M. McPherson, *Battle Cry of Freedom: The Civil War Era* (New York, 1988), 311–12, 352–58, for divisions in the North over the slavery issue.

74. Bigelow, *Retrospections* 1:370.

75. Wilbur R. Jacobs, ed., *The Letters of Francis Parkman*, 2 vols. (Norman, 1960), 1:141; Parkman to the *Boston Daily Advertiser*, 28 August 1861.

76. Charles Sumner to Russell, 16 September 1861, in Edward L. Pierce, *Memoirs and Letters of Charles Sumner*, 4 vols. (Boston, 1881–93), 4:42–43.

77. *Albany Evening Journal*, 23 September 1861.

78. See William H. Seward, 21 September 1861, in *The War of the Rebellion: A Compilation of the Official Records of the Union and Confederate Armies*, 128 vols. (Washington, D.C., 1881–1902), ser. 2, vol. 2:74.

79. Mowbray Morris to J. C. Bancroft Davis, 7 August 1861, Manager's Letter Books. The printed letter, to Charles Sumner, and dated 31 August 1861, is in the Sumner Papers. The Massachusetts senator declined to have his name attached to it, however. See Russell, *Diary North and South* 2:350–62, for the trip to the West.

80. Russell to John T. Delane, 13 September 1861, Russell Papers, News International Record Office.

81. Hankinson, *Man of Wars*, 178. See also Crawford, *Anglo-American Crisis*, 121–23, for the impact of Russell's problems upon Printing House Square's editorial policies.

82. For some tantalizing glimpses of the special correspondent's character, see Bayley Ellen Marks and Mark Norton Schatz, eds., *Between North*

and South: The Narrative of William Wilkins Glenn, 1861–1869 (Rutherford, 1976), 50; Fitzgerald Ross, *Cities and Camps of the Confederate States*, ed. Richard Barksdale Harwell (Urbana, 1958), 139–40; and Major-General Sir George Bell, *Soldier's Glory: Being "Rough Notes of an Old Soldier,"* ed. Brian Stuart (London, 1956), 309.

83. Russell to Charles Sumner, 31 August 1861, Sumner Papers.

84. See, for example, Russell diary, 2 September, 15 October, 29 November 1861.

85. Russell to Charles Sumner, 14 October 1861, Sumner Papers.

86. See Russell, *Diary North and South* 2:422; and Russell to John T. Delane, 20 December 1861, Delane Papers.

87. Russell to Mowbray Morris, 16 February 1862, Russell Papers, News International Record Office. See also Allan Nevins and Milton Halsey Thomas, eds., *The Diary of George Templeton Strong*, 4 vols. (New York, 1952), 3:200–201, 2 January 1862, for further evidence of Russell's continuing unpopularity in the North. The occasion was an incident at the New York Club which the correspondent was visiting at the invitation of Sam Ward. The invitation was bitterly denounced by two of the club's members.

88. Mowbray Morris to Russell, 6 March 1862, Manager's Letter Books.

89. John Hay, *Lincoln and the Civil War in the Diaries and Letters of John Hay*, ed. Tyler Dennett (New York, 1939), 39. For the closing weeks in the United States, see Hankinson, *Man of Wars*, 176–81.

90. See Sam Ward to William H. Seward, 7 June, 18 June 1862; Charles Mackay to Seward, 28 May 1862, Seward Papers.

91. William H. Seward to John Bigelow, 25 June 1862, in Bigelow, *Retrospections* 1:488–89. See also John Bigelow to Russell, 8 May 1862, Bigelow Papers, New York Public Library, New York.

92. See Benjamin P. Thomas and Harold M. Hyman, *Stanton: The Life and Times of Lincoln's Secretary of War* (New York, 1962), 169–71, 174–79, 182–91.

93. Thurlow Weed to William H. Seward, 13 May 1862, Seward Papers.

94. See Russell, diary, 28 September 1863, 12 June 1865, quoted in Hankinson, *Man of Wars*, 182; and Russell to John Bigelow, 8 March 1865, Seward Papers. For Printing House Square's attitude toward the American war after 1861, see *History of The Times* 2:374–91; and Crawford, *Anglo-American Crisis*, 135–37.

95. See Hankinson, *Man of Wars*, 211–26, 242–50; and Atkins, *Life* 2:160–240, 278–312.

96. Russell's final years are sensitively described in Hankinson, *Man of Wars*, 251–66.

Private Diary and Letters, 1861–1862

ONE

To New York
and Washington

March 4, 1861
Lat. 51°16. Lon. 11°50. Run 145 miles.
Breeze rather fresh—no land in sight—wind on quarter. Course
W. by S. At 8.30 most plentiful breakfast. Capt. Stone on my right
Balaklava acquaintance, when Arabia carried troops to Kin[bur]n.[1]
Reminded me of Beatty,[2] poor Kate Willans,[3] Mary[4] dining in my hut.
Says French art[iller]y of Gréard[5] best troops he ever carried. The
arrangements on board these ships most liberal as far as grog grub
cooking &c. are concerned. Excellent lunch at 12 of what you please—
dinner at 4, tea at 7.30, supper from 9.30. My berth comrade is young
Irishman going out as doctor to 2d. W[est] I[ndies] Reg[imen]t at
Nassau.[6] Few appear at meals. There is one remarkable stout young
lady who distinguishes herself by the felicity with wh. she manages
at intervals to fly like an avalanche along the deck from her seat at
the more heavy lurches. A young Sec[retar]y of legation at Peters-
burgh[7] introduces himself to me—he has left service & is going to his
State South Carolina. He is strong as to the individual sovereignty of
States & thinks Calhoun's doctrine[8] on ye subject incontrovertible.
There is a power of jaw & eye about the young man indicative of
ability. I pressed him as to this. How can you secede unless Federal
G[overnmen]t has made a breach of contract with you. Suppose you
were attacked by a great State, how wd. you act as Sov[ereig]n State.
Is it to South Carolina or to Federal Govt. you as native of S.C. wd.
look in case of outrage abroad? &c. He is persuaded the North will

3

attempt war by blockade & in that case the South must act by land—
probably in Virginia he thinks. I went to bed considerably refreshed
by reading Lyell's second book on U.S.[9] which is really worth perusal.
Wind increasing gradually & heading us decidedly. There is no fear
of ice they say at this time of year. June & July are the worst months
for the bergs. Capt. Stone gives a very high character of the "Arabia".

1. The *Arabia* was built on the River Clyde in 1852, the last wooden ship in the
Cunard Line fleet. She was over 86 meters in length and weighed 2,402 tons, with
side-lever engines generally believed to be too powerful for her wooden hull. In 1854
she was requisitioned as an army transport vessel for the British campaign in the
Crimea and in October of the following year took part in the allied attack on the port
of Kinburn.

2. James Beatty (1820–56), engineer in chief of the Crimean railways.

3. Wife of Russell's close friend Obé (or Oby) Willans.

4. Russell's wife, formerly Mary Burrowes. They were married on 16 September
1846. Mary Russell died on 24 January 1867 at the age of 43.

5. Gen. Felix-Valery Gréard (1784–1858), distinguished French soldier.

6. Assistant Surgeon Edward Joseph Bolton, 2nd West Indies Regiment.

7. Julian Mitchell of South Carolina, U.S. consul at St. Petersburg, 1860–61.

8. John Caldwell Calhoun of South Carolina (1782–1850) argued for the constitutional rights of the individual states, notably in the nullification crisis of 1828–33. His
states' rights views derived from the compact theory of the federal Constitution and
formed the basis for the theory of secession.

9. Sir Charles Lyell, eminent British geologist, visited the United States in 1841
and again in 1845–46. His two-volume work, *A Second Visit to the United States of
North America*, was published in 1849 and was notable for its extended discussion of
southern society.

March 5, 1861

Lat. 51°16. Lon. 17°7. Run 200 miles.

A strong head wind—sea cross & disagreeable. The gulls have put
back thinking the games not worth the candle or having no candle to
play withal. Deck wet slippy with incessant spray & the round shield
of which we are the troubled boss presents nothing but ups & downs
& sea horses. Breakfast not much thought of by society generally. I
find Captain does not think much of Fitzroy's prognostications as to
weather.[1] These sailors are so obstinate. He now talks of 14 days &
considers we have scarcely started yet. The British element is decidedly depressed this morning. I invest myself in great waterproof
&c. but of course I cant complete my toilet & so I retire to saloon from
sea & spray & try to write hack this diary of mine. Thinking of my

deenyman.[2] Lincoln is a "rail splitter"—hope he wont be a "Union splitter" says a young American.[3] Hear it was intensely cold this winter in N.Y. I leave deck for a moment. Lo! it flies from one end of cabin to the other like the volatile old lady. Reading is scarcely practicable. The wind blows right in our teeth & the great Atlantic rushes against us.... With diminished power however. For they—waves of the sea—are strong exceedingly. Read Olmsted's book on Slavery[4]— it is amusing. But I fear he cd. draw pictures as strong of misery & ignorance among those in our land who are neither slaveowners nor slaves. The wind rises towards night. The Captain admits it is a fresh breeze at dinner. Something more at nightfall—a wild stormy night. Ship creaking & screaming from every pore. It is very solemn to look out on the wild Atlantic thro' the drift foam & see the armies of the waters moving to battle—with a crest of lance points flashing above them. God is the only help & hope as a young man sd. to me tonight. If I have to cross the Atlantic in March I wd. do anything rather than repeat it....

1. Vice Adm. Robert Fitzroy was the commander of the brig *Beagle* on Charles Darwin's voyages of exploration to South America. A celebrated hydrographer and meteorologist, he is remembered for his Fitzroy barometer, his *Weather Book*, and his system of storm warnings. Fitzroy committed suicide in 1865.

2. One of Russell's numerous nicknames, often shortened to "deeny," for his wife, Mary. Others included "bucky" and "dot."

3. The "rail-splitter" image originated during the 1860 Republican convention in Chicago when some of Abraham Lincoln's supporters paraded in the convention hall with a banner tied to two old fence rails proclaiming him as "The Rail Candidate for President." The banner commemorated Lincoln's early pioneering activities in Macon County, Illinois.

4. In 1861 Frederick Law Olmsted, New York landscape architect and writer, republished his two-volume account of his travels in the South under the title *The Cotton Kingdom*. They were originally published as *A Journey Through Texas* (1857) and *A Journey Through the Back Country* (1860). Russell carried a letter of introduction to Olmsted from his editor, John Thadeus Delane.

March 6, 1861
Lat. 50°53. Lon. 20°40. Run 138 miles.
Well bad as it was the night might have been worse & thank God morning broke on us all right. One of our passenger is a character des plens doles. A very stout broadbacked large bellied man with short puffy legs & flabby feet worn in slippers, a big double chinned

heavy cheeked smooth shaven face—clear light blue glistening eyes, fresh complexion, mouth wreathed with perpetual smiles on everybody & thing, a head covered with curly grey hair in neat wispy twists. He goes about with a carpet bag & a cigar a foot long always in his hand in a dress black coat, cap & slippers unless when he is busied as he is for hours at a time writing as he says "law papers". He hails from Madras & says he has been 45 years in the service & that he is a lawyer bound to America on business. I shd. like to know who he is. Somehow I suspect something which I don't know how to explain. As I was in the smoking place tonight entered into conversation with Dr. Bolton 2d. W.I.R. & another who turned out to be Hall against whom a very awkward little bit appeared in A[rmy] & N[avy] G[azette].[1] His wife is on board [...]. He admitted par[agraph] was true & I explained circumstances under which it appeared in paper. There is a nice little round Frenchman a planter in Louisiana who is a very marked person of the sort.

1. A journal devoted to military affairs, first published in January 1860, with Russell as editor. It later became the *Army, Navy and Air Force Gazette* and in 1936 the *United Services Review*, ceasing publication in September 1939.

March 7, 1861
Lat. 50°48. Lon. 25°30. Run 192 miles.
There is some fun to be got out of the Captain as he seems aware of himself. I write some letters. But there is a general difficulty in doing anything well at the far end of the saloon, close to the rudder—there is great motion. I am amused to find that the Americans—at least some of them imagine I am writing about them or am going to the U.S. to "do" a book of travels. The Cunard line assuredly deserves credit for a very liberal comfortable cuisine—how they manage it I don't know. It is unspeakably superior to the P & O.[1] But all liquids are paid for & are good of their kind. Breakfast whatever you like at 8.30, lunch hot soup cold meat &c. at 12, dinner at 4 (keep a bill of fare of a windy day), very good, tea 7 or so, & then supper whatever you like from 9 or so till 10. Lights out in cabin at 12 o'clock. March is about one of the worst months of the year for the Atlantic.

1. The Cunard Line was first organized in 1839 by Samuel Cunard, Robert Napier, and other shippers as the British North American Royal Mail Steam Packet Co. It soon achieved dominance on the transatlantic route. The P. & O. was organized in 1835 as the Peninsular Steam Navigation Co., with routes to Spain and Portugal but in 1840

added Oriental to its name as its operations expanded to Egypt and subsequently the Far East.

March 8, 1861

A schooner British in sight today about noon or so.
Lat. 49°16. Lon. 30°34. Run 268 miles.
Wind hauled round to the eastward and came up fresh by degrees—set all canvas & people came up on deck & looked sociable. There is a Swedish ex. capt. cavalry (lame) whom I like very much on board. He has a hearty hatred of Russians wh. is refreshing. Chief Officer Anderson tells pleasant stories—of icebergs &c. their times seasons courses. We make up to 11 knots. But as day wears on wind comes S. with rain in drift. Miss Tracy & Miss Moss or Morse, rum old girl bored us about American constitution &c. &c. It appears to be a general complaint on part of Americans that swell English come over & make hail fellow well met, & don't notice their hosts & friends when the latter come to England. Miss Morse begs of me not to put her in my book & I assure her I have noted all her faults, & will do so unless I am bribed. "The Irish in the towns shd. not be allowed to vote as they are—mean ignorant creatures who swamp the respectable people in New York & elsewhere. The press too is over free & shd. be restrained." The Irish are useful in their way making roads &c. "But then pigs must be free also." Young Brown nephew of the W[illia]m M[ember of] P[arliament] Liverpool[1] says his father & uncle were about sailing in privateer ag[ains]t England when accident fixed W[illia]m in England where he founded the great house. He has been over to see the little house near the Giant's Causeway where his race was cradled & speaks unaffectedly & nicely about it. The Tracys also of Irish descent are proud of English connection. Both have very old relations of Celtic stock alive. Dinner passes rather pleasantly as we have plenty of conversation at our table in which Cameron,[2] Tracy, Brown, Miss Morse, the Swede who fait beaux yeux à mlle. join. The old man from India writes away as usual. Children showed today. There were feeble efforts at singing in the smoke room wh. did not go beyond bad negro melodies & worse marseillaise. And so to bed— a wild night my masters. How utterly helpless man feels even in the greatest of his works when face to face with those of his maker.

1. Clarence Brown, nephew of William Brown, M.P. for Lancashire South, 1846–57. He enlisted as a private in the 7th New York Regiment at the outbreak of the war and was later commissioned, serving as an aide to Gen. Irvin McDowell.

2. John Hillyard Cameron, a prominent Toronto Conservative politician, lawyer, and businessman. He was grandmaster of the Protestant Orange order in Canada.

March 9, 1861

Noon Lat. 47°38. Long. 34°38. Run = 184 miles.
A bitter fierce N.W. gale & very heavy sea. The "Arabia" behaves very well as to heavy seas but it is too indulgent to spray & light water & lets in so much our cabins are wettish & deck is inches deep in water. The Atlantic lashed into foaming mountain waves is really "a grand sight—that's a fact stranger." Ah indeed a sight, grand awful overwhelming. Knocked to & fro on its surface is our little world, laughing fearing thinking eating smoking chatting silent sick. Captain is restive at b[rea]kfast. An antipathy seizes me to the Germans on board, beasts I think—one selfish brute threw himself into my corner, which I was keeping for Cameron of Canada.... I waited till Cameron came up & then started him by saying "he is too selfish to move." No he said he was not & bolted with growls. Sighted a steamer supposed to be Jura[1] steering E. Wind bitter cold as we go on. Message from the sea very poor stuff. Hail now & then. Cameron wants me badly to come to Toronto. He says it wd. be of immense service to Canada to set her case plainly before England, to develop her resources, to attract emigration, expand her commerce &c. We play a rubber of whist in the evening in spite of the sea—our soup hops into our lap. The steps of ye paddlebox broken by a sea. It is terribly trying work for the officers & men of the ship to face such wind frozen & fierce on the hurricane deck. I write some of my diary & find my old friend constant in his place. He is named Orme, & is he says partner of Bruce Norton[2]— going out to America to look for some property which belonged to some remote ancestor! Can such chases of wild geese be and overcome the goose at last? I had serious thoughts last night of noting one's sensations in a cabin—during a breeze—describing the motions &c. the dipping, sliding, sinking, bowing, jerking, sloping, mounting, falling flapping grimacing darting digging, dashing crashing motions.

1. The Cunard iron screw steamship *Jura*. When launched in 1854, it was, at over 95 meters, the longest steamship in the world.
2. John Bruce Norton, barrister and clerk of the crown of the supreme court in Madras. He later served as advocate general in Madras.

March 10, 1861
Lat. 46°41. Lon. 38°13. Run = 169 miles.
We had prayers at 10.30 read by Cameron, nearly all ye passengers
of various denominations were present. I was amused to see that the
Americans wd. not pray for H.M. Prince Consort & rest of the Royal
Family. Brown & Tracy au moins. Cameron is married to a lady[1] who
is descended from Roger Williams[2] & has the land on which he first
landed. Read B[isho]p Oxford's review of Reviews & Essays in Quarterly[3] which I think a very confused very stupid exhibition of small
critical cantery. To criticize in the real style of the Quarterly as of old
is difficult. But the old Review, which was a general dissertation set
out with all the learning & ability of the writer respecting the article
treated of by the words under consideration in which the views of
the authors were taken as casual expositions of different opinions,
was a very much more instructive mode of treating questions than
that of small criticism on numerous quotations. The Bishop is much
afraid the evident piety of some of the contributors will do much mischief to the young. If his acc[oun]t of Williams be true there can be
no doubt his teaching is dangerous and disingenuous. Soapy Sam
has however much to answer for in reference to these very questions
for he undoubtedly was one of the leaders of Young England in the
church & his supposed tendency to Puseyism[4] seemed confirmed by
many opinions & acts of his earlier ecclesiastical life.
I had a long conversation today with Cameron as to Orangemen of
Canada. He lays all ye blame on Duke of Newcastle because the latter
did not stop ye preparations for ye Orange receptions of which he
must have been aware, Cameron says, from the papers. Cameron
really thinks the Prince shd. have gone under the Orange arch with
the picture of William III above it.[5] He does not know how mealy
mouthed we are in Ireland & everywhere as to our R[oman] C[atholic]
brethren—justly so at times—no doubt.

1. John Hillyard Cameron's second wife, the former Ellen Mallet, daughter of an
American soldier. They were married in 1849.
2. Roger Williams (1602–82/83), dissident Puritan clergyman and founder of Rhode
Island.
3. Samuel Wilberforce, known as "Soapy Sam," Bishop of Oxford from 1848 until
his death in 1873. His critical review of *Reviews and Essays*, a collection of seven
essays reflecting liberal theological thought, was published in the *Quarterly Review*
109 (January 1860): 248–301.
4. An Anglo-Catholic movement that sought to oppose the spread of liberal ratio-

nalist theology in England. Its leading light was Edward Pusey, Oxford scholar and theologian.

5. Touring Canada in 1860, the Prince of Wales was advised by the Duke of Newcastle, the colonial secretary, not to give any official recognition to the Orange order, which was banned in Great Britain. This infuriated Canada's Orangemen, who unsuccessfully contrived at various places to get the young prince to pass under Orange arches. John Hillyard Cameron, as grandmaster, sought to restrain Orange anger but also initiated a huge petition condemning the Duke of Newcastle's actions, which he presented in London.

March 11, 1861

242 miles in the day. When I took my first peep on deck this morning I was rejoiced to see a fair canvas spread out before a stiff breeze. Alas too stiff for it was somewhat too much on the beam & buried us. Still we ran over 11 knots & did our 242 miles. I had some fun with Miss Morse this morning. She is an admirable specimen of the strong minded, rather ill educated (in our sense) American woman— a mass of vulgar prejudices. I told her she shd. not talk of the Pilgrim Fathers. Rather she should speak of the "Pilgrim Mothers"—& I threatened her with "annexation"—with a Marquis of Missouri & Duke of New York &c. Every one reads & abuses the New York Herald. In course of discussion it comes out that at Sing Sing prison near New York there is still torture in use, ie. dripping water on ye heads of recusant prisoners, & a sort of thumb screw.[1] The irritation against ye Irish element is very strongly expressed by the New Yorkers. They swamp local elections & put power in the hands of the lowest order of citizens. Another object[io]n to them comes from ye Southerners— it is curious. The Irish form a large part of the United States Regular Army. In case of a conflict the "low Irish mercenaries" would be matched against the best blood of the South who wd. be obliged to fight like common soldiers, & these "gentlemen" would be killed by the lowest Irish whose lives are worth nothing. The Irish it appears are regarded as mere food for powder. Poor Paddy—his facility of reproduction is a wonderful natural counterpoise to his tendency to exercise the bump of destructiveness. The Southerners are determined to fight tho' they say the proprietors will be obliged in taking the field to leave their families at the mercy of slaves "who *may* be hounded on to violence by abolitionist emissaries." We eat drink sleep & play our friendly rubber as usual. And to bed at 12—wind still bowling us along. Sea very smooth.

1. Sing Sing prison was built in 1825 by convict labor on a site thirty-three miles from New York City at what is now Ossining. During its early years the prison was notorious for the cruelty and corruption of its regime. It was a favorite stopping spot for European visitors to the United States.

March 12, 1861
Lat. 44°26. Lon. 49°44. Run 262 miles.
The commencement of the page beyond refers to this day & date. We are running 11 knots & over. Bien. The fat Frenchman with the capote is lively this morning. He has never washed since he came on board—nonetheless he is gai & now delivered from his demon sea sickness has brisked up amazingly & sparkles from under his crust of dirt like a stream of corking lava. He lies prostrate for days in the gentlemen's cabin feeding in light slops & groaning consumedly. The rest of his compatriots all day work away at the Game of Horses for infinitesimal stakes. Speak Canton at 11 a.m. Bitter cold on deck ice-bergy. There is nothing particular to inquire about. Play rubber in ye evening & lose many points. Ladies named Brown[1] came up from the deep—very fierce slaveyholders who do the whole slave doctrine first rate.
Very bright star light—thermo 30°. The motion of the ship scarcely perceptible, & the great Atlantic as mild as new milk. There is not a motion perceptible at times save the tremor of the paddles.

> Alas! Alas! How sad
> that I must wash
> with water!
> The thought will
> drive *me mad*
> He lay sick for nigh
> 10 days on the sofa in
> the cabin below.

> The man who never
> washed. Français.
> For fourteen days in
> dirt he laid
> Wrapped in a furl capote
> and every day the dirt's increase
> With pleasure I did note

Until at length as thick it lay
As nap upon a coat

1. Probably the family of John Calvin Brown, Tennessee lawyer and future governor, who was returning to the United States after a recuperative visit to Europe and the Middle East. He served in the Confederate army, reaching the rank of major general. His (second) wife was Elizabeth Childress. They had four children.

March 13, 1861
Lat. 43°11. Lon. 54°55. Run 242
Wind light but right in teeth. Mr. Mitchell informs me that Woods[1] was not at Richmond at all when the Prince visited it & seems to think the acc[oun]t was a lie. *To write & inquire.*
Wind slightly on the beam—sea blue ditto sky wind very cold. Little Brown tells me awful tales of 250 ships which sailed from Liverpool & were never heard of in one year. We jog along very pleasantly. Towards evening there is scarcely any wind & the sea is so smooth as to excite ones admiration. But ye captain says it is not unusual to have fine weather in the middle of March. Cameron tells stories of good shooting in Canada—cutting off heads of wild turkeys with bullets at 180 yards right and left which except from a man of position wd. be incredible. See the force of character—no one would dream of doubting him. Grande negotium. I bought a tarpaulin hat—went up on deck off went hat to sea—a porpoise is now wearing it.

Little know the merry dolphins
What my chapeau cost.

1. Nicholas Woods was a leading descriptive reporter on *The Times*. In October 1860 he accompanied the Prince of Wales on his tour of Canada and the United States.

March 14, 1861
Lat. 42°23. Lon. 60°44. Run 265 miles.
I lose the lottery by only one mile. Breeze light & favourable—a new hat bought by me for ulterior movements.

Our jolly friendly Swede
By German irritated
Was very wroth indeed
Nearly broke his pate did
And so we jog along

In this rum microcosm
With every passion strong
As in a megacosm
The Gods delight
By day & night
To watch over
Our dear Morse
And mitigate
In her behalf
Their laws of
nature's force.

Here be Louisiana French planters
One with 500 slaves—worth
nearly £100,000.

I am obliged to hear some Yankees discussing going South say among themselves it would be very risky work just at present. It is very calm & would be pleasant but a terrible little thing called Brown of Nashville aged 16 is too strong for me. The best behaved woman on board is the wife of a performer in Montreal. I except Miss Tracy who is very nice—poor girl she suffers from some contortion of the neck. I like her very much. She is frank & cheerful. Young Brown is also very good & so is Tracy. Cameron gives a very interesting account of the saving of a man from Niagara by a blacksmith—also particulars of Canada rebellion.

March 15, 1861
Lat. 41°19. Lon. 67°17. Run 300 miles.
As calm as a millpond—wonderful weather! Sea smooth—wind favourable. Look at the result above. Sandyhook is only distant 312 miles. I am driven off into the farthest corner of the saloon by nasalism & nationality. How is it ye Americans are so aggressive? Read Dillon's[1] extracts from N.Y. Herald. It is clear to me that ye South looks forward to a career of conquest & exclusive possession in the Southern part of the continent & Mexico &c. annexation of Cuba &c. &c. All attempts at compromise to judge from speeches &c. are worse than useless & the South courts war & aggression relying perhaps on the aid the supposed necessities of France & England must afford to her. The wind which was favourable increased in violence

Lat 44°36′ Lon 49°.44 Run 262 miles

The commencement of the page beyond refers to this day & date We are running 11 Knots & over. brrr. The fat henchman with the capote is lively this morning. He has never washed since he came on board – nathelefs he is gai & now delivered from his demon sea sickness has brisked up amazingly & sparkles from under his crust of dirt like a stream of Corsij lava – He lies prostrate for days in the gentlemens cabin feeding on light slops & groaning consumedly – The rest of his compatriots all day work away at the frame of horses for infinitesimal Stakes. Speak Canton at 11 am. Bitter cold on deck iceberg. There is nothing particular to inquire about – Play rubber in ye evening & lose many points – Ladies named Brown come up from the deep – very fierce Slavey holders who do the whole slave doctrine first rate.

very bright star light – thermo 30° The motion of the Ship scarcely perceptible, & the great Atlantic as mild as new milk –

There is not a motion perceptible at times save the the tremor of the paddles

Alas! alas! How sad That I must wash with water! The thought will drive me mad

He lay sick for nearly 10 Days on the sofa in the Cabin below —

the man also never washed. Francais

For fourteen days in dirt he laid wrapped in a foul capote And every day the dirt increase with pleasure I did note until at length as thick & clay As rest upon a coal

Two entries from Russell's diary, written on board the
Cunard steamship *Arabia* en route to New York
(News International Record Office)

Lat 42° 23' Lon. 60° 44' — Run 265 miles . I lose the
lottery by only one mile. Breeze light & favourable — a
sew hat bought by me for ulterior movement

Our jolly friendly Swede
By human irri-   -tated
was very wroth   indeed
& nearly broke his   pate did
And so we pog   along
In this own   microcosm
with every   papers tarry
so   in a   megacosm

The Gods delight
By day & night
To watch over
our dear horse
And vindicate
in her behalf
the laws of
natures' force

Here he Louisiana
one with   500
nearly   £

French
slaves &c
100, 000

planters
— with

I am obliged to hear
Some yankees discussing going South say among themselves
it would be very risky work just at present — It is
very calm & would be pleasant but a terrible little
thing called Brown of Markville aged 16 is too
strong for me . The best behaved woman on board is the
wife of a performer in Montreal — I except Miss
Tracy who is very nice — poor girl she suffers from some
contortion of the neck — I like her very much She
is frank & cheerful . Young Brown is also very
good too is Tracy . Cameron gives a very
interesting account of the saving of a man from
Niagara by a blacksmith also particulars of
                              Canada rebellion

& at last blew a whole gale towards midnight accompanied by rain sleet & snow. The darkness was intense. The officers were lashed on deck. The howling of the wind like the roar of a battle—an awful night. Nantucket Shoals somewhere to the N. of us 30 miles. Pleasant stories of shipwreck in the fiddley.[2] I could not sleep a wink. "Arabia" yawed a good deal & now & then seemed inclined to broach to. As if to keep in unison with the weather Miss Morse, Mr. Mitchell, Miss Tracy, Rhedin had a good row & now wont speak. We played whist in spite of the rolling of the vessel. Our expectations of getting into N.Y. by tomorrow look very fishy.

1. John Henry Dillon, an old friend of *The Times*'s editor, John Thadeus Delane, and its manager, Mowbray Morris, was a strong supporter of the South. He had provided Russell with a large collection of articles from the *New York Herald* concerning the American crisis.

2. Iron framework around the hatch leading to the stokehole of the steamer.

March 16, 1861

Growing dark as we haul alongside Custom House.

March 17, 1861 [New York]

Bitter cold snow & frost. Martial music. Bancroft Davis[1] calls & we arrange to go out & see Broadway. Rowan[2] very kind points out sundries to me.... Great stream of women walking about in furs & pretty hats. Hotel has nice "reception" & "Ladies" Room—good dining & second dining room. Kerner[3] old Hollander who served in Wellington's wars.... Must describe house hereafter. Find my bed room is quite dark unless when gas lighted. Walked up 5th. Avenue—lined with ugly clanthus trees. Hotel fine, strait rails & cars horrid, bad pavement, snow not cleared off streets. House very handsome fine Portland carved stone fronts—handsome door way outer doors open, & basement story or stoops very nice. Ends of street unfinished.

1. John Chandler Bancroft Davis was the son of Sen. "Honest John" Davis of Massachusetts and a nephew of the eminent politician and historian George Bancroft. A lawyer by profession, he served as New York correspondent of *The Times* between August 1854 and December 1861. He later served in a variety of public offices, including assistant secretary of state, American agent to the "Alabama" Claims Commission in Geneva, U.S. minister to Berlin, and, for nearly twenty years, reporter to the Supreme Court. He died in 1907 at the age of 84.

2. Col. Henry Sebastian Rowan, Royal Artillery, was commissioned in 1832 and

served in Syria and in the Crimea at the Battle of Inkerman and the siege of Sebastopol. He was awarded the Companion of the Bath in 1857.

3. Mynheer Kerner, a Dutch veteran of Waterloo, was proprietor of the Clarendon
Hotel in New York where Russell was staying.

March 18, 1861

Oh Erin my country. A parade [illeg.] this morning in the bitter bitter
cold.... The 69th. New York. Green uniform green flag harp without
a crown Corcoran[1] commanding.

1. Michael Corcoran, born in County Donegal, Ireland, emigrated to the United
States in 1849. He entered the 69th New York Militia as a private and rose to the rank
of colonel. Wounded and captured at Bull Run, he was exchanged in August 1862 and
promoted to brigadier general. He died in December 1863.

March 19, 1861

It was very late when I got up to b[rea]kfast with a splitting headache.
Denied myself to everyone. Bigelow[1] called. Stay in all day as the
snow was heavy out of doors & day very cold & disagreeable. Wrote
a few lines to Mary & Morris.[2] Saw Mrs. Bigelow[3] [...]. I am much affected by reading my speech in the papers.[4] Oh Lord why *did* I do it?
Papers announce it. I am also invited to give a photographic sitting.
I wish I could collect in ye morning all the thoughts of the evening.
Mr. Earp came into shave me. From him I learned that a man must be
5 years in New York 'ere he gets the franchise. A paper is deliv[ere]d
to him on landing which is produced in 5 years time when he registers
as a voter. If not r[e]g[istere]d he must show by 12 householders he
is entitled. It is asserted I find by Republicans that South meditated
this "treason" a long time. But men are blinded by passion. Seymour[5]
is a man of compromise & yet even his views are rather beyond those
entertained by ultra men 10 years ago. The feeling ag[ains]t the use
of coercive means is very strong & general. As Tylden[6] said however, if an enemy were beleaguering Fort Sumpter the Federal Govt.
would soon find the means of relieving it. Seymour pointed out that
Supreme Court of United States can over rule & abrogate any law of
Congress without hesitations. I dined at J. Duncan Butler's.[7] Sherman[8] sharp snipey little swell. Tylden clever & keen. Lord[9] very good
& sensible. Gov. Seymour is a very shrewd, clear-headed ingenious
excitable man. Old Duncan.[10] B. Davis. Mrs. Duncan charming. Ban-

croft.[11] I took in Mrs. D. to dinner, splendid room. Dinner excellent appointments first rate, wine undeniable. Politics after dinner. Seymour expounded views of constitution, wh. are in effect that Govt. has no force to prevent not secession but in reality Revolution—a thing justified by principles of original compact. Went to Belmont's [12] & was introduced by Bancroft to many pretty & some beautiful girls. A splendid house—pretty collee pictures. To Club where I saw young America dicing & oathing. Drove Young [13] to hotel where was confrere of Dalys [14] member parthenon & so to bed.

1. John Bigelow, New York journalist and diplomat. In August 1861 he was appointed U.S. consul in Paris. Bigelow was Russell's closest American friend, the two men first meeting in Switzerland in 1859.

2. Mowbray Morris, manager of *The Times* from 1847 until 1873.

3. John Bigelow married Jane Poultney, whose family came originally from Maryland, in June 1850. The couple had seven children.

4. On 17 March Russell spoke as an invited guest of the Friendly Society of St. Patrick at the Astor House, New York.

5. Horatio Seymour, leading New York Democratic politician and opponent of Republican war policies. He served as governor from 1853 to 1855 and from 1863 to 1865.

6. Samuel Jones Tilden was a prominent New York Democrat. He subsequently served as governor and, in 1876, was the defeated candidate for the presidency.

7. Jane Butler Duncan, formerly Jane Percy Sargent, was the wife of William Butler Duncan, conservative New York banker and partner in Duncan, Sherman and Co.

8. William Watts Sherman, Duncan's banking partner.

9. Henry W. Lord of Michigan was U.S. consul in Manchester from 1861 to 1868. He was originally from Massachusetts.

10. William Butler Duncan's father, Alexander Duncan, who emigrated to the United States from Scotland in the winter of 1821–22 aged 17 and founded the banking firm of Duncan, Sherman and Co. in 1851. He subsequently retired to Scotland.

11. George Bancroft, historian, politician, and diplomat. He was a former secretary of the navy and from 1846 to 1849 served as U.S. minister to Great Britain.

12. August Belmont, prominent New York banker and Democrat and former U.S. minister to the Netherlands. The Belmont house, with its impressive picture gallery, was a focal point for wealthy New York society.

13. William Young, editor of the *Albion*, a New York weekly paper devoted to British interests and news. He was the son of an English admiral.

14. Judge Charles Patrick Daly, chief justice of the New York Court of Common Pleas and a leading figure in the city's social and political life.

March 20, 1861

Snow on the ground. Up at 9.30 & down to b[rea]kfast where were Bigelow, Rowan & 3 leddies. Shad not good—rice cakes & treacle better, hominy excellent, butter & bread so so. Clarence Brown tells me tariff[1] must be repealed. Stuart great dry goods[2] has counter-manded all orders & he does 800,000 drs. a year. (Visited his maga-zins very remarkable Broadway). New York will be ruined if per-sisted in. Went out with Rowan after visit from Pascoe Glyn,[3] & Rhedin—also from Alexander begging Irishman late of L[iver]pool press, Galloway ditto Scot. Left letter at Grinnells,[4] worked down to Bancroft Davis—talked politics. Sherman says Quincy Adams ad-mitted reparation as of right in 1839.[5] Tribune has article on my speech at Irish dinner. Bigelow gave me letters to Washington, visited Appleton's[6]—very fine library indeed & enormous bookbinding es-tabl[ishment] &c. They sell a million Webster spelling books a year.[7] Wikoff[8] called on return to ask me to dinner at Gordon Bennett's[9] tomorrow. Don't forget funeral French 55th. Reg[imen]t very good class carriage. Coffin with armaments, band soldiers &c. excellent effect—to inquire about order of Cincinnati(us)?[10]

1. The Morrill Tariff was passed on 20 February 1861 by the Republican-dominated Congress. Though only moderately protectionist, it nonetheless appreciably raised tar-iff duties above existing levels and marked the reversal of the long-term trend toward free trade.

2. Alexander Turney Stewart, an Irish immigrant, owned the largest dry goods retail establishment in New York.

3. Pascoe Charles Glyn, third son of the first Lord Wolverton and later Liberal M.P. for Dorset East.

4. Moses Hicks Grinnell, wealthy New York businessman and former Whig con-gressman. In 1861 he was commissioner of charities and commissions in New York City.

5. In 1839 former president John Quincy Adams acted as counsel for fifty-three black slaves who had mutinied and killed the captain and crew of the Spanish slaver *Amistad*. They were detained in Washington, while Spanish authorities demanded reparations under the terms of existing treaties between the two countries. The slaves were eventually freed by the Supreme Court on the grounds that Spain had outlawed the African slave trade in 1820.

6. A leading New York publisher and bookseller founded in 1838 by Daniel Appleton and his son William H. Appleton.

7. *The American Spelling Book* by Noah Webster (1758–1843) was first published in 1785 and by 1837, according to the author's own estimate, had sold more than 15 million copies.

8. Henry Wikoff, known as the Chevalier, American traveler, adventurer, and writer.

9. James Gordon Bennett, publisher and editor of the *New York Herald* from 1835 to 1867.

10. The Society of Cincinnati was established in 1783 as a fraternal organization of Continental Army officers and their descendents, with George Washington as its first president. The order was opposed by Republican groups for its supposed aristocratic character. In 1861 its president was Hamilton Fish.

March 21, 1861
I dined at Hurlbert's.[1]

1. William Henry Hurlbert, a native of Charleston, South Carolina, was a writer and journalist with the *New York Times*. He later became editor-in-chief of the *New York World*.

March 22, 1861
Awful morning. Snow storm &c. Dined Bancrofts.

March 23, 1861
Ground covered with snow. No attempt to clear it away. I am attacked by begging letter imposters. Visited armoury Viele[1].... Dined Ward,[2] Lambs Club.[3]

1. Egbert Ludovicus Viele, prominent New York civil engineer, who served with distinction in the war first as engineer captain in the 7th New York Militia and from August 1861 as brigadier general in the U.S. Army.
2. Samuel Ward, New York lobbyist and financier and brother of Julia Ward Howe. Ward first met Russell in the summer of 1860.
3. New York social club at the United States Hotel, particularly frequented by newspapermen, writers, actors, and musicians. It was reorganized and legally incorporated in the 1870s and derived its name from a similar club in London.

March 24, 1861
Bitter cold—frost last night. It was late when I got up & breakfasted. Visitors of course—Minton[1] & Stuart & Kerner & Gurney[2] who was hungry to take my photograph & didn't. 6.30 dined with Butler Duncan, Van Buren[3] after dinner, Rowan & Belmont as with Mrs. Duncan.

1. Robert Bowne Minturn, New York merchant and shipper, partner in Grinnell, Minturn and Co.
2. Jeremiah Gurney, New York daguerreotypist and photographer and principal competitor of Mathew Brady.
3. John Van Buren, known as "Prince John," son of the former president and a leading New York Democratic politician.

March 25, 1861

Frosty night snow & cold. Young took me off to br[ea]kfast chez Chevets at 10. Present Edmund O'Flaherty né Stuart,[1] Hon. Raymond,[2] Bayard Taylor[3] big coarse man, little nice Olmsted (lame), Editor of Courier des États Unis, Durcartier diabolish Français,[4] Dana of Tribune[5] very nice fellow. Inevitable smart Hurlbert, Irish fighting ed[ito]r of N.Y. Times.

Capital dejeuner—no speeches—great fun over after 1.30. To Hotel & began to pack up—a very serious burden. On the whole I liked the men en masse very much indeed Raymond & O. especially. Herald not admitted. Rowan & Hurlbert came and interrupted my packing. But I went on in spite of all. Sent books to Bancroft & B. Duncan. At 5 had a morsel, & bade goodbye. Off [illeg.] to ferry boat—ticket, get a lot of brass checks for baggage. Met Sanford.[6] Dark in huge ferry boat. Train all one class—stove in carriage gum drops apples & cake man. Great big yankees. Rail thro' streets of many cities of neat wooden white houses two stories high, Corinthian porticos & pillars in painted wood. Gave two bags for check before Philadelphia. Boat very extraordinary sight. City enormous extent looks very well, drove to La Pierre supper. To train at 10.50—sleeping car very strange sight extra for places. Rowdies & whiskey & fighting. "I'll sleep where I god d'm please." Foreign mission. Bosom of Uncle Abe. A good deal of real yankee fun am[on]g the rowdies. I took my top shelf & slept on very mal indeed. It is a capital plan. No changes as sleeping car is moved complete across ferry &c. &c.

1. Edmund O'Flaherty, British-born journalist and theatrical promoter, who used the pseudonym of William Stuart. He emigrated to the United States in 1854. The following year he wrote a series of highly critical reviews in the *New York Tribune* of the actor Edwin Forrest.

2. Henry Jarvis Raymond, founder and editor of the *New York Times* from 1851 until his death in 1869.

3. Bayard Taylor was a Pennsylvania-born traveler and writer, who served briefly during the Civil War as Washington correspondent of the *New York Tribune* and as a secretary of the American legation in St. Petersburg.

4. Possibly a deputy editor. The proprietor and editor of the *Courier des États Unis* from 1851 until 1871 was Charles Lassalle.

5. Charles Anderson Dana was managing editor of the *New York Tribune* and Horace Greeley's deputy. He later became the proprietor and editor of the *New York Sun*.

6. Henry Shelton Sanford, leading New Jersey Republican. In 1861 he was appointed U.S. minister to Belgium. He was a close friend of Bancroft Davis.

March 26, 1861 [Washington]

Very warm & muggy. Great change in weather. At 6 a.m. roused up from car at Washington—gave checks to man at bus Willards & Sanford drove me to Willards[1] a huge caravanserai. Proprietor in bar took down names in book & when all were come distributed keys— mine 86, lovely maid—as magnificent a woman except my own dear wife as any I ever saw in my life. Two of my bags missing. Willards menagerie enormous—crowds in bar, smoking room, reading room, 100s writing, passage crowded, great tall long nervous bearded anxious men, 2,500 dined during prepare for office. Man took my check to find bags, breakfasted late & went up & wrote. Sanford came to remind me of dinner. I went at 5.30. Truman Smith[2] large heavy headed fatter.... Anthony[3] Jew ed[ito]r clever & humourous, Foster[4] a man of ability, Seward[5] a small man who put me in mind of Douglas Jerrold[6] when in a serious mood. He talks a good deal & is very much given to raconter & badiner—a subtle quick man not quite indifferent to kudos. He intimated he wanted no extra session—"Kings who call Parl[iamen]ts lose their heads." Pres[i]d[en]t impressed by my historical parallels. Told some good stories of pressure on President. "Governor" in England. The style in Slave States is what prevailed in N.Y. &c. 50 years ago, coaches horses &c.—parallel between N. & S. usually quite unsound—did not think any inconvenience or loss of revenue would result from tariff. As to secession he & all his brothers & sisters seceded from home in early life but they all returned. So would the States. No orders given to evacuate Fort Sumter[7]—invited me to call on him tomorrow. Went home with Foster & Anthony, took a stroll—[...]. Came back in time for letters. The bottle of Madeira, the "bar" at Willards at night, water closets, barber's shop where I shaved.

1. Washington's most famous hotel on the corner of Fourteenth Street and Pennsylvania Avenue. It was enlarged and remodeled in 1850 by the Willard brothers of Vermont. The hotel was recently restored, reopening in 1986 as the Willard Inter-Continental.

2. Truman Smith, lawyer and former Whig congressman and senator from Connecticut.

3. Henry Bower Anthony, Republican senator from Rhode Island from 1859 to 1884.

4. Col. John Wells Foster was a former U.S. government geologist employed by the Illinois Central Railroad. He was the author of the widely distributed "Report upon the Mineral Resources of the Illinois Central Railroad," issued in 1856.

5. William Henry Seward, former New York governor and senator, was appointed by Lincoln as secretary of state in March 1861.

6. Douglas Jerrold (1803–57), English playwright and man of letters.

7. Brick-built Federal fort in Charleston harbor, constructed in 1828, it was the focal point for negotiations between South Carolina and the Federal government during the secession winter of 1860–61.

To John T. Delane, March 26, 1861

Willards' Menagerie, Washington.

My dear Delane,[1]

I left New York last night & arrived here this morning rather done up by a transition from frost & snow to Southern heat such as we are now exposed to. My life at New York was most profitless & pleasureless spite of the good intentions of my friends & in one respect I was like the Kingdom of Heaven for I suffered violence "at the hands of those who would have possession of me" whether I liked it or not. The absence of all good purpose in my stay arose principally from the chaos of opinions into which I was at once plunged over head & ears, all so opposite & so violent that like opposing forces they produced at the unhappy centre to which they directed their course complete absence of all motion—or more properly speaking my head was like the central space in a revolving storm where all is nullity while the furious currents whirl around it, and bear with them their placid interior. Such diversity of assertion & opinion extending even to the minutest matters of fact I never encountered before now even in H[ouse of] C[ommons] or at a meeting of the Geological Society. As far as I can make out there is no one with any faith in anything stronger than the march of events. Every man is an atom in a gale with an idea of its own & a tendency to take an independent course if it could which are overwhelmed & controled by the force which has set it and its fellows in motion & can of itself effect nothing or go beyond the blind submission to chance.

New York to my mind is exceedingly gay insouciant & even frivolous, but I am told that the great events which are going on here affected the upper ten thousand notwithstanding incessant dinner & evening parties. Politics in New York mean a trade for journalists or rather for people who use journals to enable them to assume some position as politicians whilst the rich & well educated & enlightened retire from the arena which is filled with so much dirt & nastiness to the private worship of the almighty dollar & to the enjoyment of the pleasures which success in cultivating the good graces of their deity bestow here as fully as in any part of the world. Universal suffrage seems to have frightened moral courage. It has struck a death blow even at the gallant heart of true patriotism. I was astounded when I heard confidentially that grave doubts and dislikes existed to the very principles of its existence in the part of leading statesmen of the Republic—that Liberty of the Press was a nuisance carried to its present extent, that universal suffrage demanded limitations & had outgrown the bounds set to it by the fathers of the country & that many "institutions" were utterly abominable effete or corrupted. But I dare not having regard to my future here write all this at present, for I should be hunted down by all parties. I fear I shall not be able to send you any thing by this post, but now that I am on the spot I hope to be enabled to dispatch some useful matter by next mail.

The men I have met do not much impress me. Old George Bancroft is a pedant without any firmness or faith in anything but G.B. Horatio Seymour is an ingenious gentleman who thinks the Union can be best maintained by not attempting to govern it at all. Horace Greeley[2] is the nastiest form of narrow minded sectarian philanthropy, who would gladly roast all the whites of South Carolina in order that he might satisfy what he supposes is a conscience but which is only an autocratic ambition which revels in the idea of separation from the South as the best recognition of its power. The Douglasites are angry with all parties but most of all with the section of the Republicans which came nearest to & deserted them. But when one finds Mr. Belmont—judaeus incognitus[3]—whose only claim to such high consideration is derived from his position as representative of the Rothschilds their leader in New York, he is not inclined to regard them as a national party with the highest aims in the world. Gordon Bennett is so palpably a rogue—it comes out so strongly in the air around him, in his eyes & words & smell & voice that one pities the cause which finds in him a protagonist. Our friend Hurlbert who by the by was—"Jerusalem! greased snakes Yes Sirree! It's a fact!"— a Methodist preacher & parson—is a very clever, very agreeable, & very amusing fellow but I find he has no position here, & that his line as a journalist (now cut short by secession forced or voluntary from the N.Y. Times) is supposed to be influenced by "secondary" considerations. And so on with the rest of New Yorkers—always with every regard for Butler Duncan, & Raymond & some others & B. Davis.

I expect I shall be in a very different atmosphere here. The society of N[ew] Y[ork]ers was very charming, & their hospitality was deadly. If the rapidly expanding orb which contains your stout friend's digestive apparatus had been provided with adequate masticatory apparatus & ducts he could have dined seven times a day—terapin soup, canvas backed ducks clam chowder I abhor ye. The sight of an oyster—of that huge bearded muscular mollusc which put me in mind of a wax anatomical preparation of some thing curious in tumorous—makes me sick! First I fell a victim to the Green Sons of Erin of whom I was the most verdant in as much as I was told it would be a nice little party & that I would not be asked to say a word & of which it was true that hundreds of green sons assembled & that I was all but driven at the point of the carving fork to make a speech which was duly misreported & for which I was duly punished by an elaborate account of myself in which I am described as a man between 48 & 54 years of age with grizzled grey hair, a cocked nose, blue eyes, a double eye glass, a ditto chin, an elaborate toilette &c. &c. &c. Then I was engaged literally in one day for the next fortnight & when some tormentors found breakfast was a meal I did not indulge in on the same day as dinner they invented lunches & suppers for me. Such transparent artifices as saying I was engaged or was out or locking my door they laughed to scorn—& they hunted this poor little tom cat with as much earnestness gravity ferocity & determination as if they were really engaged in the pursuit of a full grown "lion". "Of all the plagues Good Heaven thy wrath can send! Save me! Oh Save me! from a New York friend". They are really most hospitable & jolly exceedingly. But as they dont talk much at dinner, & as they bolt after dinner one does not hear much & later at night they wax contradictory. One thing I can make out. They would be all very much obliged to any power which would oblige them with a war as the most sovereign remedy for the domestic cancer. Their bad leg of 50 years standing would they think be cured in an instant by gunpowder, & men have the cheek to tell you that who admit they could not relieve Fort Sumter "unless it was beleaguered by an English Army." There are some northern men so violent as to assert the U.S. Govt. shd. regard the recognition of the Southern States by any European nation as a casus belli—& of that sort will be found some of the new ministers. They declare that the South must come back & that right soon, & the opinion is indeed growing to the effect that a strong reaction will very soon take place against the chiefs of the Secession. The wish may be father to it. The question of fighting seems to be eschewed as far as possible. Neither party likes to assume any attitude save that of the Richard Strachan or the Earl of Chatham[4] & as yet the South has got the best of her opponent by the fierceness of her air & the cock of her hat.

I shall stay here for a week & then go South whither the increasing heats summon me. I have got plenty of letters to everybody. I wish some of them would be kind enough to give me a satisfactory reply to the question of jesting Pilate. Below all the big talk there is a sense of humiliation at the spectacle presented by the Great Republic to Europe altho' they talk vain things about the moral grandeur of a conflict in which no blood is shed. I am quite certain if they should fight, & I say Lord forbid, they are quite ready for a bloody & desperate struggle. I am all anxiety about my wife. Good news about her will make me happy. Give my kindest regards to all my friends who are of yours, & believe me

Yours most truly always & ever my dear Delane,
W.H. Russell.

1. John Thadeus Delane, editor of *The Times* from 1841 until 1877. Delane visited the United States and Canada in 1856.
2. Horace Greeley, founder and editor of the *New York Tribune* from 1841 until 1872.
3. "unknown" or "unrecognized Jew."
4. Adm. Sir Richard John Strachan (1760–1828) and Gen. John Pitt, second Earl of Chatham (1756–1835), were joint commanders of an expedition against the island of Walcheron in 1809 with the larger purpose of destroying Napoleon's fleet and arsenals on the Scheldt. The costly expedition proved almost totally unsuccessful, and the two commanders engaged in bitter recriminations as to each other's responsibility for the failure, effectively ending both of their careers.

March 27, 1861

Sanford at 10.15. He has been at Bogota....

Presented to the President at interview when Chev[alier] Bertannati[1] presented letters of credence on part of the Piedmont. Power of The Times.

Dined with Mr. Seward, his daughter,[2] his son,[3] Sanford, Mr. [Goodrich] Sec[retar]y of Legation Brussells.[4]

1. Chevalier Joseph Bertinatti, Sardinian ambassador to the United States from 1861 to 1867.
2. Anna Wharton Seward, the secretary of state's daughter-in-law, who acted as his

hostess in Washington. His only surviving daughter, Fanny, who was aged 16 in 1861, lived with her mother in Auburn, New York.

3. Frederick William Seward, Seward's second son, was an associate editor of the *Albany Evening Journal* and assistant secretary of state.

4. Aaron Goodrich of Minnesota, originally from New York, secretary of the U.S. legation in Brussels from 1861 to 1869.

March 28, 1861
In all day.
Dined with President & his Cabinet ministers. Fish dinner.

March 29, 1861
Writing.
Dined with Sam Ward, Valentine[1] & officer of U.S. N[avy].[2]

1. Possibly James E. A. Valentine, Ward's secretary and horse handicapper.

2. Lt. William Nelson, a Mexican War veteran. Appointed brigadier general of volunteers in September 1861, he was the only naval officer on either side in the Civil War to achieve the full rank of major general. Nelson was killed by Gen. Jefferson C. Davis in a private fracas in Louisville in 1862.

March 30, 1861
At 11.30 Navy Yard 2 carriages.... Dahlgren.[1]
Mrs. Lincoln's bouquet flowers.[2] Reception.
Brodie[3] & Warre.[4] Lord Lyons[5] letter.
Dined Sam Ward. Little Davis[6] called to ask me if he might travel South with me....

1. Capt. John Adolphus Bernard Dahlgren, leading Federal naval officer and inventor. He was commander at the Washington Navy Yard from 1861 to 1863, when he was promoted to rear admiral and placed in command of the South Atlantic blockading squadron.

2. The president's wife, Mary Lincoln, had sent Russell a "magnificent" bouquet of flowers inviting him to a White House reception. See William Howard Russell, *My Diary North and South*, 2 vols. (London, 1863), 1:78.

3. William Brodie, 1st attaché at the British legation in Washington since 1860.

4. Frederick Richard Warre, 2nd attaché at the British legation since December 1858. He previously served in Washington from 1854 to 1857.

5. Richard Bickerton Pemell Lyons, second baron and first viscount, and Earl Lyons, British minister to the United States from 1859 to 1865.

6. Theodore R. Davis, *Harper's Weekly* artist. Accompanying Russell on stages of his southern tour, Davis apparently tried to pass himself off as being employed by the

Illustrated London News, thus disguising his connection with the northern journal. Russell was eventually forced to disassociate himself from the artist's activities.

March 31, 1861

I dined with Lord Lyons, met Senator Hon. Sumner,[1] who was the only other stranger present. Home with him.

1. Charles Sumner, leading Republican antislavery senator from Massachusetts, was chairman of the Senate committee on foreign relations.

April 1, 1861

Raining & coldish this morn[in]g. B[rea]kfast Olmsted, & then to write wh. lasted till 2.30, off to Post with No.3. Letter to Mary &c. &c. To Douglas Senator[1] with Ward at 3.50. Lives long way out, view of Capitol &c.

1. Stephen Arnold Douglas, Democratic senator from Illinois and defeated candidate in the 1860 presidential election. He died in June 1861.

April 2, 1861

Started up early b[rea]kfasted & off to Wards to visit Mt. Vernon, at 9.30 or so by steamer John Colyer with Sam Ward. See notes small pocket book under date.

To J.C. Bancroft Davis, April 2, 1861

Willards, Washington.

My dear Davis,

I think I shall stay here for a few days longer in the hope of learning what the Govt. is really about to do. I dined with the Pres[i]d[en]t on Thursday & with his Cabinet, & am not a half the wiser.... Lord Lyons is I think strong for the Union & ag[ains]t S[outhern] U[nion].

Will you send & see if any loose letters are knocking about for me at the P[ost] O[ffice]. I shall write to you in extenso next mail.

Yours always very truly with best respects & comp[limen]ts to Mrs. Davis,[1]

W.H. Russell.

1. Bancroft Davis's wife, the former Frederica Gore King, daughter of the New York financier James Gore King and granddaughter of the revolutionary statesman Rufus King. The couple were married in 1857.

April 3, 1861

A fine warm day—a contrast to the preceeding. A letter from Lord Lyons asking me to dinner this evening. Also a letter from a Mr. Clements asking me to mind my writing.

Dined with Lord Lyons. Mde. Stoeckl wife Russian M[inister][1] very fine American. Brodie, Jenner,[2] Warre, & my Lord & one man of the party talked pleasantly.

    1. Elizabeth Howard Stoeckl, a native of Springfield, Massachusetts, was the wife of Edward de Stoeckl, Russian minister to the United States since 1859. He had been secretary of the legation since 1841. The couple were married in 1856.

    2. George Francis Birt Jenner, attaché at the British legation. He was transferred to Turin and then Athens in 1862.

April 4, 1861

Visited Mr. Seward at State Dept. & was there for an hour or more with him.

Dined with Senator Douglas where were Mr. Chase Sec[retar]y Treasury,[1] Smith Minister of Interior,[2] Forsyth the Southern Com[missioner]s.[3]

    1. Salmon Portland Chase, former antislavery governor and senator from Ohio, was Lincoln's secretary of the treasury until his resignation in 1864, after which he was appointed chief justice of the U.S. Supreme Court.

    2. Caleb Blood Smith of Indiana served as secretary of the interior from 1861 to 1862.

    3. John Forsyth, editor of the *Mobile Register*, who together with André B. Roman, former governor of Louisiana, and Martin J. Crawford, former congressman from Georgia, had been appointed by Pres. Jefferson Davis on 25 February to negotiate with the Federal government on issues relating to the peaceful establishment of the new southern republic.

April 5, 1861

Gave my letter to "The Times" to mail agent at cars at depot.

I dined with Southern Commissioners at Gautiers.[1]

    1. A celebrated French restauranteur and caterer on Pennsylvania Avenue in Washington.

April 6, 1861

I rec[eive]d a letter from my darling deeny dated March 19—sight no better, primroses & violets.

I dined with Riggs banker[1] where were Capt. Jenkins,[2] Mr. Corcoran banker,[3] Cutts,[4] Carlisle,[5] very smart fellow.

1. George Washington Riggs, Washington banker and a leader of the capital's financial community.
2. Capt. Thornton Alexander Jenkins, Virginia-born U.S. naval officer. He served throughout the Civil War, notably as senior naval officer at the surrender of Port Hudson in 1863 and at the Battle of Mobile.
3. William Wilson Corcoran, Washington banker and philanthropist and former partner of G. W. Riggs. He was one of the capital's most energetic hosts.
4. James Madison Cutts, second comptroller of the treasury and father-in-law of Sen. Stephen A. Douglas.
5. James Mandeville Carlisle, prominent Washington international lawyer. From 1852 he was standing legal adviser to the British legation.

April 7, 1861

Raining all day—raw and rather cold. I wrote to my father,[1] Alice,[2] B. Davis.
I dined with Lord Lyons—present Sumner & Mr. Blackwell,[3] Warre & Jenner. Visited M. & Mde. Stoeckl Russian Minister, Tessara Spanish Minister[4] & Riggs.

1. John Russell was an unsuccessful businessman of Irish Protestant background. He died in 1867.
2. Russell's eldest child, Alice Mary, born in 1847.
3. Thomas Evans Blackwell, English-born engineer and from 1857 to 1862 vice-president and general manager of the Grand Trunk Railway of Canada.
4. Don Gabriel Garcia y Tassara, Spanish minister to the United States from 1857 to 1867.

To J.C. Bancroft Davis [April 7, 1861]

Sunday, Willards, Washington.
My dear Sir,
   Will you kindly have the clothes sent to me by express to this place. I cannot at all understand the rumours of preparations side by side with the assurances I receive from people who ought to know the facts & the intentions of the Govt. There never were such precautions to keep Govt. matters secret as there are now taken at Washington.
   I intend to go South about the middle of the week, & I shall write to you 'ere I start to give you my exact itinerary.

I do not learn much here & indeed it would seem as if all the Cabinet were living on the events of the hour. Kindest regards to Mrs. Davis.

Yours always,

W.H. Russell.

April 8, 1861

Wet all day & stormy, wrote till past 2 only going down to b[rea]kfast & being seedy rather. As there were all sorts of stories in the N. papers I wrote to S[ecretary of] S[tate] asking him facts if admissible at all. Drove to Smithsonian[1] with Sam Ward & was rec[eive]d by Prof. Henry[2] & Prof. Baird.[3] Had a very interesting march thro' the place with both. Henry's remarks about the map of North America very interesting as to slavery & extension of population & valley of the Mississippi—dream of empire fallacious. Good museum—idea of library good. The two snakes & hisses. At 5.30 home to Ward's had dinner. Rec[eive]d a note from S[eward] to say he would see me at 9. Went in, his daughter & son. He told me [...] S[outhern] Govt. [...] anecdotes of Genl. Scott[4] & his desire to be a poet & writer &c. Battle of Chippewa[5] as well as writing to National intelligencer. Showing that Buchanan[6] shd. have fortified forts by Paley[7] & Shakespeare. Then we played a rubber & in course of it S. called for his portfolio & read a very able and long despatch to [...].[8] I pledged my word to keep the paper secret & I will do so but in effect there was nothing more than a distinctive exposition of the Inaugural with fuller argument. I remained with him till 12.30 enjoying our rubber. They wd. mean war if it cd. be had. But it wd. be wicked. There is a strong belief in reaction. Invitation from Mde. Stoeckl to dinner. Wrote to Alice, Willy,[9] deeny, Thackeray,[10] father &c.

1. The Smithsonian Institute was founded in 1846 upon the bequest of an Englishman, James Smithson, for "the increase and diffusion of knowledge among men."

2. Joseph Henry, renowned American physicist, was the first secretary and director of the Smithsonian Institution.

3. Spencer Fullerton Baird was a leading zoologist and assistant secretary at the Smithsonian. He was elected to the secretaryship after Henry's death in 1878.

4. Lt. Gen. Winfield Scott, a native of Virginia, was commander in chief of the U.S. Army. A hero of the War of 1812 and the Mexican War, he retired from the army on 31 October 1861.

5. Fought between Britain and the United States on 15 July 1814 on Chippewa Creek near Niagara. The brief engagement resulted in an American victory as troops led by Winfield Scott drove British regulars from the field.

6. James Buchanan, president of the United States from 1857 to 1861.

7. William Paley (1743–1805), British theologian and philosopher, author of *Evidences of Christianity* (1794).

8. The dispatch was to Charles Francis Adams, the new Federal minister to Great Britain, and was sent on 10 April 1861. It was intended to counter any British recognition of the Confederate States and provided Adams with precise instructions should he discover that this was the British government's intention on arrival in London. Adams did not in fact leave the United States until 1 May. See Russell, *Diary North and South* 1:102–3.

9. Russell's eldest son, William, born in 1849.

10. William Makepeace Thackeray, English novelist, was a close friend of Russell.

To William H. Seward, April 8, 1861

Private, Willards Hotel, Washington.

My dear Sir,

If it were considered admissible to acquaint me with the extent & destination or with the object of the preparations & expeditions (which are noted in the papers), under any reservations I would pledge my honour to observe any conditions with which such confidences might be accompanied, & would bind myself on my faith only to use such intelligence as might be afforded to me in the dispatch which I am forwarding to The Times & of which the contents can not be known in this country till the return of the paper to this country in a month hence.

Under any circumstances I am assured that your condecension & favour will excuse the request if reasons of state or duty should forbid you to grant it. I leave towards the end of the week, & if you could obtain General Scott's permission to let me pay my respect to him 'ere I left it would add to the number of obligations under which your kindness has laid me.

I am my dear Sir with very great respect
Your most faithful servant,
W.H. Russell L.L.D.

April 9, 1861
Ward took letter. I dined with Lord Lyons.
Tremendous day of storm wind & rain.

April 10, 1861
A mail in & no letter from deenyman. One from MacDonald[1]...

1. John Cameron MacDonald was chief engineer and future manager at *The Times*.

April 11, 1861
I dined with General Scott. Seward, Bates,[1] Col. Cullum.[2] Cavalry demonstrat[io]n before dinner. He is his own butler, warmed his claret.

1. Edward Bates of Missouri, Lincoln's attorney general.
2. Maj. George Washington Cullum, an engineer, was aide to Gen. Winfield Scott. He later became brigadier general of volunteers and in 1864 was appointed superintendent of the U.S. Military Academy at West Point.

April 12, 1861
Visiting packing &c. &c. Valentine off.
Tremendous rain—left Baltimore at 6 p.m. Arrived Eutaw House at 8. Coleman.[1]

1. The Eutaw House hotel, at the corner of Baltimore and Eutaw streets, was opened in 1835. R. B. Coleman, of the firm of Coleman and Stetson of the Astor House, New York, was manager of the hotel from 1859 to 1874.

To J.C. Bancroft Davis [April 12, 1861]

Friday night, Coleman's Eutaw House, Baltimore.
My dear Davis,
   As I found I could really do nothing at Washington except sift opinions I started today for Richmond by this route which is in the present state of the rail better than by Aquia Creek & I expect to reach Charleston in three days. Will you forward me any letters &c. to the care of Mr. Bunch H[er] B[ritannic] M[ajesty's] Consul[1] there if the mail is not closed. Should it be shut perhaps some express such as Adams would take them. I am very uneasy at my wife's state of

health in the face of the silence which has not been broken by the last two mails. I will write to you at length tomorrow ere I leave.

Yours very truly,

W.H. Russell.

T.O. S.V.P.

To whom should I send letters & messages at Boston? Have we any one there to act for the Times?

1. Robert Bunch, British consul in Charleston.

TWO

The Confederate States
of America

April 13, 1861 [Baltimore]
I was very unwell this morning cd. eat no breakfast. In fact I cd. only think of my dot. I go over & over again the chances of hearing from her & wd. be easy only in her last 2 she spoke of illness. I have visitors Lee[1] & Graham.[2] Drive out & visited Mrs. Bigelow at Dr. Shencks,[3] Zouave children—it was not Mrs. Bigelow after all! Bombardment of Sumter is confirmed.[4] My friends are elated at news. No great Union sentiment. Baltimore nice city, destroyed by the tram ways in streets. Washington Monument good, handsome hall doors, large number of blacks—carriages &c. Monument & other streets nice & clean. Great number of German names & numerous Irish d[itt]o. With Lee to Maryland Club.[5] Alas! Crab salad! Introduced to files of gentlemen at ye door, & talk & lunch. I am diddled by the crab. Young Mr. Davis turned up this morning having pursued me over from Washington to sketch for Illust[rated] London News. He is a keen smart young gent. Will this be the victory of Black Republicans.

Left Baltimore for Norfolk Va. steamer 4 p.m. Georgeanna steamer. So seedy. Glorious sail. Forts, thundri, steamers distant train &c. bar on board. Doyle & friend—fierce secessionist.

1. Stephen States Lee, Baltimore coal and iron merchant, originally from South Carolina.
2. William H. Graham, director of Alexander Brown and Co., the oldest banking house in Baltimore, established in 1811, and the parent firm of Brown Bros. of New York.

3. Possibly Dr. Noah Hunt Schenk, Baltimore Protestant Episcopal clergyman.

4. After thirty-three hours' bombardment, commencing at 4:30 A.M. on 12 April, the Federal garrison on Fort Sumter surrendered to local Confederate forces under Gen. Pierre G. T. Beauregard.

5. Founded in 1857 as a meeting place for gentlemen who sought to preserve the state's civilized society, it served mostly as a dining and cards club. It still exists today at 1 East Eager Street, Baltimore.

April 14, 1861

A most uneasy night—never ceased thinking of my darling soul. I cannot banish fear & sorrow from my mind. Noises on board the steamer, whistles steam blows &c. at dawn Fort Monroe but I cd. not see it. Negro woman came in for my ticket. A fine morning, on right faced low wooded coast with creeks close at hand, anxious looking little wooden lighthouses.... Up narrow creek with wooden houses ragged wharves on both sides. Two b[ui]ld[in]g sheds, one large 3 decker Pennsylvania in ordinary never been at sea. Sloop alongside the sheds—two hulks. On right Portsmouth a very poor likeness of the shabby part of our dock—on left Norfolk. Both present many species of flag staffs. Crossed at 7 (there is a steam ferry). Ragged boat, we went in our big Georgeanna—630 tons. Wretched 'bus, drove to Atlantic Hotel spitoony place. Sumter surrendered "yes Siree!" Terrible bad pave & street railway in midst of course. After b[rea]kfast group of men to see telegram. No great excite[men]t— however, generally satisfied. One man grumbles because more arn't killed. I took a sad & solitary walk my darling Mary. No telegram open, no post leaves—nothing till tomorrow. So here I am stuck. Her little bunch of violets. The Cumberland frigate is lying off point here—a short stumpy looking old sailing ship. Sailors smart enough. No gas in bed rooms here. Gave Davis a letter to send off.

To J.C. Bancroft Davis, April 14, 1861

Norfolk, Va.

My dear Davis,

I am so exceedingly sick with anxiety on my wife's account that I must beg of you to open my letters which may arrive by next packet & telegraph to me to Charleston care of Mr. Bunch British Consul to give me the news of her. Then you can close & send them on by post.

As the Washington rail was destroyed below Aquia Creek by floods I was obliged to come round by Baltimore on Friday & thence by steam to this place & now I am stuck here for a day as there is no train for the South till Monday afternoon. I am not well but there is only one cause for it—silence from my friends & grave fears & suspicions therefrom. May you never know such anxiety.

I hear today that I am late for the fair. The news will be a great blow to Seward & the people at Washington unless they are consummate hypocrites.

Send me some information & directions about the post & the sailing of vessels if you can. Do excuse all this trouble. Charge the expenses of telegraphs &c. &c. to The Times. Give my kindest regards to all my good friends at New York & present my remembrances to Mrs. Davis.

Ever yours most truly,
          W.H. Russell.

April 15, 1861
At dawn up & off to Portsmouth & thence across the dismal Swamp by Roanoke rail 5.30 a.m. Robinson engineer very civil & very intelligent, took me on engine. Stopped negro shanty, shed of wood several large chests of wood locked, deal planks to lie on, fire of logs on hearth hot as it was. Dismal Swamp truly wonderful & very interesting place—but it lasts for miles & miles. Bridges are exciting in size & frailty, great skill engineer. Wild turkeys tortoises deer I hear sometimes seen. Visited Blackwater station & steamer.... Narrow stream very curious. 3 N.C. hogs to make a shadow. N.C. here is most miserable, but people at stations are wondrous respectable—see rail guide for names. Our food quaint & curious. Confederate flag flying from many. Staff ofttimes before two or three log houses. The poor whites here are rabid to have a class below them, ergo they are all for slaves. Soldiers in cars here & there. At Weldon a civil gentleman wanted me to stay & see the antiquities. It is amenable place. We changed our carriages here at all events. Dined at Goldsboro' table waited on & dinner cut by slaves, 2 nice looking women. The master stood in hall to take the money. He wd. not sell them for a good bit I was told. At Goldsborough & elsewhere much excitement & a good deal of drink. State volunteers going out to seize the U.S. fortresses Macon & Caswell[1] & of course ungarrisoned. Ladies waving kerchiefs from

public house to drunken men, arms bad, splendid long legged chaps tho' very often handsome faces. Griswold's Hotel centre of life. All line to Wilmington either swamp or forest or tracks of dead & burned trees inexpressibly wild & desolate and stumps in ground & withered arms twisted aloft crying for foliage. Grand names of stations. Lincoln's proclamation calling 75,000 out is all laughed at & derided.[2] As long ago as 3 months cannon were sent to Charleston & shot & shell in any quantity. Pigs on the rail very funny, caught some in cow lifter. There is no stove whatever. Conductor of our train called "Captain" Lyall by all passengers. Presidents house very neat little backwoods settlement in cleared spot amid trees, at one station negroes going fishing farewell, group happy enough. Excitement at stations increasing. White blossoms of dogwood & magnolias beautiful in forests wh. ring with mocking birds, pine everywhere.

1. Federal forts in North Carolina that were ordered to be seized by Gov. John Ellis on 15 April. Fort Macon, situated on Bogue Banks opposite Beaufort, had already been occupied by local volunteers under Capt. Josiah Pender. Fort Caswell, on Oak Island in the Cape Fear River, thirty miles south of Wilmington, was seized together with neighboring Fort Johnson by Col. Josiah L. Cantwell. Both masonry forts dated from the 1820s.

2. President Lincoln's proclamation calling for the mobilization of seventy-five thousand ninety-day militia to suppress the rebellion was issued on 15 April, having been presented to the cabinet the previous day.

April 16, 1861
(Left Wilmington at 5 a.m. crossed river ferry to rail). When arrived last night at Wilmington walked across platform to room where rude supper was spread & slaves waited—asked whether we wanted separate beds & had to sleep 2 in a room. Vigilance Comm[itt]ee wd. not permit my telegraph to go. They were all drunk. I refused to see them. Davis came in pale & agitated rather. As we left supper last night the family came in to feed off remnants. Dreary breakfast, gas however. Wilmington looked well across broad Cape Fear River. Shell on pier, coarse jokes about old Abe, some s[ai]d Anderson[1] cd. not help defending Sumter. Our journey much same as before. Pinewoods awful jungle great rivers, trestle bridges & causeway, swamps.... On entering South Carolina our baggage exam[ine]d by Custom House officer. Nichols station detention of passengers. At Peedee river bridge & trestle 2 miles long. The dismissed employé at Washington, his lan-

guage. Ere we arrived at Charleston the country improved. In distance we see Fort Pickens[2] with Confederate flag waving. Troops en route to Virginny.

Drive to hotel where is Sam Ward. Mills House.[3] Get a decent dinner late at night in l'hotel & am introduced to Governor Manning,[4] Senator Chesnut,[5] Colonel Lucas,[6] Porcher Miles,[7] an accueil cordiale. Went to General Beauregard[8] who late as it was rec[eive]d me very graciously & arrangements were made for him to send his ass[istan]t Engineer Major Whiting[9] with me to Sumter next day. Bunch in bed, to club.

1. Maj. Robert Anderson, a native of Louisville, Kentucky, was commander of the Federal garrison at Fort Sumter, which surrendered to Confederate forces on 13 April.

2. Russell means Fort Sumter. Fort Pickens, in Pensacola harbor, remained in Federal hands for the duration of the Civil War.

3. Charleston's leading hotel on Meeting Street. In April 1860 it housed many of the delegates to the Democratic party convention.

4. John Laurence Manning, a wealthy planter, was governor of South Carolina from 1852 to 1854. He held extensive plantation lands in both South Carolina and Louisiana. In 1861 he served as voluntary aide to Gen. Pierre G. T. Beauregard.

5. Former senator James Chesnut, Jr. Elected to the U.S. Senate in 1858, he served on the committee that drafted the South Carolina secession ordinance. He was the husband of the celebrated diarist Mary Chesnut.

6. Col. James J. Lucas, aide de camp to Governor Pickens of South Carolina.

7. William Porcher Miles, leading Charleston planter and politician. He was a former U.S. congressman and mayor of Charleston.

8. Brig. Gen. Pierre Gustave Toutant Beauregard of Louisiana, a Mexican War veteran, was commander of Confederate forces opposing Fort Sumter. He subsequently commanded the Confederate army at the Battle of Bull Run.

9. Maj. William Henry Chase Whiting of Mississippi was engineer in charge of Confederate emplacements in Charleston harbor. He was promoted to brigadier general in July 1861.

April 17, 1861 [Charleston]

I visited Fort Sumter at 7 o'clock in great state after a visit to Bunch who was very civil & seems a very nice fellow. Governor Manning, Senator Chesn., Hon. Porcher Miles & Colonel Lucas a.d.c. to Governor Pickens[1] accompanied us to Genl. Beauregard where I was introduced to Major Whiting late U.S. Engineers as my guide. After respects we went to tug steamer specially prepared & as it appeared provisioned for us. De Fontaine of some N.Y. paper[2] with us, & a local of a very dirty colour. Steamer first went to Morris Island long

spit of sand, on beach was a guard rough looking long haired gents, with crossed bayonets who only let those who were vouched for land. Visited sandbag batteries—well made enough & strong. The iron battery not worth much I think ag[ains]t a really heavy fire. Officers & men strolling all over ye island, the fine dirt flying before ye wind rendered a visit to the face of the works very unpleasant, & nearly blinded us. Many wore dust spectacles. Saw few traces of damage anywhere next to camps which were straggling here & there pitched in among the sand hillocks with odd names painted on the poor tents—smell very bad in places, no latrines, bones & bottles strewn about. Entered one mess hut where great preparations were being made to give a dinner to some swell general & his staff—& the officers were making & drinking huge jugs of badminton, some rather cut. We partook thereof, drank toasts none of a party character & were introduced to & shook hands with hosts of people.
Dined with Ward late at hotel.

1. Francis Wilkinson Pickens was elected governor of South Carolina in December 1860. He had formerly served in both houses of the U.S. Congress and from 1858 to 1860 was U.S. minister to Russia.

2. Felix Gregory de Fontaine, a Boston native, was a prominent southern war correspondent and editor of the *Columbia Daily South Carolinian*.

April 18, 1861
Hotel crammed with men in uniform. I am introduced to shoals of them. We dined or breakfasted as the meals are alike save in point of time & drinks at the table d'hote. Coloured men fine, waiter Irish, flies the devil. Ladies in white & well dressed very fine—nice women. Tables crowded with uniforms. We have a pleasant chat at breakfast—all the swells take their meals at the table d'hote like the rest. The coloured servants wait outside yee lobbies as in India. Charleston not a bad sort of place. At least it looks well. Major Whiting called for me at hotel & Ward he & I started for Customs House stairs & then we tried to get to Ft. Moultrie[1] in a "model steamer" about 6 tons burthen, our boat having been taken over by Baron Sternberg Russian[2] to visit works and batteries. It blew hard & strong, nasty sea in harbour, little steamer made no way, rolling & taking in water. Whiting talking of Thackerays writings on which he is lunatics. At last we came into actual danger, & so 'bout ships was the word, &

with lots of water on board back we went after 3 hours trial—re infecta.[3] "I'm glad we turned back" quoth ye Captain.

We dined with Bunch in the evening. Present Manning, old Mr. Huger,[4] one who shook hand with ye framers of independence, old Rose,[5] Preston[6] &c. Very wonderful Madeira & very pleasant evening. Old Huger pronounced Hugee in great grief & distress at break up of the Union. Conversation was general, strong for the South of course. At night about 8.30 there was a bell sounded which was warning to all coloured people to get home. If out after 9 unless with special passes they are put into prison. On way from Bunch passed City Watch house where was a policeman doing sentry & armed like a soldier outside. There is said to be a large force of men inside always ready to turn out. Patrols of cavalry traverse the streets all night. There are precautions against the negro population.

Charleston has broad streets lined with trees, houses detached with gardens, very dusty except where there are plank roads laid on the sands. A fine red sandstone b[uil]d[in]g with a crownless Irish Harp marks the St. Patricky elementary temple. They do much hard work here. Market in city is not bad, large numbers of turkey buzzards are always charging about among ye dogs for ye offal & they are protected by law. The negro servants are well dressed—in the market all the stalls are kept by coloured people, but they are slaves for the most part if not altogether. There was an incessant rattling & rolling of drums & a good deal of marching all day. Fine looking fellows mostly.

1. Fort Sumter's powerful companion at the north entrance to Charleston harbor, it was seized by southern forces in December 1860. Built in 1811, Fort Moultrie survived devastating Federal assaults in 1863.

2. Baron Ungern Sternberg was on an unofficial observation tour of the southern states on behalf of the Russian government.

3. "without accomplishing our object."

4. Alfred Huger, Charleston planter and postmaster.

5. Possibly James Rose, planter of Christ Church Parish.

6. John Smith Preston, South Carolina lawyer, legislator, and art collector, whose wealth derived largely from his Louisiana sugar plantations.

April 19, 1861
I wrote today.

To Lord Lyons, April 19, 1861

Charleston, South Carolina.

Dear Lord Lyons,

. I arrived here the night before last via Baltimore, Norfolk & Wilmington. North Carolina was in revolt—that is there was no particular form of authority to rebel against, but the shadowy abstractions in lieu of it were treated with deserved contempt by the "Citizens" who with flint muskets & quaint uniforms were ready at the various stations to seize on anything particularly whiskey which it occurred to them to fancy. At Wilmington I sent a message to the electric tel[egraph] office for transmission to New York but the "Citizens" of the Vigilance Committee refused to permit the message to be transmitted, & were preparing to wait upon me with a view of asking me what were my general views on the state of the world when I informed them peremptorily that I must decline to hold any intercourse with them—which I the more resolved to do in that they were "highly elated & excited" by the news from Sumter. I went over the works the day before yesterday with Genl. Beauregard's A.D.C. & the Chief Engineer, Major Whiting a most intelligent man. The military injury done to Sumter is very trifling, but Anderson's defence negative as it was must be regarded as exceedingly creditable to him. He was driven off the parapets at once & cd. not work his barbette guns by wh. alone he cd. hope to silence the batteries opposed to him, & then he was reduced to the light guns à fleur d'eau[1] in the casemates of which he cd. only work a few—4 I think at most—& these without elevating screws—he had 100 fuses for shells or he cd. have done great damage to troops in support of the batteries, his magazine was in great danger from the furious fire which has gutted the fort completely of all that could burn. They are busy at work repairing it now, & it would be a very formidable obstacle to a naval force. The shore batteries are not very formidable excepting Fort Moultrie which wd. be mischievous to a fleet, but even now 5,000 men well led landed on the islands below the range & covered by boat guns cd. take the works in reverse, & probably clear away the mass of armed companies wh. fancies itself an army even tho' it has in its ranks many most gallant fellows who would fight like demons. There seems to be about 7,000 to 8,000 of them about but they are badly armed—miserably equipped & ill provided for a campaign. If they are obliged to keep on these sand islands they will rot like sheep in summer between their want of cleanliness & the climate. They have no field artillery whatever as far as I can see. If the fleet had come in after Anderson had surrendered they cd. have done much damage, & if they cd. have landed 2,000 men they might have taken the whole line of batteries on Morris Island. In a weeks time the place will be a hard nut to crack. One thing is certain—nothing on earth will induce the people to return to the Union. I believe firmly their present intention is to march upon Washington if it were merely as a diversion & to carry the war away from their interior which is rather a delicate one. This is a very hasty scrawl which I beg your Lordship to excuse on the ground that I will be better next time. Believe me dear Lord Lyons with many thanks for your kindness.

Your faithful ser[van]t,

W.H. Russell.

May I ask your Lordship to remember me to Warre & Brodie?

1. "at water level."

April 20, 1861

No boat to Pringles.[1] Visited Courier & Mercury[2]—also Mure,[3] also Trenholm[4] &c. &c. I dined with Reed,[5] (Miles), Manning, Pringle &c. at hotel.

1. John Julius Izard Pringle, a leading Prince George district rice planter. In 1860 he owned two hundred slaves.

2. The *Charleston Daily Courier* and the *Charleston Mercury* were the two leading newspapers in the city. Founded in 1803, the *Courier* was the spokesman for Charleston's mercantile interests. Edited in 1860 by Aaron Willington, it had initially opposed secession. The *Mercury*, on the other hand, edited since 1851 by Robert Barnwell Rhett, Jr., was one of the leading advocates of radical secessionism within the state.

3. Robert Mure, Charleston merchant. In August 1861 he was arrested by Federal authorities in Louisville while en route to London but was subsequently released. His cousin William was British consul in New Orleans.

4. George Alfred Trenholm, Charleston merchant and financier and one of the wealthiest men in the Confederacy. In June 1864 he became Confederate secretary of the treasury.

5. Col. John Harleston Reed II, planter and legislator, of Belle River plantation near Georgetown, owned over five hundred slaves in 1860. Educated at Harvard, he held the record for nine consecutive legislative sessions before the Civil War.

To J.C. Bancroft Davis, April 20, 1861

Charleston, South Carolina.

My dear Davis,

I am going to visit some sea side plantations & then on Wednesday or Thursday next I proceed to Pensacola, New Orleans, Montgomery where I look around & watch events for some time—unless they are urgent at some concentrated focus of action elsewhere. Yours of 17th. April was only received by Bunch for me this morning. Will you if possible tell me the date of the dispatch & the addresses of the letters you sent to me? I have not received one except that from Morris— none from Delane, only one from Aldershot. Any which arrive here- after please send me to Bunch H[er] B[ritannic] M[ajesty's] Consul here till further orders. In view of the great derangement of the postal service it would be as well perhaps to send in future by Adams Ex- press tho' they tell me there is no safety in that mode of conveyance in these times against scrutiny. For that I do not much care, as I pre- sume no party would like to incur the odium of intercepting letters to The Times of London.

I wish you would send me a good cypher for use in case of necessity & all the postal information as to dates of sailing &c. &c. you can. There is no great excitement here. But there is immense resolution & determination to fight to the last. They are on a mine however. Two regiments march for Virginia this morning—2000 men.

Yours always in much haste,
W.H. Russell.

I send a letter for "The Times" to go by the "Persia" by Adams Express this evening directed under cover to you.

April 21, 1861

Writing.
Letter to The Times sent off by Sam Ward to British Consul Rich- mond[1] for Washington Lord Lyons—per Adams Express Company.
With Porcher Miles to Crafts small farm & plantation.[2]

1. George Moore, British consul at Richmond.
2. George I. Crafts, a planter in St. Andrew's Parish.

April 22, 1861

Started at 7 in Georgetown steamer. Pringle, Ward, Col. Reed, self—
on board Nina. Mitchell[1] nice fellow also with us, a lawyer. Coast
very low, see letter to the Times.
Georgetown 3 seedy. Reids House. White House Plantation 5 o'c[lock].
Mocking birds.

1. Nelson Mitchell, Charleston lawyer. In 1863 he defended the rights of black Union
soldiers captured at the siege of Fort Wagner to be treated as prisoners of war.

April 23, 1861

A nice library. Our walk. After dinner conversat[io]n—a general
desire expressed for the rule of a Prince of England! If it cd. be done?
It was past midnight when horses came to, & we started in a lovely
moonlight to Georgetown. Crossed the ferry—negro s[ai]d river was
full of alligators. Arrived at wharf about 3 a.m. Capt. just to start off.

April 24, 1861

Seedy enough & knocking little about in seaway Nina going to
Charleston. Up at 9½ talk to our Captain a first rate specimen of
keen tall intelligent seaman in inland waters—told us of Cap. Buck[1]
from Maine who came to Wacamaw river worth 1000 drs., found out
nice land at 20 cents acre & cotton lands & is now worth million dollars nearly—lives on estate all year round. Captain goes up & down
river all year round, says he can buy enough pork from niggers on
one plantation to last his ships men for the winter. Man on board has
bought himself & family out.
Charleston about 3 p.m. Find that Petigrus[2] dinner is postponed.

1. Henry Buck, originally of Bucksport, Maine, built the world's largest sawmill on
the Waccamaw River. By 1860 he possessed over three hundred slaves and was one of
the wealthiest planters in South Carolina.
2. James Louis Petigru was a leading South Carolina Unionist who had opposed
both nullification and secession. He died in 1863.

To J.C. Bancroft Davis, April 24, 1861

Charleston, South Carolina.

My dear Davis,

I have just returned or rather I am now returning from Julius Pringle's plantation & I shall go on my way to New Orleans—& Montgomery. I fear it is hoping too much to get letters. But if there is any mail communication with the British Embassy pray forward my letters from England under cover to Lord Lyons our ambassador at Washington. We absolutely know nothing of what is taking place in the North & judging from the papers you are equally ignorant there of the state of things in the South. My letters to The Times have small chance of having reached which I regret only to a certain extent as up to this they have not been very novel or interesting. I don't see how war can be avoided. Here there is intense resolution & overwhelming unanimity. As to the Govt. at Washington it wd. seem that destruction is something forced on & preceded by folly as well as madness.

Yours always truly,
W.H. Russell.

April 25, 1861
Sent off letters by Cavendish Taylor[1] who travelled as Bunch's messenger with dispatches for Lord Lyons. Spent the day in writing them till 1 o'clock.
Dined at Mr. Petigru's—Judge King,[2] Genl. Beauregard, Mrs. King,[3] Mrs. Carson.[4]

1. George Cavendish-Taylor, son-in-law of Col. Charles Carroll of Doughoregan Manor, Maryland.
2. Judge Henry C. King of Charleston.
3. Mrs. Susan Petigru King, daughter of James Louis Petigru and author of several books, including *Busy Moments of an Idle Woman* (1854). Her husband, Henry, a lawyer, was killed at the Battle of Secessionville in June 1862.
4. Mrs. Caroline Petigru Carson, daughter of James Louis Petigru and wife of Col. William Augustus Carson, prominent Cooper River rice planter.

April 26, 1861

Left Charleston at 9.45. Ferry. At Pocotaligo at 12.20. Trescot[1] there in the flesh. Tom Elliot[2] & Cuthbert.[3] The Rain-crow. Drive from Heywards.[4]

Boat to island—home. Mrs. T.[5] The boat & 4 negroes singing oh my soul oh your soul. We're going thro' the churchyard to lay this body down. The fires on the banks.

1. William Henry Trescot, Charleston lawyer, historian, and diplomat. In early 1861 he played a leading role in the negotiations surrounding the Charleston forts.

2. Thomas Rhett Smith Elliott, eldest surviving son of William Elliott, Jr., Beaufort planter and author of *Carolina Sports by Land and Water* (1846).

3. Possibly George Barnwell Cuthbert, St. Helen's Parish planter.

4. Edward Barnwell Heyward, Richland district rice and cotton planter.

5. William Henry Trescot's wife, Eliza Cuthbert Trescot. They were married in 1848.

April 27, 1861

Trescots. Drum fishing. Barnwells island.

April 28, 1861

Trescots. Describe the day, the house the grounds. How we loiter. Drive to see a tree—the cottages. Edmund Rhett.[1] My walk. Sunset. Thunder clouds. The incident.[2] To bed.

1. Edmund Rhett, planter and state legislator, was the son of Robert Barnwell Rhett, the South Carolina secessionist leader.

2. Russell's published *My Diary North and South*, 2 vols. (London, 1863), 1:214–15, does not describe any particular "incident," mentioning only that the correspondent went out into the garden to watch the thunder and lightning flashes before retiring to bed.

April 29, 1861

Up at 6 or so, incident last night. Heyward. Snake Hawk. Pocotaligo. Train 12.20—lovely object. Savannah 3. Davies & Green[1] at platform.

Quiet dinner sole. General Lawton[2] & cartridges. Walk in park.

1. Charles Green, British-born Savannah merchant. In July 1861 he was commissioned by the Confederate secretary of war to purchase arms in England. Green was arrested in Detroit in November on his return but released in February 1862 after the intercession of the British minister, Lord Lyons.

2. Brig. Gen. Alexander Robert Lawton, former Georgia legislator. He served as Confederate quartermaster general from 1863 to 1865.

April 30, 1861 [Savannah]

Today drove to Bonaventure at 1.30.

Dust.... Wrote to the Times a good deal.

Grand dinner. Deasy,[1] Ward Chinese Minister,[2] Sam Ward, Locke Editor newspaper,[3] Judge———, General Lawton, Commodore Tatnall.[4]

1. Henry E. Decie, English sailor and owner of the renowned racing yacht the *America*, which, renamed the *Camille*, was employed in running the blockade.
2. John Elliott Ward, former mayor of Savannah and U.S. minister to China, 1859–60.
3. Joseph Lorenzo Locke, a former engineer and soldier, was editor of the *Savannah Republican*.
4. Josiah Tatnall, a native of Savannah, was a veteran naval officer who served in the War of 1812. In March 1861 he was commissioned captain in the Confederate navy.

May 1, 1861

At 12.30 drove to Station find Commodore Tatnall, B[rigadier] General Lawton in full figg & proceeded on board the steamer. River muddy. Camilla—banks low, rice fields. Visit to the Fort. Pulaski.[1] Returned at 8. Dinner. Gourdin called here Godine,[2] & old man unknown.

Letters from Mary, Alice & Oby.[3] Thank God.

1. A huge masonry fortification on Cockspur Island in Savannah harbor, built in 1829. It was captured by Federal forces in April 1862 and held for the remainder of the war.
2. Henry Gourdin, a leading Savannah and Charleston merchant.
3. Obé Willans, Russell's close friend from school days. A colonel in the Army Pay Department, he acted for many years as Russell's financial agent and adviser.

To J.C. Bancroft Davis, May 1, 1861

Savannah.

My dear Davis,

I had to draw 250 dollars at Charleston on James G. King's Sons[1] for which & a surplus to be placed to my cr[edit]. I enclose these bills on Coutts.[2] I leave tomorrow for Montgomery. I have had letters at last from home, but those sent to Washington are still missing. There is a great change in the tone of men here since the news from N.Y. has been made public. The swagger & exultation have disappeared N.Y. is abused roundly, but it is obvious that they are surprized to find they are not going to have it all their own way. *Now* they all disclaim the smallest intention of marching on Washington, "the idea never entered into our heads"! &c. &c![3]

I have been a little feverish but am now all right. Write & send letters to Bunch as heretofore.

They are in great hopes that G[rea]t B[ritai]n will not permit a blockade & they swear they'll keep every bale of cotton for a year to try how Lowell & Manchester can stand.

> Yours ever t[rul]y,
> W.H. Russell.

1. James G. King and Sons, leading New York finance house, founded by James G. King (1791–1853), the son of the revolutionary statesman Rufus King.

2. Coutts and Co., London bankers, founded by the sons of James Coutts (1699–1757), banker, merchant, and lord provost of Edinburgh.

3. See Russell's reports in *The Times* of 28, 30 May 1861 for more detailed accounts of the perceived change in southern opinion.

May 2, 1861

Breakfasted with Mr. Hodgson,[1] present Locke, Ward (Chinese minister), Sam ditto, Green, Miss Telfer awful rum old girl,[2] Mrs. Hodgson ditto.[3] Talk de omnibus. Breakfast silver service very fine. Good house badish pictures.

1. William Brown Hodgson, leading Savannah planter and former U.S. representative in Algiers, Constantinople, and Cairo among other places. He was an internationally known oriental scholar.

2. Mary Telfair, sister-in-law of William Brown Hodgson. She was the daughter of Edward Telfair, former governor of Georgia.

3. Margaret Telfair Hodgson, wife of William Brown Hodgson and youngest daughter of Edward Telfair.

To J.C. Bancroft Davis, May 2, 1861

Savannah.

My dear Davis,

I have at length rec[eive]d here the p[ac]k[a]ge of letters addressed to the care of Consul Bunch which appear to have come over by the Asia & preceding steamer. But I regret to say that the letters from Delane and from Aldershot which with others you announce as having transmitted to Lord Lyons have not yet come to hand.

Nor have I any letters from you particularly in reply to my suggestion of a cypher. What a melancholy disorganization your P[ost] O[ffice] department exhibits. Before these troubles its arrangements were in but an infantile state of development. I had no comfort out of it in Washington and since then infinite misery. I feel that my dispatches are hardly safer to hit a steamer than if they should be thrown into the sea in a sealed bottle—and yet Franklin was y[ou]r first P[ost] Master general![1] Strange that the author of Poor Richard & the lightening rod should fall below Cadmus[2] who first introduced letters into Greece whence Mr. Rowland Hill[3] is supposed to have gathered the seeds of our postal civilization.

My next halt will be at Montgomery. From there I shall skip to Pickens and jump to New Orleans. Pray address me at the Post Office Montgomery for a week after you receive this. I shall advise you of my subsequent postal desires. Let me suggest that the addition of Mr. Archibald's Consular seal[4] might entitle your envelope to a respect which your great merit, unappreciated in this region, may possibly fail to command. On second thoughts pray send letters &c. as before to care of Bunch under cover.

Yours very truly,
W.H. Russell.

1. Benjamin Franklin (1706–90) was Philadelphia postmaster for fifteen years before his appointment as joint deputy postmaster general for the colonies in 1753. He held the post until the Revolution.
2. Cadmus, the son of Agenor, King of Tyre and Telephassa, was the founder of Thebes and reputedly responsible for introducing into Boeotia the art of writing with Phoenician letters, from which the Greek alphabet is derived.
3. Sir Rowland Hill, inventor of the penny postage.
4. Edward M. Archibald, British consul in New York since 1857.

May 3, 1861
Sent off letters to The Times by vice consul Savannah[1] per express
to Bunch. Took one seam hatbox 1 coat roll 1 handbag 1 portmanteau 2 black bags & 1 writing desk. Railway fares 18 dollars. Leave
Savannah. Slept at Macon & our supper negro child describe.

　1. Edward Molyneux, British consul in Savannah. He was a merchant.

May 4, 1861
Left Macon at 9.45. Drove thro' environs. Hodgson joins us.
Arrived at Montgomery at 10.55. Supper.

May 5, 1861 [Montgomery]
Describe hotel. Dined at hotel. Night with Deas[1] &c.

　1. Col. George Allen Deas was acting adjutant general of the Confederate States.

May 6, 1861
A day of great heat in the town. Wrote.
Visit Legislative Body[1] chaperoned by Wigfall.[2]

　1. In May 1861 the provisional Confederate Congress was a unicameral legislature
consisting of members originally chosen as delegates to the Montgomery Convention
that met in February to organize the new republic. It would be replaced after elections
in November 1861 by a new bicameral legislature on the Federal model.
　2. Louis Trezevant Wigfall, fire-eating former Texas senator and, in the spring of
1861, an aide to Pres. Jefferson Davis.

To J.C. Bancroft Davis, May 7, 1861

Montgomery.
My dear Davis,
　I have not received the missing letters, but I have got thank goodness some letters from home which were sent to Bunch for me. It
appears that there is almost no chance of letters or telegrams going
south now. However I shall try from time to time & leave the rest to
Heaven. It is rather disheartening however & takes the stuff out of
me very materially. There is no use in my trying to send you news,
because the n[orthern] papers are always in advance of letters.

If there are any letters or papers after this reaches you send them to me please under cover to the care of Lord Lyons at Washington.

I am my dear Davis faithfully yours,

W.H. Russell.

May 7, 1861

Declaration of state of war & issue of letters of marque[1] in the Montgomery papers. Wigfall, Cobb,[2] Henningsen[3] at ye same table at b[rea]kfast this morning. Wig. comes with me to State Dept. introduced to Davis[4] who is interview[in]g several citizens. Large airy plain room. "Pres[i]d[en]t" on door. He is a very calm resolute man— slight spare a lean Cassius with extremely wrinkled puckered skin on thin intellectual head, eye corner tic. Dressed in drab slate colour. Plain in manner, said but little, admitted military spirit of people, which exposed them to ridicule for our colonels &c. Ordered a protective letter from Sec[retar]y of State for War[5] to whom I proceeded with Wig. He is a tall fiery impulsive yankee looking man—chews & speaks, spits & knaws. Promised order. Next visited Benjamin Att[orne]y Gen[era]l.[6] Israel of diverse orbed brightness. Clever keen & well yes! What keen & clever men sometimes are.

I dined with Benjamin, Wigfall & brother in law[7] there.

1. On 17 April Pres. Jefferson Davis, in response to President Lincoln's call for seventy-five thousand volunteers to suppress the rebellion, issued a proclamation avowing the Confederacy's determination to repel the northern invaders and inviting "all those who may desire, by service in private armed vessels on the high seas, to aid this government in resisting so wanton and wicked an aggression, to make applications for commissions or letters of marque and reprisal under the seal of the Confederate States." James D. Richardson, ed., *The Messages and Papers of Jefferson Davis and the Confederacy 1861–1865*, 2 vols. (New York, 1966), I:60–61.

2. Howell Cobb, leading Georgia politician and former secretary of the treasury. He was chairman of the Montgomery Convention that organized the Confederate States.

3. Charles F. Henningsen was a Scandinavian soldier of fortune who came to the United States as Louis Kossuth's secretary in 1851. He married into a wealthy Georgia family and fought with William Walker's filibusters in Nicaragua in 1856–57.

4. Jefferson Davis of Mississippi had been inaugurated as provisional president of the Confederate States on 18 February 1861.

5. Leroy Pope Walker of Alabama. He resigned in September 1861 and was replaced by Judah P. Benjamin.

6. Judah Philip Benjamin, a distinguished Louisiana lawyer, planter, and politician, was the Confederacy's first attorney general. He subsequently served as secretary of war and, most notably, as secretary of state.

7. Jules de St. Martin, brother of Benjamin's wife, Marie Nathalie.

May 10, 1861

[...] Uneasy sleep, wooden beams of engine creaking & high pressure engine throbbing....& whistle screaming uneasily. When I dress b[rea]kfast is over. Negro stewards & ladies are taking their meals pleasantly—latter well dressed. Go out in balcony. River same as usual, long cane brakes trees on banks continuous. Now & then some wooding station high bank wooden huts, cotton slide negro children an overseer or planter on horseback visible occasionally. Talk with Captain. His story. Irishman fish on Friday no body or soul to be saved but yourself. "Collector at Mobile. What do you think. Ship full of negroes coming in, Sheriff gone U.S. Marshal away & up she goes to the devil up the river." Calls up two negroes. Boy named Bully marked scars on face—"plenty belly full," "come from Carolina" don't know how old. A man d[itt]o....

May 11, 1861 [Mobile]

It was early 'ere dawn when Southern Republic got up to wharf at Mobile. It was 7 when we landed & walked to Battle House[1]—a quay bounded with stores & ships Irish German French Spanish Italian names & language. Battle Ho[use] very good hotel—much spit tho'. Magee[2] & Dr. Nott[3] dined with us in parlour for which they did lay on—20/– a head wine & brandy 50/– very fair of its kind however.

1. Mobile's largest and most prestigious hotel, opened in 1852 on the site of the old Waverly Hotel at the corner of Royal and Francis streets. The Waverly had burned down the previous year.
2. James Magee, acting British consul in Mobile.
3. Dr. Josiah Clark Nott, eminent Mobile physician and ethnologist, best known for his theories on race.

May 12, 1861

A remarkable & pleasant day. Steamer chartered by citizens Forsyth &c. Dr. Nott, Stein,[1] Col. Hardee.[2]

1. Albert Stein, a native of Germany, was a slaveholding merchant and hydraulic engineer who operated Mobile's waterworks system in the 1840s and 1850s. He had earlier designed and directed the construction of waterworks in several southern cities, including Richmond and New Orleans.

2. William Joseph Hardee, a Georgia native, was a Mexican War veteran and author of a widely used textbook on rifle and infantry tactics. He served throughout the Civil War, achieving the rank of lieutenant general in October 1862.

May 13, 1861

I felt very shaky today & had a vague notion that I drank rather too much last night & did not act as I ought to have done, but there is always great excitement in arguing with Americans.

In the evening Forsyth elected Mayor & Mr. Ravesies[1] who is to go to Pensacola dined with me in parlour—dinner high. First rule Bienville Club[2] "No gentleman shall be admitted in a state of Intoxication."

1. Either Frederick or Paul Ravesies, Mobile cotton factors.
2. Mobile private club named after Jean Baptiste Le Moyne, Sieur de Bienville (1680–1767), the founder of New Orleans and a pioneer French administrator in the Gulf of Mexico.

May 14, 1861

Sent off letters to "The Times" (Mobile) addressed B. Davis by express—Hamden. About 5 o'clock get down to wharf where Diana was ready & with fair wind loosed & flew down Bay to the sea for Pickens & Pensacola.

May 15, 1861

Letters 13 & 14 sent by Archibald per Arabia from Boston. It was just dawn as we made out spars of blockading squadron.

Back to wharf on Bragg's[1] horse with intelligent guide fierce South. After a little chat to bed below in cabin.

1. Brig. Gen. Braxton Bragg, born in North Carolina but residing as a planter in Louisiana since 1856, was in command of Confederate coastal forces from Pensacola to Mobile. In June 1862 he was appointed as commander of the Army of Tennessee.

May 16, 1861

It was night as we passed out to sea, & about 12 we were chased by Oriental[1] as we believe.

1. U.S. Navy schooner commanded by George W. Brown.

May 17, 1861

About 5 o'clock I landed & walked to hotel. Had a nice room. Went out with Ward for a walk.

May 18, 1861

Very hot indeed. The handsome Irish maid from Co[unty] Tip[perary] persecuted by Mr. Davis not the president but the artist.

I dined at Dr. Nott's where were Judge Campbell,[1] Forsyth, Sam, charming Miss Eausé,[2] Hardee in love & much chaffed, Mrs. Nott,[3] another lady, very fair grub, very hot wine, very long talk. Campbell long winded but clear headed & legal.

1. John Archibald Campbell, associate justice of the U.S. Supreme Court from 1853 to 1861. He later served as Confederate secretary of war and as commissioner to the Hampton Roads peace conference in February 1865.
2. Adele Auzé, Dr. Josiah Nott's sister-in-law.
3. Sarah Cantey Nott, wife of Dr. Josiah Nott, was a cousin of Sen. James Chesnut, Jr., of South Carolina.

May 19, 1861

Venit summa dies.[1] At 2 or so cometh Magee & chariot & we are out to Springhill—to Stein. The lads of the village my eye what scarecrows. What laughs I had at them—negroes going to church &c.

The scuppernong grape native of N. Carolina. The stalk seems to grow rather as a branch than as a vine with a smooth close grained grey bark. Cherokee plums magnolias.

1. "The great day has come."

May 20, 1861

Letter to The Times per Hoskier.[1] 2 d[i]sp[at]chs. At 8¼ started per steamer Florida from wharf for New Orleans. Nice steamer, rule no. 6 in cabin "All slave servants must be cleared at Custom House." No 7. "Passengers having slaves will please report them as soon as they come on board." Lake Borgne, Grants Pass, Horn Island, Round Island, Pascagoula, Ship Island, Mississippi City, Cat Island, Pass Christian, Fort Pike, Rigolets, pronounced Rigolase, Lake Ponchartrain & musquitoes, duel & the drunkymen.

Kept awake all night by the Colonel & his friend & baffling musqui-toes.

1. A courier for Brown Bros., leading Anglo-American merchant bankers.

To J.C. Bancroft Davis, May 20, 1861

My dear Davis,

I am going on to New Orleans today having had a very interesting visit to Pickens & to Bragg at Pensacola. I think Pickens will not be taken & it must be attacked if they can keep their men quiet. They hope to starve & fever them out but the garrison will be better off than the men on shore. I had to draw yesterday per Hoskier Brown Bros 250 dollars on James G. King's Sons. Pray see the draft is met please & let them draw on Coutts thro' me at New Orleans. I will write at length when I get there. This goes by Hoskier—private hand & I hope will be safe.

> Yours always & ever truly,
> W.H. Russell.

May 21, 1861 [New Orleans]

To town by 7 train—describe lake platform & the bathing boxes. To Mure's consul.[1] Letters. Morris nasty. Two from my soul. One 20th. April other 26th. not so well when she last wrote. I was very unhappy indeed....
Wrote & read.

1. William Mure, British consul in New Orleans.

To Lord Lyons, May 21, 1861

New Orleans.

My dear Lord Lyons,

I avail myself of a few lines by private hand half dazed as I am by long & heated travel to tell you what I have seen—in part at least within the last few days at Pickens & Pensacola. The further I travel the more satisfied I am of the terrible results of the struggle which seems quite beyond the reach of evasion. There is on the part of the South an enormously exaggerated idea of its own strength & of its faut vivre for the rest of the world which nerves its sinews & there is also the desperation of position which one must feel who sits on a barrel of powder & who is menaced with a hot poker. They are resolute & unanimous to a most extraordinary degree—they are stronger than I expected to find them—but they—I speak of the men—not of the South as an "it"—will I think discover that they are ill fitted for a defensive & protracted contest & more especially will they lose heart when or if the sheet anchor fails them, & England & France permit the blockade for a year or more. Their ideas of political economy are enough to drive the venerable A. Smith out of his quiet resting place with a fresh ed[ition] of the Wealth of Nations in his claw.[1] There is so far as I can observe by no means as many armed men as the papers say but there are still enough to make fighting them no easy work, & if they get time & arms & powder their position in their own dunghill will not be easily cowed down.

I visited General Bragg & his batteries on Wednesday & Colonel Browne[2] & his Fort & the U.S. Squadron on the same day & on the preceding afternoon. Your Lordship will understand the necessity imposed on me by the very courtesy of the officers on both sides not to make any communication public in America of matters which cd. only be known by reason of that courtesy, but to you I may say that if Bragg opens fire on Pickens as he stands at present he ought to receive a most tremendous hiding—whipping on dit here. Bragg's batteries with three exceptions are very poor affairs—his guns are nearly all light—he has however some five or six mortars wh. wd. do much harm if P. was like Sumter. McRae[3] wont do much. Barrancas[4] ought not to be able to fight the Fort plus the shipping for two hours, but there are two strong works at the Lighthouse which will give trouble. *If* the garrison stand well I am sure the sailors will do their duty & *if* they are well led, I consider such a landing cd. be effected of marines &c. as wd. suffice to retake the whole position. Pickens is strong with some weak points. There is a want of heavy guns, but it has been put into a good position of defence, & if Bragg does not get lots of mortars & heavy pieces it has nothing to fear. The fleet shd. take off much of the converging fire which is au reste too far to do battering damage, but nothing has been left to burn inside from shells & the men are so well protected I firmly believe they will suffer less than the Confederates who are encamped on the same hills. The fleet is in fine order & men full of fight.

The soldiers of the C.A. are wild splendid dare devil ill armed men without uniformity of uniform or of anything except sacred thirst which they slake by a call to the bar whenever they can. There are about 7,500 over a very weak wide position. The Fort can destroy the Navy Yard in half an hour. The Force I think wd. do better by taking it which might be done in a day if—I am obliged to use many ifs—their fire—fleet & fort—has the effect I think it ought.[5] By destroying McRae wh. the fleet can readily do they can draw off much of the converging fire & take up positions to rake the batter[ie]s & they can throw shell quite over the island. Whichever side has most dash must win for the fort might be taken by a bloody escalade at night & the fleet wd. then have to fly. I shall write again if you permit me & r[e]m[ai]n dear Lord Lyons.

>   Yours very faithfully,
>   W.H. Russell.

1. Adam Smith (1723–90), Scottish philosopher and economist, whose *An Inquiry into the Nature and Causes of the Wealth of Nations*, published in 1776, provided the intellectual foundation for economic liberalism in the nineteenth century and beyond.
2. Col. Harvey Browne, 5th U.S. Artillery. A veteran of the Seminole and Mexican wars, he was in command at Fort Pickens from April 1861 until February 1862.
3. Masonry fort, built in 1834, on the west shore of Pensacola Bay.
4. Masonry fort, built in 1839, two and a half miles northeast of McRae, on the site of the old Spanish fortifications of San Carlos.
5. Russell added here a crude sketch of the harbor area, noting the relative positions of the various fortifications.

May 22, 1861
Write & visit club which is quaint—describe interior, Irish waiters &c.
At 6.30 left my parcel for Mr. Wood to take with him to New York. Writing all day like blazes (it was taken charge of by Mr. Hoskier of Brown Bros & Co. from Mobile—ie. letters 18, 19, on 20th).
Briggs & Ward dined at Mure's, capital claret, & persons came in during the evening.

May 23, 1861
I finished a despatch for the Times no. 20, letters to Quain,[1] Bancroft Davis, Olmsted &c. Sent in consular packet by Mr. Ewell of Dennistoun & Co.[2] who came to grief in Tennessee. The grey doctor, dyed Randall,[3] Morse[4] &c.

I dined with Major Ranney[5] excellent table, Morse, Moise[6] Jew, Hunt[7] sombre fierce, Eustis[8] very nice also, Hunt like Jew swivel eyed black bearded—wines good. One of the slave servants at table was a son of General Jackson—so Ranney told me, must inquire about this. Much talk of New Orleans. Morse denied cotton bags. It is certain that a citizen claimed damages for 72 at all events used by Jackson's troops.[9] We had hot & at times fierce debate at times & I shut up old Morse's barbette guns & prevented him from spouting out Randolph's speeches[10] & had the gratitude of the comp[an]y I believe in consequence. It was very late when we broke up.

1. Richard Quain, Russell's doctor.

2. Dennistoun, Cross and Co. were leading Anglo-American exchange brokers, with branches in Liverpool, Glasgow, New York, and New Orleans.

3. Possibly David A. Randall, Democratic politician from Ascension Parish.

4. Isaac Edwards Morse, attorney general of Louisiana.

5. Maj. Henry Joseph Ranney, president of the New Orleans, Jackson, and Great Northern Railroad.

6. Edwin Warren Moise, a Charleston native, was justice of the Louisiana state supreme court.

7. Randall Hunt, leading New Orleans Unionist. He was related by marriage to Lincoln's secretary of the treasury, Salmon P. Chase.

8. George Eustis, Jr., New Orleans lawyer and Democratic congressman from 1855 to 1859. As secretary to John Slidell, he was taken prisoner in November 1861 from the British steamship *Trent*.

9. During the siege of New Orleans in 1814–15, cotton bales were used by Gen. Andrew Jackson to strengthen American breastworks along the Rodriguez Canal, the theory being that cotton could absorb bullets better than could earth.

10. John Randolph of Roanoke (1773–1833), Virginia congressman and outstanding advocate of states' rights principles in the early republic.

May 24, 1861
Awoke this morning rather dazed no wonder, too much talk smoke & brandy & water last night. Old Sam came in very seedy. I went to work & tried to write but good South could not do much. We were puzzled & angry as it appears Davis had gone. News is exciting, rumours of war in Virginia—on 23d. invasion took place. Colonel Ellsworth assassinated by keeper of hotel named Jackson at Alexandria for taking down his Secession flag.[1] Walked out with Ward to Ranney's, left him to go to bed & sleep as he was quite done up. To Charles Hotel[2] huge place lots of men sitting reading in part of bar, found Davis was not gone. This hotel famous for difficulties, also for assault by filibusters of Walker's gang[3] on Capt. ———R.N. Streets

quite full of uniforms. Went to Mure's & wrote there—curiously well the women of lower orders dress very French in all respects. Davis came in, & I drove scamp to rail. He is a mysterious young fellow. Has made friends here & one of them gave him a bear wh. he keeps in his room. At 4.30 went down to train to Lake where was delicious dinner—Eustis, Johnson,[4] Josephs,[5] Hunt, a very nice sort of place— the New Orleans Richmond or Trafalgar. Terrapin soup excellent, fish bouillabaisse very good, soft crab, pompinoe, &c. wines capital very good service, French cooking—glorious sunset over the waters of Ponchartrain—yachts & fishers stealing about gardens full of rose laurels in full bloom & the most wonderful sand flies. Josephs has travelled with Bruce[6] in Europe. Came home at 9.30 in car drawn by horse along the rails & got to bed very nicely at 11.30 or so.

1. Col. Elmer Ephraim Ellsworth, former law clerk in Abraham Lincoln's office and commander of the 11th New York (the "Fire Zouaves"). He was killed at Alexandria, Virginia, by the proprietor of the Marshall House hotel, James T. Jackson, as he was hauling down a secessionist flag.

2. The St. Charles Hotel on St. Charles Street was completed in 1842. Destroyed by fire in 1851, it was rebuilt and reopened in 1853. The hotel was again destroyed by fire in 1894.

3. William Walker (1824–60), Tennessee-born filibuster, who was executed by Honduran authorities after a failed invasion attempt.

4. Frederick A. Johnson, commissioning and furnishing merchant of Magazine Street, New Orleans.

5. Aaron Keppel Josephs, attorney of Canal Street, New Orleans.

6. James Bruce, eighth Earl of Elgin, was governor general of Canada from 1846 to 1854.

May 25, 1861
Writing all day, Ward came in after b[rea]kfast at 10, & I prepared acc[oun]ts, letter to Times under date, Delane, Mary, Morris, Lord W. Hay,[1] Bigelow, Bunch, Bates, Justis &c. I also drew bills on Coutts under date June 1st for £50 at 3 days sight in favour of J.G. King's Sons. Acc[oun]ts of invasion of Virginia not much fuller. I incline to think it's all up with Richmond as I say in my letter. Sam Ward came in wrote something & vanished at 3 to go with the Major Ranney to see an encampment. Davis also arrived to bid good by. He is certainly as keen a lad as I know. I charged him with dispatches & Mure gave him others for Lord Lyons & Archibald Consul at New York. When Mure came in he had letters from my father May 2nd, & one

thank God for my own soul of May 1st better far than the last, but sad & low in tone. God comfort her & spare her to me & make me worthy of her. It was a comfort however to get it late as it was. I used to get letters in India almost as soon. It is very strange that Oby did not write. It makes me uneasy. I wish too Lizzie[2] had written. I dressed after dinner & went off to Slidells[3] with Mure, found parlour full of ladies carding lint. Slidell, Mrs. Beauregard[4] &c. He is a "remarkable" man. He has fine thin features, a cold keen grey eye—an elderly grey haired man of medium height, stout, lips resolute, manner pleasant like Spring Rice or Monteagle[5] somewhat. Sat there till 10.30. To club where were 2 Englishmen most bitter slaveholders & secessionists. Davis took charge of letter no. 21. He pretends to be in fear of a bodily chastisement from some enemy of his.

1. Lord William Hay, third son of the Marquis of Tweedall, was a civil servant in India and later member of Parliament.

2. A cousin of Russell's who often looked after the children during his wife's illnesses.

3. John Slidell, U.S. senator from Louisiana from 1853 until 1861. He subsequently served as Confederate envoy to France.

4. Gen. Pierre G. T. Beauregard's second wife, Caroline Deslonde, a sister-in-law of John Slidell. She died in 1864.

5. Thomas Spring-Rice, first Baron Monteagle of Brandon, British chancellor of the exchequer from 1835 to 1839.

May 26, 1861

Sent off note by cabman to steamer to say I cd. not go to Mr. Roman's[1] today as I really was seedy & did not feel up to it at all—& then turning round slept soundly. Breakfasted late with Mure....

1. André Bienvenu Roman, planter and governor of Louisiana from 1831 to 1835 and from 1839 to 1843.

May 27, 1861

Visits & purchases—driving about.

We gave our dinner party at the Lake to Mure & Ranney, Genl. Lewis,[1] Mure, Duncan Kenner,[2] Claiborne,[3] bill 56 dollars.

1. Maj. Gen. John L. Lewis, head of the Louisiana state militia.

2. Duncan Farrar Kenner, prominent Louisiana sugar planter and legislator who, in the closing months of the Civil War, undertook a diplomatic mission to Europe with an offer to abolish slavery in return for recognition of the Confederacy.

3. John Francis Hamtranck Claiborne, Natchez-born New Orleans planter and editor and former Mississippi congressman.

May 28, 1861

I dined at ye Lake as before with a large party who invited me down for the purpose—viz Misses Slidell,[1] ex Gov. & General Hebert[2] Mr. Hunt, Mr. Norton,[3] Mr. Fellows.[4]

Slidell curiously cut. We adjourned to the Boston Club[5] afterwards. Harrison[6] drunk escorts me home & wishes to become still more drunk.

1. Rosina and Mathilde Slidell.
2. Paul Octave Hebert, former governor of Louisiana and Mexican War veteran. He was commissioned colonel of the 1st Louisiana Artillery and in August 1861 was appointed brigadier general.
3. M. O. H. Norton, New Orleans commission agent and member of the 1861 Louisiana secession convention.
4. John Quincy Adams Fellows, Louisiana Unionist. In 1864 he was a defeated candidate for governor.
5. Founded in 1841, it was the earliest and most famous of New Orleans's private clubs, with membership restricted to the city's most prominent citizens. The club was named after a well-known card game.
6. James O. Harrison, New Orleans attorney, with offices in Commercial Place.

May 29, 1861

I dined with Aristide Miltenberger[1] this eve[nin]g & met there Governor Moore of Louisiana[2]—afterwards drove out 2 carriages to see shell road, lake canal &c. Old fort. Musquitoes diabolical. They are in the waters of canal. With Moore was his military Secy Mr. ——— who told me he knew nothing whatever of military matters. There is I find great jealousy of South Carolinian Jews such as Moise, Mordecai,[3] Josephs &c. Men of ability like Benjamin get over it.

1. Aristide Miltenberger, a merchant and one of the leading members of Creole society in New Orleans.
2. Thomas Overton Moore was governor of Louisiana from 1861 to 1864.
3. Moses Cohen Mordecai, known as M.C., Charleston merchant and steamship operator.

May 30, 1861

Dined with Miltenberger & visited scene of the defeat of the British in the attack on New Orleans in 1815 with Mrs. Miltenberger[1] in the carriage.

Had a tutulia in the evening at which I met Mon[sieur]s brother[2] & we had a wonderful mint julep.

I wrote & finished dispatch to Times no. 22. Local sketches, description of Camp Moor, write to Mowbray Morris, Delane. Sent by friend of Mure's private hand. Live oaks & balls, 3 miles of trenches. Lafitte & his pirates[3] defending cotton bales. Trial of Lafitte &c. Fire at Club at night. Incendiarism rife. Dr. Rushton[4] declares they must put down universal suffrage & tapage of that sort after revolution. M. Berger is au contraire.

1. Catherine, wife of Aristide Miltenberger.

2. Either Gustave or Ernest Miltenberger.

3. Jean Lafitte (1780–1825), French-born privateer who assisted in the American defense of New Orleans in the winter of 1814–15 having earlier turned down British offers. Lafitte's artillery was particularly useful in repelling the British assault of 8 January 1815.

4. Dr. William Rushton of Canal Street, New Orleans.

May 31, 1861

After breakfast I visited the jail with Mure—had some talk with Sheriff. He is appalled by the crimes wh. are committed in N.O. & says nothing will put a stop to it till it is made highly penal to carry arms. Around jail which is a common whitewashed b[ui]ld[in]g with cracked walls & barred windows were seated men in chains read[in]g papers & smoking. What do you want—order produced—enter hall, in face is iron door, & warder taking down keys ushers us into court yard. It is a noisome place filled with men of all ages all sorts, guilty of murder & charged with larceny—mingling together. A verandah runs along one side. Shown place where one Gordon, who was sitting in cell with only shirt on, irons on legs playing cards smoking, tried to escape—desperate fellow. Men lounged about as they pleased, felt a little uneasy. Warder in shirt hat & drawers, smoked & talked pleasantly. There's where we hang them, said he, pointing to a door & two hooks below it in the wall. They are hanged inside prison, and gaolbirds are shut up in their cells all ye time, but crowd to bars to look out. "They some of them die very brave indeed." Some 70 fellows, murderers, pirates, thieves, violators, burglars were together—some condemned for a few months, others wait[in]g merely for trial. Passed stairs—debtors rooms, 90 days makes free if board be paid for. In one was sitting Withers who had murdered his son in law & shot his wife—wicked and gloomy.[1] The condemned cell was marked by the words & death's head & cross bones. In it were 6 men under sentence—none believed they would hang. I shuddered as I walked in. Two rooms in one of which were religious books, a crucifix—books but little used I fear. The wall was covered with most curious crayons, Christ walking on water, Resurrection, corpses in ye grave, and angels visiting them &c. by a Frenchman who was executed some years ago for murdering his mistress. Opposite good god men madwomen glaring across & with indecent gestures shouting to the wretched men so soon to die—two were to do so next day. This was very horrible indeed. As was also the women's gallery. This is not a very sweet place, s[ai]d gaoler. Heavens it was not. Such miserable creatures—huddled together in one verandah—5 to each cell generally—no beds to sleep on, no blankets. Thence I went to yard for smaller criminals, shortest sentences, very little different from ye other. Two sailors made applications to Mure as British Subjects complaining of their sentences, & he promised inquiry & attention. One was a very bad looking boy & to say truth I did not feel proud of either of my countrymen at all at all.

Mure & self went down by 5 train to Pontchartrain where I gave him a dinner & 2 bottles of wine or so. On our return went to Club where Ward was & he unfortunately introduced me to old ——— & Nixon New O. Crescent,[2] & a talk with Ranney & others. Mure & Ward went home. I visited "Crescent" office with Nixon, saw proofs &c. thence drove with him to see a friend of his named Macdermott or Montgomery, I forget which, & we went out & had a very late supper at a place called Lake ——— —5 or 6 miles out—sang songs & did not come home till daylight did appear. Kind old Mure came to let me in as he was distressed about my being out so late.

1. A. P. Withers had shot and killed his stepson, A. F. W. Mathew, during an argument over the Washington Artillery, which had been about to depart for service in Virginia. See Russell's report to *The Times*, 19 June 1861.

2. James O. Nixon, owner and editor of the *New Orleans Crescent*, founded in 1847.

June 1, 1861

I was not by any means all right & well today & could not go out from
sheer nervousness. Lost my pocket book containing notes & dates,
very annoying as I fear it will fall into people's hands. Nixon has
already told Mure a lie in saying I proposed visit to Lake.

Mure after dinner went to see his brother[1]—& W. & self remained
talking for some time. He is very anxious to be retained on the staff
of The Times & I will do my possible for him if it is to be done at all.
Ward & I visited Custom House Street, & it was late when I got home.

1. William Mure's brother, John.

June 2, 1861

Good Mure up this morning to see me off. I am seedy but not so sick as
I ought to be. Gave Louise a sov[ereig]n. "Dieu vous garde Mons[ieur].
Soyez heureux ayez tout joie".[1] She is really a very pleasant well behaved person. Alas I wish her prayers were heard vous esperez! A
good girl—a [...]. Gave Mary 10/– Cook 10/– Henri 30/– Carriage cost
10/– Coat 16/–. Breakfasted. There came on Sheriff free black British
sailor sent by Magee from Mobile for passage to Halifax. He had his
trunk on a cart & was in much terror lest police shd. arrest him if
found in City. Mure gave him a letter to Hospital, & some relief. It is
too bad. This state of things ought not to be tolerated at all. We drove
together to boat "J.L. Cotten" where were Morse. Roman Jnr.[2] cd.
not come as his comp[an]y was out. It was quite pitiable to see them
going to church in powder blue & silver uniforms. They will do no
good. Shops open French fashion. Drumming going on. Make resolve
never to travel again on a Sunday. Cotten a nice boat. Tired & lie
down & thereby avoid talk on statistics with friend Forstall[3] who is
very rich descended from Irish near Rochestown. Southern Chancellor of Excheq[ue]r & Baring's agent. He is more French than English
or Irish or American. Burnside[4] also on board with his friends preceding me to the plantation. Lingham[5] item, M. Lavillebeauvre & his
wife who is daughter of Govr. Roman.[6] He seems nice fellow. A dinner on board middling good. It was about 3 'ere I arrived at Romans
sending on things by Ward to Burnside. Leaving landing & nearby I
am sorry to say talking with us Morse who was busy proving there
were only 70 or 80 cotton bales at B[attle] of N[ew] O[rleans], plunged
into Mrs. Sippy. Not wider here than Thames at Gravesend & muddy

& strong. Kept from flooding town by levee. It is now 9 ft. higher than level of streets. A few British ships alongside wharf where all is now quite lifeless. Houses on quay very poor & vast streets lined by little houses d[itt]o indicate great conceptions not realized spite of prosperity of New Orleans because grass is on the streets. General effect not unpleasant however. Spires domes &c. rising over a sea of very flat roofs & low houses painted white. Beyond is a green forest. On the other side river is a series of low houses shingle roofs around green just rising above top of levee! The steamer floats about here & there carrying the soldiers food parcels for we can see them all busy drilling & can hear the firing as we move along. Soon reach open country beyond the bounds of city & find it is very flat & very fertile for it is lined by regular rows of houses close almost as villas on banks of Thames white & glistening with pillars porticoes & veranda & white palisade in front. Then rows of small Crimean huts more or less white & all pastured up behind which far as eye can reach to the forest edge are field of sugar cane & Indian corn. Few persons save men in uniform are to be seen—tops of buggies now & then just shows above the road which is hidden down below levee & is not itself visible on either side. No boats to be seen. Met only 2 steamers in 62 miles so blockade even admitting regular trade is now even for season of year begins to tell.

Uniform breadth of river remarkable & dull, no shelving banks, no shoals no pebbly margins. It is a huge canal like trench draining a continent. The steamer discharged us about 3.30, at Ducks Sleeping Place "Cahabanooze" Governor Romans who rec[eive]d me very kindly, Lingham & M. Lavillebeauvre & wife. Part of his garden was carried off by Mrs. Sippy. House 2 storied square verandah all around, hall centre plain furniture. In a detached house of four bed rooms library &c. one storied I took up quarters. Went out for a walk with Governor surprized to see nice dresses of two or 3 negro women servants on door who were going over to sugar house to have a dance. In negro quarters were 2 divisions that for house servants—other for plantation blacks, old women a third children—houses pretty good. Hospital poor, beds common. Sickness chiefly of lung diseases. Detached house, a good deal of poultry.

1. "God bless you, sir. I wish you every happiness and joy."
2. Capt. Alfred Roman, son of former governor André B. Roman, was appointed

lieutenant colonel of the 18th Louisiana Infantry in October 1861. A lawyer and news-paper editor by profession, he served from 1862 to 1865 as inspector general on the staff of Gen. Pierre G. T. Beauregard, whose military memoirs he later assisted in writing.

3. Edmond John Forstall, leading New Orleans banker and financier and, from 1832 until his death in 1872, agent for Baring Bros. of London and Hope and Co. of Amsterdam.

4. John Burnside was the largest sugar planter in the South, with five plantations in St. James and Ascension parishes. In 1861 he owned over thirty thousand acres of land and over nine hundred slaves.

5. J. G. Lingham, commission merchant with William H. Haynes & Co. of New Orleans.

6. Elie Lavillebeuvre and his wife, Jeane, daughter of André B. Roman, a prominent Creole family.

June 3, 1861

At 5 awake mockies d——d noisy. Governor mounted & I am on nice chesnut, went off to inspect plan[tation] with man open[in]g gates. Corn one side, cane another, when cane is bad corn sowed with it—when corn d[itt]o peas ditto. In regular drilled rows fields ran back bounded by forest wild uncleared, bayous alligatory. Distance white figures like rebels in morn[in]g marches in India on fields of grain. Came at last to hoeing grounds about 36 men & 15 women hoeing cane to clear it from weeds, laborious enough. In path a cart with water, & bucket of molasses, a tub of milk, & a mass of hominy with pans for their breakfast, overseer with lash by his side inspecting a black man, power up to 10 lashes. Sugar very expensive, cane requires care—& then frost comes & withers it in Dec[embe]r. Negroes well clad enough, but did not look up or speak—only few nodded to me. Rode to another place where mules were drawing ploughs between furrows of cane. Altho' still early I felt heat as considerable. It must be tremendous in August. Close crops, no air—got back breakfast—quite large circle—cakes various. Lingham—"I'll tell you a curious thing. He was a German you know shed old Pole—Eh you know whom I mean. Didn't want her. So I was at Grenville at the time &c. &c." After breakfast started off with Governor to visit some planters. Potier sugar refinery[1]—fine gardens & hot house…. In refinery heat considerable, naked blacks working windows barred to prevent steal-ing sugar. Price falling, profits generally 15£ to 20£ per h[ogs]h[ea]d. Potier grave fierce man like Jerome B[onapart]e,[2] great Catholic.

Back before dinner. Several strangers in billiard room. Pres[i]d[en]t
Jefferson College[3] &c. &c. Forstall came also, long statistics. Banks
p[ai]d in North. His projects &c. Dinner very nice—de trop if possible. Lingham & Forstall went off to town. Gaudet[4] et alii capital
claret. Banquet hall finally deserted, cigars & grog & talk in the open
& flies gleaming. I resolved to pack up & send things by steamer
tonight to Burnside. I like Alfred Roman sad story. God help him &
us! As I go in at night to superintend packing find Moses asleep over
portmanteau.... I walk about. It is very late when I get to bed. Watch-
man has to light a fire for big steamer to come up to river bank. I
must go back in memory for my reflections on this day.

1. In his *Diary North and South* 1:382, Russell refers to Potier as Governor Roman's
brother-in-law. However, Roman's wife's maiden name was Parent, and none of his
sisters or brothers appears to have married a Potier. The only Potier listed in the 1860
census was Alex Potier, a planter in St. Martin Parish.

2. Jerome Bonaparte (1784–1860), brother of Napoleon, who presided over the
French Senate for eight years before his death. He was married to an American woman.

3. Jefferson College was the oldest institution of higher education in Louisiana.
Incorporated in 1831, it closed after bankruptcy in 1855 but was purchased at auction in 1859 by François Valcour Aime, a wealthy St. Charles Parish planter and
philanthropist, who presented it to the Marist order. It finally closed in 1927.

4. Possibly Dr. Felix B. Gaudet of Bourbon Street, New Orleans.

June 4, 1861
My friend Moses 6 a.m.—any absinthe or any thing stomachy. Up
rather late, a heavy clouded sky. The 2 children at drill of course. At
breakf[as]t Dr. Laport or Leport[1] ancien rep[resen]t[ative] sent off
by Louis Nap[oleon][2] whom now he admires, passport for abroad or
adhesion, pref[erre]d former. Roman very nice & kind. Mde. Lafille-
beauvre & husband going to Mass for repose of soul of Valchareme's
wife had our little smoke in my rooms—our chat, & at last came the
great word. God bless you good old man, victim of position child of
necessity. The carriage is ready—farewell. Drive along the r[oa]d by
r[igh]t bank—lined with plantations uniform fence cypress staves
pointed. Sometimes whitewashed—wooden gates, shrub & rugged
garden in front. Occasionally wretched, men making 80 or 90 h[ogs-
hea]ds. sugar miserable.... Convent on other side sacré coeur. 24 out
of 30 died of yellow fever in the year. Such poor places interspersed,
remarkable want of life. River flows on desert—cows & mules graz-

ing. No boats not 1 in view for miles.... At 16 miles or so stop at Manning's overseers,[3] grim big man rec[eive]d us in a house uncarpet[e]d destitute of furniture. Spurgeon's sermons[4] on table, gave us negro to ferry over. Rain & thunder, crops good, to boathouse.... Chickens & hen around fire, woman blear-eyed & cross, child playing 2 beds, covered coarse ragged blanket, sulky. Wd. not get key boat house. Boat filled water, no oars but stumps, no good for angry Mrs. Sippy. Waited hour while negro got key. Bade Alfred Roman adieu & after traject[ory] in charm[ing] little skiff landed at Burnsides. As we walked up brick avenue host came out hearty welcome. Good room Gaines,[5] Gasket &c. describe place. Whitewashing paling on river.... Gateway with an avenue of trees, house square fine verandah, 6 pillars in front 3 stories high view from verandah. Different from Cahabanoose or Ducks sleeping place. Excellent wine at dinner. Gaines a cross little man. Says "we dont want recognition. Take our cotton. That's all we want." Politics as usual quite material.

1. Possibly Jean Baptiste Laporte, originally from Tarbes, who came to New Orleans in 1851. He died in France in September 1892.

2. Napoleon III, emperor of France from 1848 to 1870.

3. W. W. Bateman, overseer for former governor John L. Manning. In 1860 he owned twenty-five slaves with a personal estate valued at $30,000.

4. Charles Haddon Spurgeon was a celebrated London Baptist preacher, famous for his oratory and wit.

5. Possibly Charles C. Gaines, New Orleans hardware merchant.

June 5, 1861

This morning Gaines & Gasket are off to N.O. As to former his loss was our gains. Very good breakfast after which we take to the saddle & view this saccharine principality. Mr. Seal[1] is my guide—ride thro' broad street lined with fields of cane & corn just going into tassel to new sugar house wh. negroes are putting up—good masonry & carpentering. Seal talks of colour & complexion before them. They shake hands very familially, are well dressed enough. Seal says they dont mind being spoken of before their faces. "That yellow fellow is a good carpenter" &c. Heat is considerable. There is a carpenters & smith's shop where ploughs are repaired & all work required on the estate done, brick is also made by negroes. Machinery is from Cincinnati, that efforts are made to get it from N.O. where factories have been established. We next go to negro plantation where nearly 80 children are in charge of old women nurses & children of both sexes too young to work—ie. not 12 to 14. It was a curious sight. They seemed glad to see Seal & came round to shake hands with us all. Morrow, Mas' Seal. No education—no idea of God. The dead are buried in a field by their own people. Once a month they have prayers read to them. Their holiday is on Saturday afternoon. They get about 5 lbs. pork a week, plenty bread made & Indian corn—or fish at breakfast, molasses &c. Reading & writing not approved of—children fat & healthy. Nursing women at times allowed to go from work daily to suckle the young ones.

1. H. M. Seale, overseer on John Burnside's Houmas sugar estate. He owned six slaves in 1860.

June 6, 1861

Late to b[rea]kfast & did nothing afterwards till 1 when I rode out with Lee to visit Orange, the farm so called from a few orange trees. Overseer Seal salutes, visit Boatswain who says he dont recolleck nothins of Africa. God gave him 14 children & took them all away again. Orange grove plantation is magnificent land, cane & crops wonderful. Overseer Gibbs or Gibson,[1] a grim man big beard & eyes, meets us. He is not very bright, takes us into cane brake—shows where Irish have been working, a gang under one 'John Laughlin', they are very quiet, he says, & are fed on regular rations more stingely than the negroes are. A fair child looks out of a hut, it is a slave son of an overseer. The child always partakes of the status of mother. The overseer who got this child bought another of his own out of slavery & carried it away with him. Johnson is his name. Forty bushels to acre a good crop here I am told & 1½ hogshead of sugar very good. Visit some cottages, sick old woman. "My children quoth Gibbs are healthy." At dinner were Cottmans[2] (one has been in Russia), McCaul,[3] Bringier,[4] Colon,[5] Kenner (sporting man).

1. Benjamin Gibbs, overseer at John Burnside's Orange Grove plantation.
2. Dr. Thomas E. H. Cottman, Louisiana planter and leading Unionist. In the mid-1850s Cottman lived in Europe where, among other roles, he acted as surgeon to the Grand Duke Constantine. In 1855 he undertook an unofficial mission to the United States on behalf of the Czar of Russia.
3. John McCall of Evan Hall plantation in Ascension Parish. He owned 233 slaves in 1860.
4. Marius St. Colombe Bringier of White Hall plantation in St. James Parish.
5. Octave Colomb, sugar planter of St. James Parish.

June 7, 1861

At 6 Joe summoned me to a bath of Mrs. Sippy water a glass iced d[itt]o a cup of coffee & as horses were ready away we sallied, Lee, Ward & self to view Gov. Manning's, B[urnside]'s neighbour. Way thro' splendid crops waving corn—to negro quarters wh. pleased me more than any I have yet seen. Street very wide & green filled with poultry, some sheep & ox & calf of the Brahminee cross. House doors open & people moving about, more signs of life in fact than I have yet seen on plantation villages. Some doors were closed, at others were old men & women boys children &c. Trees before doors, close behind poultry huts, most of ye houses are of brick. A fine stable being built by negroes further on. Thence to saw mill & water wheel for draining ye land. On by the forest side thro' land in which Indian corn was waving amid stumps of forest trees to see process of clearing land. Overseer Bateman—poney specs & quid. Knife in belt wh. however he keeps "to cut his way thro' the cane brake." The forest smouldering marked scene of labour, huge trees grim sycamore, live oak &c. The mules yoked 3 abreast drag plough painfully thro' gnarled roots & rigid earth but it yields its gold at last & next year will be fit for sowing with Indian corn. With 120 negroes & mules to match 450 acres will be cleared this year & the balance of a thousand next year. Manning has 1800 acres. This work is death on negroes & mules "Generally get it done if we can by Irishmen." The same is true of canals & ditching. Friend Lee talks learnedly of slaves breeding &c. 500 acres is enough for a man to make a fortune with say of a million dollars. All materialism in its most painful form. To breakfast amid a shower wh. deepened into thunder & rain to great delight of ye planters. Burnsides good soul leaps with joy at every drop. He is not a naturalized citizen yet.

June 8, 1861

Did not ride out this morning....
At McCauls at last, usual white house, 1 story high above ground, another hid by glacis. Riverferry adventure.

June 9, 1861

Packing up à quoi bon? Birds singing cheerily & deliciously. About 12 thunder storm which lasted & lasts till 3 or more.
The mocking bird screens her young. "No truth outside these gates."

June 10, 1861
After dinner leave Burnside who with Lee accompanying us in his carriage to ferry. Wonderful clouds & glorious sunset. Perambulate town. The chief of Donaldsonville police.

June 11, 1861 [Baton Rouge]
5 a.m. Acadia for Baton Rouge, where we arrive at 2 p.m.... Walker & his introductions. Dine at Mrs. Meers.[1] Creole.... Conrad[2] calls. Judge Avery[3] ditto.

1. Mrs. Augustine Mears, who ran a boardinghouse in East Baton Rouge.
2. Frederick Daniel Conrad, East Baton Rouge planter. In 1860 he owned 248 slaves.
3. William H. Avery, planter of Iberville Parish.

June 12, 1861
Awoke by 4 a.m. Pargoud, "Mary T." takes us at 7 a.m. Rush on to Natchez which we reach at 11.30 p.m. too late for Marshalls.[1]

1. Levin R. Marshall, prominent Natchez district sugar planter.

June 13, 1861 [Natchez]
Marshall going off commends us to his sons.

June 14, 1861
Cross river & view plantations.
Take "General Quitman" for Vicksburg at 10. Supper.

June 15, 1861
Breakfast on board, Vicksburg in sight. Washington Hotel. McMeekan[1] singing out names of dishes. Citizens meeting & punch at Station. Cars at 3.
Jackson 5 p.m. Russell's[2] horse & carriage. Our walk in the city.

1. T. C. McMeeken, proprietor of the Washington Hotel, Vicksburg.
2. Dr. M. C. Russell was a Jackson city alderman.

June 16, 1861 [Jackson]
Write at Jackson....
Start at 6 for Memphis. Change cars at Canton. Drunk recruits all
night screaming. Sick in the m[or]ning.

June 17, 1861
Gayoso House Memphis at 1.30 p.m....
Pillow[1] calls to take me to Fort Randolph[2] 65 miles up.

1. Gideon Johnson Pillow of Tennessee, a Mexican War veteran, was senior major
general of the state's provisional army. In July 1861 he was appointed brigadier general
in the Confederate army but was relieved from duty after the loss of Fort Donelson
in February 1862.
2. Tennessee fort on Mississippi River north of Memphis.

June 18, 1861
Visit Randolph....

June 19, 1861
Start at 4 a.m. Humboldt 82 miles from Memphis.... Arrive at 9.
To Columbus 72 miles.
Boat to Cairo reach at 6 p.m.

June 20, 1861
Visit Prentiss[1]
Visit camp. Make speech.... Flies in hotel.

1. Brig. Gen. Benjamin Mayberry Prentiss, a Mexican War veteran, commanded
Federal volunteer forces around Cairo, Illinois.

June 21, 1861 [Cairo]
Cairo. Write all day.
Send off letter 29 by steamer of Wednesday.

June 22, 1861
Cairo—write all Saturday.
See men embark for exped[ition].

To J.C. Bancroft Davis, June 22, 1861

Cairo, Illinois.

My dear Davis,

I have at last got out of the land of Dixie & whiskey, & am speeding on towards Washington where I hope to be by July 2d. & I have written to Brodie to take rooms for me by the week. If there is any large movement of troops going on I shall probably take the field with them as soon as I am fit for it. I have resolved since I saw some paragraphs in the Chicago Tribune & other papers here attributing to me the most ludicrous statements to have no words with any representative of the local press as the falsehoods & misrepresentations which are the certain results are monstrous. Did you see what I allude to? By this mail I send a letter to Harper's Weekly respecting the blackguard part played by their artist Mr. Davis of which I have just been made aware. If they do not publish it I must send it to the New York papers.[1] Now as for the war. If the North is as anxious & as resolute as the South you will have a most tremendous conflict for there can be no doubt of the spirit, resolution & *unanimity* in a military sense of all the States I have been thro'. I doubt their lasting powers, but they have thrown their soul into the question, & it will take more than one fight to conquer them. It is perfect madness to trust brigades under Schenks[2] & Sickles[3] [illeg.] ag[ains]t the adroit skilled & cunning Southerners commanded by men who know *something* of war & fighting. The absurdities I have seen in the New York papers about military matters are enough to drive a soldier mad. It does seem to me as if your contractors are in a bad way. In the South they swear they will hang any contractor they find cheating the men. It would "encourage les autres" very much. You want cavalry & field artillery to make decisive & short work & to secure the fruits of any victories you may win. Depend on that. I have seen enough of armies to know there is nothing wd. astonish the Southerners so much in the field as some good cavalry.

When I get to Washington there will I hope be a perfect mail bag of letters. I got one from my wife 15th. May in which she gave me better accounts & cheered me up greatly. I am told I am very unpopular with the North & in New York. I can't help it. I must write as I feel & see & I believe I may have the consolation accorded to the impartial of finding myself still more unpopular in the South 'ere I leave America. I wd. not retract a line or a word of my first letters on the cross....

> With kind regards to Mrs. Davis, believe me yours very truly always,
>
> W.H. Russell.

1. See *Harper's Weekly*, 20 July 1861, where Russell's statement was published together with depositions from Davis and other witnesses.

2. Brig. Gen. Robert Cumming Schenk of Ohio, former Whig congressman and U.S. minister to Brazil. He resigned from the army in 1863 and returned to Congress. From 1871 to 1876 he served as U.S. minister to Great Britain.

3. Brig. Gen. Daniel Edgar Sickles, controversial former Democratic congressman from New York, who in 1859 was sensationally acquitted of murdering his wife's lover.

June 23, 1861
In evening start for Chicago.
4 p.m. Camps on way. Prairie.

June 24, 1861 [Chicago]
Arrive at Chicago 9 a.m. Richmond House. Dickens[1] &c.

1. Augustus Dickens, younger brother of Charles Dickens, whom the novelist nicknamed "Boz," later to become his own pseudonym. In 1858 he deserted his wife, who had gone blind, and ran off to America with another woman. He died in Chicago in 1866.

June 25, 1861
Dined with Au[gustus] Dickens.

To J.C. Bancroft Davis, June 25, 1861

Chicago.

My dear Davis,

Here is a letter for Saturday's post. I am on my way to Washington by July 2d. I have just seen a file of "The Times". My letters have all gone to pot apparently. I miss one from Charleston—one from Savannah, one from Montgomery. There were two from the first two & three from the last. This is going to be a very terrible war if it be fought out. It must end in a compromise I think. The South is not as strong as the North but its defensive power is enormous. I have a little touch of fever which weakens me but do not say anything about it to them at home.

In haste yours very truly,
            W.H. Russell.

June 26, 1861
Cheque James G. Kings Sons cashed at hotel 250 drs.
Colonel Turchin Russian[1] sent orderly to me.
Dined at Fosters.

  1. Col. John Basil Turchin of the 19th Illinois Infantry, formerly Col. Ivan Vasilo-vitch Turchinoff of the Tsar's Imperial Guard, who emigrated to the United States in 1856. He was commissioned brigadier general of volunteers in July 1862.

June 27, 1861
At 8 a.m. left Chicago for Niagara—sent letter 30.

June 28, 1861 [Niagara]
Niagara. Our morning walk towards the Falls 3.30 a.m.

June 29, 1861
Visit Streets Island. Lundys Lane. Chippewa.

To J.C. Bancroft Davis, June 29, 1861

                                                    Clifton Niagara.
My dear Davis,
    I arrived here last night & start for Washington via Elmira tomor-row. Will you kindly send me a line to say if you have received a letter from me sent by Express from Chicago & instructions as to anything I can do for you in Washington in the way of news for the paper. It is stated that an immediate move will take place. I hope not for I dont think an advance can be made down Southwards in the present posi-tion of things without great danger of the right flank of the U.S. army being cut in two & turned. That such is the design of Davis I have

little doubt, & with such raw ill disciplined troops as there are in the field combined movements in line are always difficult & uncertain— routs are fatal, & even small checks often prove most mischievous. As I told Ward the other day Picton[1] said "War was the science of precautions" & I have more confidence in Scott if he is let alone than I have in Davis who is however the man for a daring sudden desperate dash suited to the temperament & exigencies of his troops. Entre nous do you think our friend Ward would be a good man to trust in the field? He is plucky as steel & as true I think, but there would be a great responsibility on me if anything became of him after he had gone on a campaigning exped[itio]n at my solicitation. He is ready & willing but I dont feel inclined to ask him to undertake such a risk.

I am sorry to see the hostile spirit which is growing up between England & the States, I believe on the side of the latter. The dispatch of troops to Canada[2] I am satisfied is [torn] Canada than America. You have 300,000 in arms. If they do their work speedily here it may not be so easy to [torn] them at the close of a short campaign & besides we are threatened with an invasion of runaway negroes. There is not now [torn] in all this part of Canada, & in the whole provinces there is only one regiment of British infantry some 700 bayonets. In view of your enormous force an addition of three regiments is not unreasonable considering that there is a strong element of discontent in Canada which might take occasion in the disruption of local power & authority at your side to do us mischief.

 Ever yours truly,
  W.H. Russell.

1. Lt. Gen. Sir Thomas Picton (1758–1815) served under Wellington in the Peninsula campaign and was killed at Waterloo.

2. In the spring of 1861, in response to the American crisis, the Palmerston government acted to strengthen its military forces in British North America. Three new infantry battalions were sent in May and June, with over two thousand troops alone sailing on the "Great Eastern" in what Americans regarded as an overly provocative gesture. Significant munitions reinforcements were also made, while the North American squadron also received six new vessels.

June 30, 1861
Go over to Goat Island—drove back Niagara....

July 1, 1861
Engaged George coloured boy at 20 drs. a month & advanced him
9 drs. on acc[oun]t.
Falls splendid—great grey column hidden in a grey cloudy morning.

July 2, 1861 [New York]
At early dawn looking out on ye Hudson crossing Albany Catskill
Mountains enveloped in mist & scenery much bedeviled thereby generally. Steamers &c. West Point &c. At 9 a.m. Duncan's carriage
awaits us. Bath breakfast &c. into town where to my great pain but
not surprize I hear of Charlotte's death.[1] I felt I never would see her
again at ye last time. Poor soul. Peter Burrowes[2] wrote it casually in
a letter to me. Imagine my horror otherwise misery profound if I had
been told as I was by Davis "a letter in deep mourning has been sent
on to you". Thank you kind angels. The Lord be praised. Ever & ever.
Talk with Davis—draw on Coutts £100 King's Sons & draw check.
Order things. Sit for portrait. Write a letter Harpers Weekly & post
it. Mathew [illeg.] & consul[3] comes in & we talk together de omnibus
& other things. He is crapulous. A good story. During ye excitement
on enlistment question a young attaché amused himself by sending
telegrams which he signed Mathew for sport. These came into hands
of U.S. officials & Marcy[4] with great delight declared he had proofs
of Mathew's complicity. Mathew never knew reason of his recall till
long after & too late. A pleasant dinner party at Duncans. Evarts[5]
cute lawyer, Rowan. Barlow[6] came in & fierce argument thereon.
They seem to think Hurlbert is in danger. Evarts fierce man on ye
subject of ye blockade. I was very tired & not at all sorry to get off
to bed by singing a song. If I had not seen Peter's letter what shd. I
have done? And so to bed but if one has to rise early one never sleeps
well I think.

1. Possibly an elderly relative or companion of Russell's wife, Mary.
2. Peter Burrowes was an Irish lawyer and close friend of Russell. It was through
Peter Burrowes that Russell met his wife, whose father was Peter's cousin.
3. George Benvenuti Mathew, British consul at Philadelphia from 1853 until May

1856, when his exequatur was revoked by the president of the United States as part of the Crimean enlistment controversy. He formerly served as consul at Charleston.

4. William Learned Marcy of New York was U.S. secretary of state from 1853 to 1857.

5. William Maxwell Evarts, a prominent New York Republican lawyer and grandson of the Revolutionary statesman Roger Sherman. He had a distinguished political and legal career after the Civil War, including service as attorney general and secretary of state.

6. Samuel Latham Mitchell Barlow, leading New York Democratic lawyer.

July 3, 1861

Lounging no longer than needed to twist out of bed I uped & downed to breakfast at 5 &, starting at 6.15 I with difficulty reached train or boat rather at 7 a.m. & so bashed off & away for Washington. N.Y. looked well in early morning—not so well pleased with vegetable carts in streets. Warn George not to say who I am. Country in N.Y. well cultivated, houses numerous see notes of various sorts in note book. Baltimore guarded & kept down by force, camps all along the road men looking tolerably well. At Washington about 5½ found Lord Lyons in garden & Monson.[1] A lot of letters, I drive over at once. There were my wondrous deenyman's. Such a lovely lot of them I never seed in all my life before, & each showing she was getting on in spite of the terrible shock. I showed my gratitude in a peculiar way oh Lord. Luggage a long time coming. My quarters were 179 Pennsylvania Avenue. 2 small cribs indeed, & a privey in a small y[ar]d below with a big smell. Well Sir it was nasty & for 30 dollars a month! I walked towards Gautiers & met Sumner who told me most important news for wh. see note book as to relations between France & England & the dirty little mountebankism of my weeny friend in office. Sumner makes it appear he saved the whole concern from going smash. Maybe he did—maybe he didn't, any how he kept me an hour outside Gautiers—& no mistake & I so savagely hungry & sick. I lodge in house owned by [illeg.] Irishman with 4 daughters next to Jost.[2]

Letter to Times posted last night Duncan.... Wrote to Mary ere I left.

1. Edward John Monson, the son of Lord Monson, was attaché at the British legation since 1858 and private secretary to the minister, Lord Lyons. He was transferred to Hanover and then Brussels in 1863.

2. The Josts were Swiss "wine merchants" on Pennsylvania Avenue with whom Russell lodged after his return from the South.

THREE

Bull Run and After

July 4, 1861 [Washington]

Breakfasted with Johnson, Cecil Queen Messenger,[1] an old acquaintance scarce remembered of the City of the Sultan, very jolly. I had first however made a rude meal of tea & toast. Wrote to Lord Lyons for seat in diplomatic part of Senate which opens today, but he said he was not going nor were any of his staff. I may mention by the by that next evening I brought him a copy of the Message,[2] the first he had seen wh. rather amused him as proof of activity of staff. I dined there in ye evening & only Johnson was present beside self, good dinner. Afterwards off we went to see camp of 12th. N.Y. Col. Butterfield[3] a very nice fellow. Fireworks illuminations flags &c. describe officers tent, freedom of men, only 2 U.S. soldiers out of 12 &c. Monson told me tonight the condition of things with Lord Lyons & Seward had been very bad, so much so Lord L. wd. not go near State Dep[artmen]t for fear of being insulted by the tone & manner of little S. My goodness I forgot I went to see S. yesterday & he seemed quite happy at being able to inform me poor little man that a passport system had been established now & that my passport had been signed by Lord Lyons but was no good till he signed it & then it must be signed by General Scott. When I went to the Senate I had the honour of being introduced to floor by Sumner & Wilson.[4] I sat at Sumner's desk & sent off letters. I despatched a host of correspondence per Monson, British Legation also on Friday morning for Saturdays post.

1. Capt. Cecil Godschall Johnson, Queen's foreign service messenger since 1839. Formerly a midshipman in the Royal Navy, he also served with the British Auxiliary Legion in Spain in 1836–37.

2. Abraham Lincoln's message to the special session of Congress, which convened on 4 July, in which the president attempted to define the central issues in the conflict with the rebel states.

3. Col. Daniel Butterfield of the 12th New York Militia. He was appointed brigadier general in September 1861 and was wounded at Gaines Mill. He composed the bugle call "Taps."

4. Sen. Henry Wilson of Massachusetts was Republican chairman of the military affairs committee.

To J.C. Bancroft Davis, July 4, 1861.

179 Penn[sylvani]a Avenue, Washington.

My dear Davis,

Where will you put up at Washington? If you like I will look out for a logement for you. I am here in two furnished clothes chests over a watercloset facetiously considered apartments. Relations with England & France better than they were. Message not to be had by me. Write as to the lodgings &c. &c. I hope you will come—& that soon.

Yours always,

W.H. Russell.

July 5, 1861

I visited the Senate today Bigelow, Sumner. Breakfasted very quietly on dirty water & toast at my lodgings. Mails in & I read papers & write. How beautiful my darling Mary's letters are. I read them over with pleasure. She is a true woman, never was finer courage more tender love in this wide world, never, never. There is no movement forward yet. Bigelow came & sat with me & at his suggestion I went in & saw if old Scott was visible. Quarters are quiet, a few officers in a.d.c.'s room. I met Cullum, & we went over positions &c. Scott was with Mansfield[1] & was very sorry but too busy to see me. I am not to be caught calling on old Vanity again but he really is a fine old lump of martial glory. Dressed & walking over with Johnson to Lord Lyons to dine saw the General yellow lappels sewed to coat & walking between his two aides & we spoke to him in order not to hurt him. "You see I am trying to hobble along quoth he. I will cause it to be intimated to you when I can have ye pleasure of seeing you &c." At Lyons after long time in came faded beauty Lady Georgianna

Fane[2] & her escort Mrs. Clifford. She must have been a gay & very spanking woman in her day. She is proslavery to the backbone & talks about English labourer & negro &c. & in a way wh. shows influence of her friend who has been for years in South. Weary evening rather. Afterwards talk of fire flies anglice lightening bugs.... Called on Riggs, found there Madame Stoeckl, Mon[sieur] Le Baron, &c. &c. & so to bed after a time & home to my chimney. George is I fear a loose fish, verrons nous.

1. Brig. Gen. Joseph King Fenno Mansfield, a Connecticut native, was in charge of Washington's defenses. He was killed at the Battle of Antietam in September 1862.

2. Lady Georgianna (or Georgina) Fane, daughter of John Fane, M.P. for Wormsley, and wife of Joseph Warren Henley, president of the board of trade in Lord Derby's government. She died in 1864.

July 6, 1861

Breakfasted with Bigelow & coming later was B[rigadier] Gen. McDowell,[1] 42, grey & iron tuft, broad jowl and smooth face, keen blue eye, good brow, block head, square stout clumsy figure & limbs, talked a good deal against political generals &c. Beauregard was he said always studious at West Point, g[rea]t muscular strength. Some officers suspected of selling rations &c. Regular Army never. We walked back together to my lodgings, & did not stir out till towards evening when I went out with Johnson & Brodie & listened to an excellent band playing in Presidents garden. The sight pretty, foliage green, the hills covered with tents, artillery practising at Potomac, citizens & soldiers walking about or lounging in the lawn under trees. News agents & rush for newspapers on the grass. Then go back & drive with Thermistocles who is not let go home by Lord Lyons & is losing money, very unfair it is by the by. I wrote many letters today, had good dinner & in ye evening Warre & Irvine[2] came in & we sat till it was late. There were disturbances in city, a Zouave had been murdered outside or in a house of bad repute & his comrades burned it & others down & were only delivered by charges of cavalry from doing worser. Soldiers came knocking at door & beg for drop of whiskey or money to get some. Soldiers uniforms not well made. Mr. House of N.Y. Tribune[3] a nice fellow called on me. Harpers which I bought today states that my letter will be published next week. I have thus put a finish I think to my clever young friend & taught him a lesson which cannot fail to be useful for the term of his life. As I told him honesty was the best policy. I fear my new servant is rather a scamp, too fond of liberty & gadding to suit my taste exactly. Go he must then.

1. Brig. Gen. Irvin McDowell of Ohio, commander of the Federal forces in Virginia.
2. William Douglas Irvine, secretary of the British legation since 1858 and son of Lord William Douglas. He resigned from the foreign service in September 1862.
3. Edward Howard House, correspondent of the *New York Tribune*. He later had a successful career as a journalist in Japan.

To Frederick W. Seward, July 6, 1861.

179 Penn[sylvani]a Avenue.

My dear Sir,

I looked in at you thro' the door yesterday when I called on Mr. Secretary but you had an air of such "work to be done" about you I could not bring myself to intrude upon you, altho' I would gladly if permitted renew the pleasure of your acquaintance. The Secretary of State informed me that it is now necessary for foreigners to be provided with passports, & I herewith beg to enclose mine which I took when I was going South with the prospect of more peaceful & extended travels, for the purpose of securing the countersignature or visé of the Secretary of State & would feel obliged if you could obtain it for me. May I ask you to present my respectful compliments to Miss Seward[1] & to believe me to be my dear Sir,

Your very faithful servant,
W.H. Russell

1. Russell again probably means Anna Wharton Seward, Frederick Seward's wife.

July 7, 1861

Breakfasted wi' Bigbelow where were Thurlow Weed,[1] oh such a wily old card, King[2] Senator & Stomach, the pooping elegant N.P. Willis,[3] Wilson ex shoemaker now a member of Senate & head of Military Com[mitt]ee, a member from Missouri, a professor from West Point, Olmsted. Politics. Wilson inveighed ag[ains]t regular army & its officers, he wants politicians at ye head. Scott is too old. Army obstructives. Would not take cavalry & artillery. Now they want them—

Scott does—in ye same way they wd. not occupy Harper's Ferry & Manassas Gap Junction. It was curious. He is furious ag[ains]t McClellan[4] for talking of slaves as property & is of opinion no officer shd. hold give up or impede any slave. Meigs[5] is now the able & much praised Q[uarter] M[aster] G[eneral]. Both parties urging forward the fighting. The leaders hanging back till they are ready—a thousand cav[a]l[ry] are wanted. Conviction is great that they must conquer. Difference between them & South was they were not fighting. In South all would have been. Civil to me, no wit or fun tho'. Walked home with N.P. Willis. Very hot, wrote to Oby, father, Duncan, &c. Sent off parcel for Times under cover to Thompson & nephews. Olmsted called talked of sanitary matters. They are all anxious to push on & talk of conspiracy wh. existed Breckenridge[6] &c.

1. Thurlow Weed, influential editor of the *Albany Evening Journal* and a close friend and political associate of William H. Seward.

2. Preston King, Republican senator from New York from 1857 to 1863.

3. Nathaniel Parker Willis, celebrated essayist, short story writer, and editor.

4. Maj. Gen. George Brinton McClellan of Ohio was appointed general in chief of the U.S. armies on 1 November 1861. During the early months of the war, he successfully commanded the Federal forces in what is now West Virginia.

5. Brig. Gen. Montgomery Cunningham Meigs, a Georgia native, was appointed quartermaster general of the U.S. Army in May 1861 and served with great distinction in that capacity for the duration of the war.

6. John Cabell Breckinridge, prominent Kentucky politician and vice-president of the United States from 1857 until 1861. He was Democratic candidate for the presidency in 1860. Breckinridge remained in Washington after Lincoln's inauguration but afterward fled to the South, where he subsequently achieved the rank of major general, participating in many of the leading engagements of the war. In March 1865 he became the Confederate secretary of war.

July 8, 1861
Visited Arlington Heights.

July 9, 1861
Sick all day nearly.
Dined with General Scott. Fremont.[1]

1. Maj. Gen. John Charles Frémont, western pathfinder and Republican candidate for the presidency in 1856. In early 1861 he commanded the Department of the West.

To William H. Seward, July 10, 1861

4 p.m.

My dear Sir,

I have only just returned from a trip on the sacred soil of Virginia & therefore did not receive your kind invitation to dinner in time to send my acceptance any sooner. It will give me much pleasure to avail myself of the opportunity you are so good to offer me of renewing my acquaintance this evening. I have been so busy in camps that I have neglected somewhat the observances of civilized life I fear since my arrival in Washington.

Yours very faithfully,

W.H. Russell.

July 12, 1861

There is no news today at all of any kind. I write with energy all day up to posthouse hour but Woods takes it for me at 2.30 per hands of Sam Ward. Little Woods[1] is app[oin]t[e]d Q[uarter] Master by Blair's[2] influence to Fremont who is I think no great shakes—& is said to be unpopular in California tho' he made a good run for President. I wrote to my deenyman &c. Congress passed act to close ports, commercial intercourse unlawful, customs established for all ports in C[onfederate] S[tates] to be collected on board ship or in secure place. Ships liable to forfeiture if disobeying orders.[3]

Sent off dispatch per Woods for tomorrow steamer to New York....

1. Col. I. C. Woods. He later testified about the Blair-Frémont relationship before the Joint Committee on the Conduct of the War.

2. Francis Preston Blair, Jr., leading Missouri Republican congressman. He served as a major general of volunteers from 1862 to 1865.

3. In June 1861 a "Southern Ports Bill" was introduced in the U.S. Congress in order to strengthen the Federal blockade. The bill passed both houses on 12 July, accompanied by protests from the British and French governments.

July 13, 1861

Raining. Sam Ward crept into my crib with news of McClellan's "victory" over rebels. The curs fled with small loss but left 6 guns & no end of provisions behind them. McClellan in 11th attacked & defeated Sec[essio]n[ist]s at Laurel Hill[1] taking 6 guns camp equipage &c. &c....

1. On 11 July 1861 Federal forces under the overall command of Gen. George B. McClellan made concerted attacks upon Confederate positions at Laurel Mountain and Rich Mountain in western Virginia. The movement was only partially successful, however, with McClellan himself failing to attack on time, thus permitting a significant portion of the southern forces to escape.

July 15, 1861

Dark gloomy day. Six miles an hour up the Chesapeake—wind & tide ag[ains]t us....

July 16, 1861 [Annapolis]

Called this morning. No inclination to arise & so slept on, huge nigger gave me tub & breakfast in room. I wrote an acc[oun]t of Fortress Monroe. Baffled citizens by remaining in my room. Dined there also. At 3.30 walked to State House[1]—door open—in hall cannon raised from river bed s[ai]d to belong to original colony. Young officer s[ai]d he wd. send gate keeper, waited, he did not come. Cd. see two very poor gaselier figures Law & Justice at foot of stairs. As I walked to rail wedding, grave black faces looking at ye Chapel. At train bride & bridegroom came followed by crowd of girls all of whom looked important. Paid fare & at 4.15 started [illeg.] Annapolis. Very difficult ravinous woody country. At Junction officers were good enough to ask me into Station to rest. Talked with them, cheery fellows opened a bottle of claret, all ye men Germans. On to Washington & at Station saw M[ajor] Gen[era]l McDowell who was looking after 2 batteries of artillery Barry's[2] & another wh. had gone astray. He told me he had moved out his camp 6 miles & wd. advance tomorrow, drove me home in his carriage & s[ai]d Beauregard had advanced towards Fairfax or was said to have done so & that there was a regular levee en masse by force in Virginia. Gave me a photograph of himself & said jokingly. He did not know what sort of general he wd. make, wd. be very happy to see me at H[ea]dq[uarte]rs but was afraid of being under my silver microscope. I said as I parted I wished him success. Cd. I help doing so, & yet I wished the same to Beauregard. I was in time at Johnson's for dinner après tout. Monson came in Brodie was there found a lot of letters & thank God one from Alice saying Mama was going on very nicely. Went out with Warre, and talked on balcony.

1. Construction of the Maryland State House had begun in 1772 on the design of an Annapolis architect, Joseph Horatio Anderson, but in 1784 its original dome was

replaced with a much larger structure by a local merchant and builder, Joseph Clark. The interior of the State House was rebuilt in the 1870s.

2. Maj. William Farquhar Barry of New York was Gen. Irvin McDowell's chief of artillery. He was appointed brigadier general of volunteers in August 1861.

To J.C. Bancroft Davis, July 16, 1861

Annapolis.

My dear Davis,

Arrived at Monroe at 6. General[1] not visible till 9. He was civil too much to me to please the Sanitary Com[missioner]s[2]—ordered a steamer & took us up to Newport news. Returning Olmsted was left behind by mistake. Bellicose Bellows[3] & I dined with him & then we went forth to visit Hampton the steamer being ordered to wait till 8 o'clock for us. When we went down to the quay at 9 steamer was gone. Butler angry ordered the slow sailing feeble old screw Elizabeth to prepare—at 11 a.m. I embarked *alone* in her under the delusion that we wd. overtake the other or be on time at Baltimore for train. Suffice it to say I was glad to get in here last night after 20 hours of starvation & dirt. Oh my eye! Wasnt it a rough time.

How did Taylor get on. If he can send back the glass he took care of for me very kindly it may be of use but there is no hurry about it.

Yours ever very truly,

W.H. Russell.

1. Maj. Gen. Benjamin Franklin Butler of Massachusetts commanded Federal forces at Fort Monroe in Hampton Roads, Virginia. He later achieved notoriety as commander of Federal troops occupying New Orleans, and subsequently served in Congress and as governor of Massachusetts.

2. The United States Sanitary Commission was a civilian agency organized to assist the Army Medical Bureau in providing for the care of soldiers. Based on the British Sanitary Commission of the Crimean War, it received official War Department recognition in June 1861 and made an outstanding contribution to army health conditions throughout the war. In July 1861 its secretary and chief executive officer was Frederick Law Olmsted.

3. Henry Whitney Bellows, prominent New York Unitarian minister and founder of the United States Sanitary Commission.

To J.C. Bancroft Davis, July 16, 1861

Washington.

My dear Davis,

Butler detained me at his quarters 'till after the steamer sailed—& as I was greatly disappointed he made a shindy, & at 11 o'clock at night started me off solus in a damned old steam tug screw with a promise that I should be in Baltimore at 3 o'clock on Monday. Suffice it to say that with difficulty the screw aforesaid after a passage of twenty odd hours deposited me at Annapolis last Monday night late for everything. There was a train in the morning, but the people at the hotel did not tell me of it, & I cd. not get away from the City of Anna till 4.15 yesterday & arrived here late last night.

I found McDowell had started off his column that very morning— a short march. This morning he was to march again at dawn & as Beauregard was reported to have moved out from Manassas to Fairfax Court House or in that direction it is likely a battle—a real one, may be fought today or tomorrow. However, the telegraph will tell you faster than I can.

Will you then look out for a horse of the price you mentioned because I must have two. Something over 15 hands not *white*—strong forelegs particularly up to 15½ stone, a good walker. I must get a light tax or tilt cast also. The glass may be sent by Taylor at convenience per Adams Express. I will attach myself to McDowells column as soon as I am quite ready. Maps I cannot get & campaigning without them is terrible work.

Yours always,

W.H. Russell.

It is very curious how little we saw of each other whilst in Washington which was my fault rather than yours. I think you would have liked Fortress Monroe, tho' the troops there are not first rate. Duryea's Zouaves[1] are a set of scarecrows. The regulars are very good. I haven't seen the Reviler. If it's very spiteful send me a copy.

---

1. Col. Abram Duryee of the 5th New York Infantry, known as "Duryee's Zouaves." Zouave regiments were common on both sides in the Civil War and were modeled on original Algerian light infantry, distinguishable by their bright uniforms and baggy trousers among other things.

To John T. Delane [July 16, 1861]

Washington.

My dear Delane,

I believe after all as soon as I can get any sort of equipment I shall be in the field again—any where better than this infernal pandemonium of excitement lies bar roomery & carmagnolism in which the press assumes a mien & attitude not to be understood by one who has not seen them. The Indian press is really respectable journalism compared to the section of the New York papers which are generally quoted in England, & I find that no one of any weight in society attaches the least importance to the opinions or leaders of such a paper as the N.Y. Herald for example tho' they read it for the news. If it were not so often quoted in England & Europe it wd. not be so well known & therefore would lose something of the life blood which keeps it going. I can not as you will easily understand go in on the same terms as the American correspondents who generally live with some officer or are actually on his staff, & I must therefore be quite independent before I enter the field & be able to live by myself. I have set people a bank to provide for me & I hope to be present malgré prudence per instructions when any thing great really occurs. They are fast churning up a great fight—no doubt of it. If McClellan can get down on the main line between Richmond & East Tennessee, cutting off Wise[1] as he has cut off Garnett[2] the Confederates can only relieve themselves by giving fight to McDowell first & then turning on McClellan. They are getting into a very tight place in Virginia, but I suspect they have some coup in preparation of which we shall hear more when the Federalists have got further into Virginia. I suppose you saw Mure's letter. Lest you did not I send it to you. I am glad to tell you that on a point whereupon I have encountered no little ridicule I am amply sustained by Bunch at Charleston, & he has—keep this a secret pray—written a letter to Lord John Russell[3] substantiating every word of what I said which was in fact not half of what I had reason to state in reference to the pro-monarchy sentiments—or expressions of the Carolinians. Now they find the Border States are angry with them & they are frightened accordingly, & several of my "friends" called on Bunch to beg that I would not urge the controversy or give the proof of which I spoke. There is a strong feeling ag[ains]t England even now, & Seward told me with bitterness the other day that she was within four days of recognizing the Confederation. Lord John's use of the words "belligerent rights" without defining his meaning irritated them greatly, & I can positively assure you that only for Sumner who went direct to the President Seward would have sent a dispatch of such a character that a breach of relations would have been inevitable. You wont let me say what I think about Cotton. If we must have it I think the old island is doomed for our weakness is so apparent that all the plate annum in the world wont make the thing seaworthy or shot proof. Writing to you now is like shouting to the sea—even that has something to say for itself....

There is do you know a real & prodigious energy in this people in spite of all their bunkum, but they are so very French I can not cotton to them. I wish I cd. have remained in the South, but the place was not fit for me. I really cd. not have managed it unless en garçon. What will you do with me when my time is up? The poor old soul at home cries out to me now & then. In one of your evening rides you might go out & see her & say to me how you thought she looked. But I am asking too much. I fear the A[rmy and] N[avy] G[azette] has found it can get on now without myself. I cant find time to write here with damnable faces of visitors.

Yours ever & always in spite of your ker-ruel-tie,
W.H. Russell.

1. Brig. Gen. Henry Alexander Wise, governor of Virginia from 1856 to 1860, who commanded part of the Confederacy's forces in western Virginia.

2. On July 13 Brig. Gen. Robert Seldon Garnett's retreating Confederates were overtaken by an advance guard of McClellan's troops at Carrick's Ford on the Cheat River. Garnett was killed.

3. Lord John Russell, British foreign secretary from 1859 to 1865. Created first Earl Russell in 1861, he had served as prime minister from 1846 to 1852, a post he would resume after the death of Lord Palmerston in 1865.

July 17, 1861

Boat from New York. I hope my letters went all right. Papers begin to arrive. Saw Cullum who explained beaucoup de choses to me. McDowell moved this morning again. His batteries came up. He found Fairfax Court House almost a myth occupied it with little loss taking tents equipage food &c. but cd. not push on to Centreville on railway at Bull Run river.

Excitement in Washington as they say rayther loud. My bag which had been out of the way was delivered today all right. I sent off a telegram to Davis but it was too late. I wished him to advertize The Times of my being alive oh for the sake of dear deenyman. Why should I not be able to have a steamer of my own always. I walked out for a little with McJohnson. Read in ye papers ye acc[oun]t of ye great fire of London[1] which is almost worthy of Defoe.[2] Poor Woods what a fine facile pen he has & what would I not give to be able to do his blue blisters. Hear of Lord Campbells death[3] & of Lord Abingers[4] also—at least read biography. Monson dined with us—so did Brodie, dinner was very late Johnson very cross cursing & swearing like a boat full of bargers on First Trinity after a bump. A great change in Washington, streets quite empty. Brodie came in so did Warre & we all sat up till all was blue. There is a curious delusion in ye minds of multitude that Genl. Winfield Scott will take ye field in extremis. Truman Smith called before dinner.... A nice old man.

1. On the evening of 22 June 1861, a huge fire engulfed properties in the Cotton Wharf district of London, near London Bridge. The fire, which persisted for several days, destroyed many warehouses containing valuable merchandise, including large stocks of silk and cotton, and resulted in the death of James Braidwood, head of the London Fire Brigade.

2. Daniel Defoe (?1661–1731), English novelist and journalist, who wrote vivid descriptions, supposedly derived from memory, of the Great Fire of London of September 1666.

3. John Campbell, first Baron Campbell, a prominent law officer, legal biographer, and lord chancellor in Palmerston's government. He died on 22 June 1861 at the age of 82.

4. Robert Campbell Scarlett, second Baron Abinger, former M.P. and minister to Florence, died on 24 June 1861.

July 18, 1861

Letters from Deenyman &c. Johnson not quite so bad as he is sometimes. A man named Morrill Montreal Gazette came in to see me. Cullum sent me letters with details as to army. McDowells advance on Fairfax Court House not said Cullum. The advices I asked for were actually in the N.Y. papers. You might as well he said try to keep cats out of a meal tub as reporters from the archives. Johnson & I drove out to see reported fire & at Capitol Hill we halted & saw nothing whatever. Johnson cursed of course. In the forenoon Monson—afternoon came in with the Order of Release for Johnson but he showed no signs of joy, cursed the rather & would not dine with Lord Lyons. Rum & wonderful Inglizman. What a curious study for travellers. I wrote letters part of the day to all sorts & conditions of men. My

deenyman tells me some one Lizzie told her she had Brights disease.
A strange thing to say. What could Lizzie mean by it? Alice wrote me
a wild sad merry sort of letter. I dined with Lord Lyons at 4 p.m.—
Warre, Brodie, Monson. Went into garden & saw most curious cater-
pillars with feelers like fine feathers in plume, knobs of yellow on
back & long tail. Young racoons out climbing. Went back to Johnson
who was cursing as usual. Recalled in Mahon[1] & Grant[2] 2 men who
were outside, talked of Union &c. I made up my acc[oun]ts for The
Times this evening & find I am short a good deal of money. How can
this be? Read when I got back most spiteful & amusing article on
The Times Special in The Saturday Review. As a proof of the very
thing being in their blood which they lay to the paper as circulating
medium the papers contained in very same mail some very pretty
like criticisms à propos of my letters!

1. Capt. Thomas Mahon, Royal Artillery.
2. Capt. Robert Grant, Royal Engineers. Mahon and Grant were acting as observers
for the British army in North America.

July 19, 1861

Rose at 8, old Johnson cursing fearfully at 9. Breakfasted a little
seedy. A fine troop of regular cavalry passed thro' the streets, great
excitement of orderlies &c. I wrote into Cullum for news who told me
in a note that fighting was going on & that 69 & 70 had been attacked
at Bull Run. Went in afterwards & learned that in fact McDowell
found Beauregards left too strong to attack & was brought up on the
roads. All sorts of rumours at wh. C. & self laughed. I rec[eive]d some
few lines from Oby. Johnson cursed all day very much—packing up
quite awful. Storm of imprecations. Met Genl. Mansfield who seemed
quite pleased when I told him I was merely calling to pay respects
to him. Grim old chap straw hat uniform coat &c. Gave letters to
M. Morris, O. Willans, The Times &c. cover to B. Davis to Johnson—
drove with him to rail. Telegraphed to Davis as to what I had done
& wished. Mde. Jost charming us. Dined on flies at old Frenchman's
Boulanger.... Crowds at Adj[utan]t Generals office, all sorts of lies.
At Phelps who told me Davis lied & showed me a letter from Purly
Poore[1] saying his letter was not intended for publication. Despatch
5 hours coming from McDowell at Centreville. Mr. Morrill called &
after delay made request for letters. I gave him one to Beauregard,

one to Porcher Miles, Manning, Brown,[2] Wigfall & saying he was for Montreal Gazette fine British subject. He promised to write me a weekly letter. In evening met Wise[3] & Warre & walked to see Stevens Ram model.[4] Guns curious, vessel 480 ft. long, speed 25 miles. Turns on its length...shell proof. Curious scene at Navy Office, no guards old man in shirt. Went on to Carrolls[5] where family sat in porch & talked with Warre & Monson for some time & so to bed. American women very free. I wrote a few lines to darling. Oh Lord! How different.

1. Benjamin Perley Poore, Washington correspondent of the *Boston Journal*.

2. William M. Browne, English-born assistant secretary of state for the Confederacy. He later commanded Confederate defenses at Savannah.

3. Lt. Henry Augustus Wise, naval officer and author of *Los Gringos* (1849) and *Tales from the Marines* (1855). He later became head of the U.S. Navy Bureau of Ordinance. His books were written under the pseudonym of "Harry Gringo."

4. A land battery faced with iron developed in early 1861 by Clement Hoffman Stevens and first established on Morris Island opposite Fort Sumter in Charleston harbor. Later promoted to brigadier general, Stevens was killed at the Battle of Peach Tree Creek in July 1864. He also invented a portable field oven for keeping bread fresh.

5. Either the family of Charles Carroll or his younger brother John Lee Carroll, a future governor of Maryland. They were the eldest sons of Col. Charles Carroll of Doughoregan Manor.

July 20, 1861
Went over to Lord Lyons.
Arranged with Warre to drive to battle. Hired carriage.

July 21, 1861
Battle of Bulls Run.[1]
It was late when Warre & I started.
My ride. To Long Bridge 33 miles at 11 p.m.

1. Fought between Union and Confederate forces under the respective commands of Gen. Irvin McDowell and Gen. Pierre G. T. Beauregard near Manassas Junction, Virginia. The southern victory was achieved with combined losses of nearly nine hundred killed and over twenty-five hundred wounded.

July 22, 1861
Writing like fury still I cd. do little as I was so much tired by my ride. Wrote on.

Dined at Lord Lyons at 4. Went over about 5.30 & wrote having secured special courier 30 drs. for fare 25 for expenses 10 for self. Schleiden's[1] man he is called. Attachés came over & sat also. Paid 36 drs. for carriage & horses.

1. Rudolph Matthias Schleiden, Bremen's minister to the United States from 1854 to 1862.

To J.C. Bancroft Davis, July 22, 1861

Wash[ingto]n.

My dear Davis,

I sent off a special messenger last night (4 a.m. this morning rather) with letter to Boston. I had a very trying day of it, & being foolish enough to interfere with runaways I was nearly murdered—once had a very narrow escape. I would never have got away only I was well mounted. I never shall forget my ride to the Long Bridge. A more disgraceful rout was never witnessed. I have sent a long letter to B. Duncan. I attribute the disaster first to deficient morale of officers, & want of discipline of men—ie. inferiority to their opponents. Second to the superiority of Confederates in their position. They led the attack to the very points they had selected for defence. Thirdly— want of judgement in delaying reinforcements too long & deficient arrangements as to ammun[itio]n. The repulse the day before had something to do with the men also. A squadron of steady cavalry wd. have stopped that much scandalous causeless panic, saved 30 pieces of artillery, 1000 primers & the honour of the U.S. army. However there is no use in saying more. Bad behaviour in the field became most miserable cowardice & disorder out of it.

Will you let me know if I owe you anything of a personal kind?— other things may go down to The Times on my account. I have James Brown[1] apply to you for money to pay fares & expenses of himself & horse to Washington, pray let him have enough for the purpose. Will you send me a list of sailings arrivals &c.

Yours always in much dampness—rode from Manassas—my *asses* is awful in consequence.

W.H.R.

1. Russell's groom and messenger.

July 23, 1861

Courier started at 3 a.m. How tired I was on going to bed.

Dined at Merciers[1]—nice place at Georgetown. Baroche,[2] Lord Lyons & Monson. Baroche & Mercier nearly fought at dinner about something.

Mde. de Stoeckl came in during evening.

1. Edouard Henri Mercier, French minister to the United States from July 1860 until December 1863.

2. Ernest Baroche, French agent in the United States and the son of Jules Baroche, French minister of justice.

July 24, 1861

Rode out & saw McDowell at Arlington with Monson. Got back & b[rea]kfasted late.

Dined with Monson at Lord Lyons—very so & so, only Brodie. Ret[ur]n[e]d home.

July 25, 1861

Dined at Lord Lyons. Lady Georgina Fane, Mrs. Clifford, Mde. de Stoeckl, M. le Baron de Stoeckl, Monson.... Sumner, attachés. Lady G. bored me awfully.

July 26, 1861

Letter sent off to Times at 2....

Called at Lord Lyons & read letters in Times. Dined at home. Wise, Wright,[1] Meigs, Macomb,[2] Monson called.

To bed not be[in]g quite pert at 12.30.

Messenger returned from Boston. Paid Monson 20 drs.

McDowell called & we talked for some time as to disaster.

1. Maj. Edward H. Wright, 6th U.S. Cavalry, aide de camp to Gen. Winfield Scott and subsequently to Gen. George B. McClellan.

2. Capt. John W. Macomb of the U.S. Topographical Engineers.

July 27, 1861

Awoke at 7 and lo bowels were unsatisfactory, pain &c.

Continued & sent for Miller[1] who ordered powders & *mint julep*. He always does.

1. Dr. Thomas Miller, Washington physician whose patients included Stephen A. Douglas.

July 28, 1861

Here am I in bed still broken. Doctor called & ordered acid drink—nasty.

The papers are beginning to say there never was such heroism as at Bulls Run! Letter from deenyman. Alice not so well—also father. Edge of Star & Dial called.[1]

1. Frederick Milnes Edge, correspondent of the London *Morning Star*. He was formerly with the *Morning Herald*.

July 30, 1861

Mieux. Sent off letter to The Times.

Brodie & Monson dined avec.

Presidents in evening. Stoeckls.

July 31, 1861

As I lay in bed this morning in came a man to my side. "I am Hart" Queens messenger—friend of Johnson. We fraternize. Cometh one also James Brown with big horse—Sam Ward's New York. Puts up at Roe's.[1] Breakfast—ill somnolent heavy, read papers. Cometh one Morrill also who hath visited Federals—a lousy crapulous would be Cassius of an evil eye. Too cometh Charles not less the Tollemache bearer of my depêches to whom I gave cheque for 25 dollars making in all 65 for message to Boston. Dismissed is he by Schleiden for message bearing. And so on to dinner. I tell Mrs. Jost to give my servant food. We fare not ill. And out to walk after dinner.

Such a difference no drunkies in ye streets, no rabblement of soldiery. By the lightening the tall unfinished plinth of marble work stands grand over Potomac[2] & the roll of drums in distant Arlington mingles with muttered thunder. As we return Wise comes in & much descants.... We had a drink at a bar in front of wh. lay a turtle gasping.

My friend left his handkerchief. On going back waiter drew it from pocket. "Guess we must pick up such fixing quick or they go."

1. Sammy Wroe's livery stables.

2. The uncompleted Washington Monument. Begun in 1848, its progress was greatly impeded by the often destructive opposition of Know-Nothing sympathizers angry at a papal gift of marble. In 1861 it was a square stub 150 feet high, its outer courses clad in Maryland marble. The monument was finally completed and opened to the public in 1888.

August 2, 1861

There came in a nice young fellow named Ritchie[1] s[on] i[n] law of J. Wadsworth[2]—with little Olmsted & they ret[urne]d to dinner with me at 5. Ritchie gave me most admirable acc[oun]t of battle. He did not leave Centreville till late at night, & slept at Fairfax C[ourt] H[ouse] whence he did not move till 8.30 a.m. & Wadsworth remained till 10.30. Panic was terrible, disgusting sickening & in his mind all ye fault of ye officers of whom he spoke in harshest terms. We dined nicely & Olmsted whom I like so much & self chatted with Ritchie & talked de omnibus till Warre came in & Vizetelly.[3] Ritchie talked rather strongly of the snobbery of English high society of wh. he gave some strong proofs, & also said hard things of poor Sam Ward.

1. Montgomery Ritchie was married to Cordelia, daughter of James S. Wadsworth. He served in the army for two years and died in 1864.

2. James Samuel Wadsworth, leading New York Republican, served as an aide to Gen. Irvin McDowell before his commission as brigadier general on 9 August 1861. He was killed in the Wilderness in May 1864.

3. Frank Vizetelly, war correspondent of the *Illustrated London News*. He disappeared, either killed or captured, during the massacre of Hicks Pasha's army in the Sudan in 1883.

August 3, 1861

Breakfasted seedily. There came a nice letter from Mary who complains poor soul of nervousness—& hints the girls are too much for her. They are I fear most difficult to manage & I hope they will become better instead of more difficult. I wrote to her & sent off many letters for "Gt. Eastern" wh. sails on Friday. For a wonder there is nothing about Russell in this days papers. There is no report of any move[men]t on the part of the troops tho' H. Wise the half cracked Governor of Virginia seems losing ground before Federalist Cooke[1] &

there is a report that Ben McCullough[2] will have annihilated Siegel.[3] McClellan is ordering regular parade drills. Young Meagher of the Sword[4] is busy writing a long account of the disgraceful little campaign of the veterans. Is it not curious. I shd. not be at all surprized if I got into trouble on account of my reporting in a very mild form. House of the Tribune stated that T.F. Meagher ran away & appeared in Centreville at the end of the day declaring that "We're whipped like dogs! Sirs we're whipped."

I had a solitary dinner at 5. A certain soup, baked not roast beef, pigeons wh. I forbid for the future. A solitary meal is hard to digest. I would say my own thoughts were better company & then all were well—if Deenyman were so. Rode out at 6.30. Met Mercier & Plonplon[5] driving to Presidents. Prince looked unusually dark, wants Nap's eyes—is sallower also. Went round by Georgetown, some good old brick houses. Heat very considerable. Coming back amused by officer drinking whiskey from flask of his men. Several drunken soldiers about.... Wounded men also marching about before their hospitals. Rode round by Willards & saw N.P. Willis escorting females for the wh. he is not unsuited at all. Ret[urne]d after dusk. Sat down to write, in came Warre & Vizetelly & sat till I turned them out in the evening so late that it was near second small hour. For first time ice is scarce tonight. Mde. Jost tells us amusing & motly stories. The maid who saved her mistress & also of the magnificent Spaniard who wd. not pay anything.

1. Col. Robert McCook of the 9th Ohio Infantry, who commanded a brigade under General McClellan and subsequently Gen. William B. Rosecrans in the western Virginia campaign. He was promoted to brigadier general in March 1862 and was killed by Confederate partisans in August of the same year.

2. Brig. Gen. Ben McCulloch, a former Texas Ranger and a veteran of the Texas and Mexican wars, commanded Confederate troops in Missouri. He was killed at Elkhorn Tavern in March 1862.

3. Brig. Gen. Franz Sigel, former German revolutionary, who arrived in the United States in 1852. On 10 August he played a critical role in the Federal defeat at Wilson's Creek, Missouri.

4. Thomas Francis Meagher, Irish radical politician, known as "Meagher of the Sword," who was banished from his native country to Tasmania in 1849 and escaped to the United States in 1852. In 1861 his "Zouave" company fought with Corcoran's 69th New York Militia at Bull Run. He was appointed brigadier general of volunteers in February 1862, having organized an "Irish Brigade" in New York City. Meagher died after falling from a steamboat during a drunken spree while acting governor of Montana Territory in 1867.

5. The nickname of Prince Napoleon who arrived in New York on 27 July for a two-month tour of the United States. He was the son of Jerome Napoleon and a cousin of Napoleon III.

To J.C. Bancroft Davis, August 3, 1861

My dear Davis,

It really looks as if neither side had much stomach for going on just now. Have both been cowed at Bulls Run? McClellan is doing his work well. A great change in Washington at all events, but there will be much difficulty in licking the unruly elements sent by the States into the form of an army. There is a great deal of fierceness left but I think the Union can not be patched up.

I am ashamed of my remissness & on the other side you will find a cheque for moneys. Does the Army & Navy Gazette reach you now for me? I rarely receive it. The horse & groom arrived all right & I have picked up a pretty good sort of a beast for 195 here so that I shall be ready for another run if news be. I am becoming rather blazé about Washington, however I must say & almost wish we were attacked. Everything shows how severely the Confederates were hit on 21st. I had no idea of it. It was nearly all done by superior artillery fire in which I always said U.S. were superior. Am I as much abused as ever. I should like to see the Southern papers. With kind regards to Mrs. Davis believe me,

    Yours always,
        W.H. Russell.

August 4, 1861

Ere I rose came a man "Meyrick Beaufoy Feild introduced by J Milton Esq War Office"[1] whom after detaining & again calling I saw. Formerly H[er] M[ajesty's] 30th., wounded Redan.[2] Real object to get letters from me in order to take service in either army. A blazing hot day. Shut door & thus repel all visitors. Wrote some letters for The Times to go by Wednesday d.v. Bulls Run about known by this time.

1. John Milton, assistant account general of the army. He had served in the War Office since 1840 and was knighted in 1878.

2. One of the defensive forts protecting Sebastopol during the Crimean War. It was finally taken by British forces in September 1855, leading to the end of the siege of Sebastopol.

August 5, 1861

A letter to The Times posted this evening for Wednesday Boston steamer.

August 6, 1861

Breakfasting with ye newspapers—heat atrocious. I set out about 12 in carriage to pay visits, left cards at Sewards, Bates, Cameron,[1] Blair, Breckenridge, &c....
I dined solus cum solo. Monson came in to see me.

1. Simon Cameron of Pennsylvania, Lincoln's secretary of war. He resigned in 1862 and was appointed U.S. minister to Russia.

August 7, 1861

A letter from my darling soul from Mayall's shop. So she is not so bad. Praised be God, wd. that my life praised him. Little Herrisse[1] came & wrote from 1.30 to 4.30. Rum little Frenchman. A letter from Dillon rather spiteful in tone I think. A day of intense heat. Moved horses from Wroe's to Irvine's stables. Herrisse dined with me & as I received cards from Seward for the reception I had to dress after dinner, awful heat, & went over about 9.30. Seward asked me if I knew the Prince. "No". So I was introduced. He wore his Bath—is very like Nap[oleon] only taller. I said the last time I saw him was at ye Alma & he asked me if I had not been in India & had travelled a good deal. He had been to Mt. Vernon & 2 of his horses dropped dead from heat en cheminant. He had a fierce little hussard with him & also a nice fellow with Legion &c.[2] He dined with Lyons & corps diplomatique were invited but it was considered that I was not good enough company tho' I am good enough or have been for Lord Lyons. I shall certainly show my sense of this not on my own acc[oun]t for I dont suffer but on that of my position as a journalist. I surely stand in as high a position who have been called the unaccredited ambassador of the people as some of my Lords guests that day. Dahlgren, Kennedy[3] &c. had talk with me. I saw little Davis & had satisfaction of cutting him dead, going up purposely to talk to a young lady with whom he was conversing. But it will do him no good. Lady Georgina there. I want her to hook on to Prince who asked me a great deal as to Fairfax & F. Court House. He is going to Manassas or at least to Beauregard whom I praised much to him. Lady G. was very near going but finally said she would not & then decided it was wrong of ye Prince to go. Such a hot night, a big bowl of whisky punch in room. Seedy Senators, Mrs. Grimsley[4] & so home where were Ward, Bing, Brodie mad drunk, Vizetelly, Barros.[5] Kept it up till past 3 a.m.

1. Henry Harrisse, French bibliographer and historian. Coming to the United States in his teens, he taught French at Chapel Hill and Georgetown and also studied law in order to make ends meet. He later returned to France. Among his many publications is *The Discovery of North America* (1892).

2. Prince Napoleon's two accompanying aides in the United States were Lt. Col. Camille Ferri Pisani and Lt. Col. Ragon.

3. John Pendleton Kennedy, Maryland politician, novelist, and secretary of the navy, 1852–53.

4. Elizabeth Todd Grimsley, Mary Lincoln's cousin, who was staying in the White House. She was the wife of Harrison Grimsley of Springfield, Illinois.

5. A secretary at the Spanish legation.

August 8, 1861
Heat again. Ritchie & Olmsted breakfasted intending to go to hospitals—too hot & too late just now. No news in papers except of cheeky C.S. privateer firing on St. Lawrence off Charleston wh. at once sunk her.
Went to Alexandria with Olmsted & Ritchie at 3.
Returned & dined. In the evening rather an orgie again.

August 9, 1861
Writing like fureyes.

August 10, 1861
Searing boiling maddening.
Monson came in with Dyer Genl. of Havana[1] & Vizetelly &c.

1. Russell possibly means William Ryder who was appointed British arbitrator in the Mixed Court of Justice at Havana in 1855 under the terms of the treaty with Spain. He had served as acting commissary judge at Havana since June 1859.

August 11, 1861
Rode out this broiling day or morning.
Saw Beaufoy Meyrick Feild at door of steps.
Such a night—nearly drowned getting in.

August 12, 1861 [Baltimore]
Death of Feild,[1] horror. Baltimore Sun. Ryder. To Baltimore at 2.45.
Rain. Eutaw House. Supper. Bed.

1. See Russell, *My Diary North and South*, 2 vols. (London, 1863), 2:279–80, for
the circumstances of Feild's death. He had suffered a fatal seizure at the Baltimore
railroad station. Russell was clearly upset by the cavalier and insensitive manner in
which the event was handled by city authorities.

August 13, 1861
Breakfasted at hotel.
I dined at clubabble dinner at hotel. Bitterly cold. Walked about.

August 14, 1861
Breakfasted in room.
Dined with J. Brune.[1] Secessionist evening.

1. John Christian Brune, Baltimore merchant and member of the Maryland state
legislature. A leading secessionist, his arrest was ordered in September 1861, but he
escaped the city.

August 15, 1861
Oh! so seedy. Cavendish Taylor. Lady Georgina Fane.
Left Baltimore at 4 p.m. Washington.
Dinner. In came Haworth,[1] Sam Ward, Vizetelly, Monson, Warre,
young Sheffield.[2]

1. Capt. Martin Edward Haworth, Queen's foreign service messenger since 1859.
He retired from active military service in 1842.
2. George Sheffield, attaché at the British legation and the son of Sir Robert Sheffield. He was transferred to Washington from Munich in June 1861.

August 16, 1861
Up & had a ride, Haworth—self camps, at 7. Groom James very
anxious about that wee brown horse. Letters.
Bigelow. Childs.[1] S. Ward. Sewards talk.

1. George William Childs, Baltimore publisher and future philanthropist. In 1861
he worked for J. B. Lippincott and Co. after the dissolution of his own firm of Childs
and Peterson. He later purchased and revived the Philadelphia *Public Ledger*.

August 17, 1861

This is a bad way to keep acc[oun]ts. I let James have 3 drs. by way
of advance on his wages. On waking found Ward asleep on ye sofa.
Dieu sait how he got in. Cold & rainy. He left early. Edge who says
he is a great man of "Star" came in trepidat[io]n to know address
of a doctor because "he felt as hif he were going to be hill" a thoro'
snob & very complete cockney. I packed up in petto[1] for a little excursion to do me good & indeed feel in want of it, besides Maryland is
in an interesting condition pregnant with political questions. I said
to Revd. Bellows some time ago it was. Maryland & B[altimore] the
Warsaw of ye United States. He did not like it. Drove to Stat[io]n &
found it guarded by soldiers to stop people without papers in uniform.
Train to Baltimore 2.30—filled with ye usual rough lot of volunteers
& rowdies spitting &c. A lady in America can have no idea of the
heartlessness of these cars. On arriving was met by C. Taylor 4.15.
Drove to Maryland Club & had hasty dinner. Off by train at 5.40
to Ellicotts Mills. Taylor & Tucker Carroll.[2] Thence in carriage thro'
rolling country past manse pasturing streets to Drohoregan Manor
a nice old place with wide front & chapel on one flank & a good avenue of trees. Colonel Carroll[3] a nice old fellow very like the Marquis
Wellesley[4] or James Guthrie Russell. Mrs. Cavendish Taylor[5] a clever
little brunette witty & sharp & feminine. Her sister[6] a pleasant girl
pining into old maidery. Young Carroll[7] & his wife[8] completed ye
circle. In one room we were shown where George Washington, Carroll of Carrolton[9] & others used to talk over their great treason. The
old gentleman is fond of antiquity of family. One of the family married Lord Wellesley[10] & thus the greatgrandaughter of the man who
left Ireland as a proscribed traitor & rebel returned to it to sit in the
throne of the Queen "(King)". Talked smoked whiskeyed & watered
& to bed in a snug fine old room. Attended by darkies.

    1. "in haste."
    2. Charles Tucker Carroll was the nephew of Col. Charles Carroll of Doughoregan
Manor. Born Charles Carroll Tucker, his parents both died when he was young.
    3. Col. Charles Carroll of Doughoregan Manor, the grandson of the Revolutionary
statesman Charles Carroll of Carrollton. He died in 1862.
    4. Marquis of Wellesley (1760–1842), governor general of India from 1797 to 1805
and lord lieutenant of Ireland, 1821–28 and 1833–34.
    5. Louisa Carroll Cavendish-Taylor, second daughter of Col. Charles Carroll.
    6. Louisa's younger sister, Helen Sophia Carroll.

7. Albert Henry Carroll, third surviving son of Col. Charles Carroll. He died in 1862.

8. Albert Henry Carroll's wife, the former Mary Cornelia Read.

9. Col. Charles Carroll of Carrollton (1737–1832), Maryland revolutionary patriot leader and signer of the Declaration of Independence.

10. Charles Carroll of Carrollton's granddaughter, Mary Ann Caton, married the Marquis of Wellesley in 1825. Her first husband was Robert Patterson, brother-in-law of Jerome Bonaparte.

August 18, 1861

A steady day of rain. Mr. Carroll's family after breakfast slipped into ye little chapel for a mouthful of prayers & I was very much pleased with ye sight of ye negroes trooping in to the service in all possible varieties of costume. The priest[1] a very agreable old man dressed in ye French style. Somewhat belongs to an ecclesiastical establish[men]t founded by one of the Carrolls in the neighbourhood where gentlemen's sons are educated. He had been up in ye North & says there is much secession feeling wh. is not shown in N[ew] York & ye large cities. As Taylor & self were heretics & Tucker was not inclined to go to chapel we sauntered about & walked to ye slave quarters wh. were better than in ye South tho' tattered & dirty eno'. The niggers seemed more independent than in the South. Their little village is right in front of the manor house quarter of a mile off at the entrance of the avenue but at ye other side of ye pike road. There was the usual multitude of poultry some pigs & goats & little children. The old people peered out of their glassless windows at us. After chapel more negroes principally young grinning & curtseying came in to Catechism. At dinner wh. was early several neighbours came in—good board & plentiful. None of our diners à la Russe when you always feel as if dining à la carte at a restaurant. More talk with Priest. He says ye people wont enlist for ye North, it is ye foreigners who do so. Every one present as we sat out in ye porch & talked freely denounced ye North as the source of all evil. They admitted slavery was not profitable in Maryland, but still they cd. not free their slaves. Where cd. they get labour? What is to become of ye slaves? They had come to them from their fathers & had a right to protection. They did not sell & breed them as ye Virginians did. I found they were all connected with officers at ye other side. The ladies declared they were dying to see Beauregard. Old Carroll not well. At night rain cold & fog very strange making ye old tree before ye manor loom enormously.

1. Rev. Hugh F. Griffin of nearby St. Charles College.

August 19, 1861
More rain—dismal in a country house. Had breakfast at 9.30. It was arranged to drive after ye papers came in. They were brought in by a little nigger on horseback from Ellicotts Mills who was threatened with a hiding by the Colonel for being late. No news of importance tho' it was said "battle expected tomorrow". Had a closed carriage & pair of horses & as rain moderated drove out with C. Taylor. Saw tobacco fields in full green—visited store in wh. it was placed in hogsheads.

August 20, 1861
The exped[itio]n to Harpers Ferry. Drove to Ellicotts Mills.
Return to Washington.

August 21, 1861 [Washington]
Writing.
Diner solus. Late evening Haworth & Waller.[1]

1. Possibly George Henry Waller, eldest son of Sir Thomas Waller.

August 22, 1861
Rage in New York. Expecting Johnson, in at Johnson's or rather Haworth's lodgings. Sheffield sick.

To J.C. Bancroft Davis, August 22, 1861

Washington.
My dear Davis,
    As I telegraphed to you I only returned from Maryland yesterday, but had you come you could have walked straight into rooms here & I am sorry you c[ou]ld not. There is every chance of my being the best abused man in U.S. & that means the world—for telling the truth as I see it. I don't like those mobs in the north at all—a very bad sign of

The Times indeed. I hope you will enjoy yourself & find an occasion now & then to write a line to me.

    Yours very truly always,
        W.H. Russell.

Did Morris ever ask you any question about Sam Ward? Some one has been poisoning his mind ag[ains]t the poor fellow.

August 23, 1861

In walked Johnson this morning! He was fresh & very noble looking, his front serene, his visage redly monarchical, his suit superb. There is a mischief in leaving one day of a diary open. The memory is ruined by keeping it & does not collect itself in the writing, & so I forgot much of what Johnson had to say. It was all grand & great. But-ler Duncan is an American & Johnson finds fault with him because he is not an Englishman. To me with all his good qualities John-son is rather a bore with prejudices. At 1.45 gave my letter for The Times to Haworth who started off with Miller for New York whence it will go on Saturday with Edinburgh. I had done my best to write. But I cd. get very little off indeed. I rec[eive]d an invit[atio]n from Monday dated Thursday to dine with L[or]d Lyons today *after* I had asked Johnson. So I stated the case & the result was an invitation to Johnson also & thus our difficulty was solved. Haworth is to exe-cute lots of commissions for me. His friend Waller formerly lived in Florence married to an American. Knows Lever.[1] He was a swell on dit in Firenza. Knew Wise &c. How these waifs & strays float about ye world. I suspect W. is now rather Bohemien. The weather is very feverish. Johnson & I walked out before dinner & showed ourselves. We dined with my Lord—a family party. Dinner was of the usual sort, conversat[io]n slack afterwards I think & my Lord not at all well looking—worn & sickly & very nervous & fidgetting. Afterwards adj[ourne]d to Johnson's with Monson—& smoked & talked there for some time in Irvine's old lodgings—very nice. Sheffield not well—a course of Brodie finished him in a few days or rather nights. He is not strong poor boy tho' he is full of work & quite anxious for fun & duty also. He is a gentleman. Went to Vizetelly's—a great deal of dropping shots as we came home. What they do who can tell. Sentinels who were amusing themselves probably. Well Sir after we left B. called at Vizetelly, & kept him up till 4 a.m.

1. Charles James Lever, Dublin-born physician, novelist, and diplomat, who, like Russell, was educated at Trinity College. He was British vice-consul in Spezzia from 1856 to 1867 and consul general in Trieste from 1867 until his death in 1872.

August 24, 1861

James roused me out of bed with the news that ye horses leg was broken, he had fallen suddenly & broken it! It was perhaps as well I was not on him for he might have broken my neck. Johnson came in. Fat vet. A great sight. He declared all that remained for the poor brute was to kill it. Alas! alas! I was writing at my accounts nearly all day—finished them at last & sent them off by Adam's Express in a parcel to B. Davis. Is there any evil for me on St. Bartholomew's day. I have quite lost appetite for breakfast, no pleasure in my grub at all. Ordered cigars from Chagournes,[1] offered Gregory[2] & others by letter to revise my own letters which the scoundrels are publishing by the hundreds without leave or license. Childs has not in spite of my application returned my cuts from The Times nor photograph. What a do the fellow must be with all his soft silky ways about him. The want of honesty is rather a feature in America. I fear it came from the Puritans who in their doctrine of faith could well dispense with works. At all events cuteness in the New England States is said to flourish. I am compelled to see too that there is great recklessness of life. A scoundrel today shot a negro boy dead because he asked him for a chew of tobacco. Infernal! Johnson dined with me & in the evening we had quite a tabaks consultum in concilium,[3] & also a great private circle of which were Brown Clarence U.S., Wise U.S.N., Bertadano,[4] Monson, Vizetelly, Brodie, Barros, a conclave who sat rather late & drank not undeeply. Before dinner I rode over to the Navy Yard & found Dahlgren & Senator McDougall[5] of whom see an acc[oun]t transferred to the next page by accident. The Navy Yard is very prettily kept & is a very neat little establishment. I was rather amused at the smart way in wh. McDougall attacked Blair.[6] See how the Scotch element comes out. McDougall, Blair, McClellan, McDowell, Cameron, Seward &c. &c.

1. A New York cigar store situated at 79 Cedar Street.
2. James C. Gregory, New York publisher. He published a "Household Dickens" in 1861.
3. i.e., a smoking circle.
4. A secretary at the Spanish legation.

5. James Alexander McDougall, originally from New York, was Democratic senator from California from 1861 to 1867.

6. Montgomery Blair, Lincoln's postmaster general. A moderate Republican, he resigned from the cabinet in 1864.

To J.C. Bancroft Davis, August 24, 1861

Washington.

My dear Davis,

Herewith a parcel to go with yours please to Morris. There is literally no "news" here but McClellan is working to get his army into shape & he is *succeeding*. His great advantage is that defeat has taught moderation & forbearance to the civilians & he has everything his own way. There will be no pressure—no precipitate councils now, & he can act at his leisure & as he thinks best. I dare not ask you what you think of the Bulls Run letter because it was not fairly treated. By that I mean that when I said I wd. leave the American journals to describe the fight & then distinctly said I only would give a description of the retreat as I saw it I left Delane to precede my letter by such accounts from the American papers as could be best formed into a narrative of the fight to *precede* my letter. Instead of wh. it was made to do duty for that it was not meant for—an account of the battle. I feel it is my doom to be the best abused man in America on both sides. It is hard to tell the truth without shaming the devil of vanity & cognate demons. I hope you are enjoying yourself. I need not say I am not & that there is no great attraction just now at Washington.

Yours very truly,

W.H. Russell.

I see there are three or four publishers tearing away at my unhappy letters. Will you never adopt an internat[iona]l law of copyright?

August 25, 1861

Mail in & letters, God be praised from Bucky darling & one from Johnson in wh. were golden letters. Every chance of "complete recovery". Poor Meyrick Feild's mother also wrote to me enclosing letter for her son. I went to Monson & showed him Delane's anxious letter as to the protect[io]n of the Legation. Only to be had inside the walls. Walked to Johnson, next visited admiralty where Wise and business were in full sway. Some rather interesting portraits of Decatur,[1] Hull,[2] Perry[3] and others on the walls, room simple but comfortable, one long passage on the first floor, with rooms on each side for the public offices, bad engravings and water colors, curious painting of the attack on Algiers in Fox's[4] room, the flag of Ward's[5] boat completely riddled also medals very coarsely executed, grant by Congress to naval officers. The models of shots and shells not numerous, sauntered about in the room, looked at the books, talked with Wise, Fox very civil, said he would give me order for steamer whenever I required it. The civility of attendants here is wonderful compared with our own. Here in small room is dedicated the whole business of Navy without any status or ostentation. The internal expenses must be small. "Hull" they say is first man who ever made a British frigate strike her colours! Bosh. Van Trump[6] et alii. About 4.30 rode out with Johnson thro' the woods out on Georgetown road—met Lord Lyons, Riggs &c. &c. When I was at ye Navy Yard yesterday I omitted I think to say that Dahlgren introduced me to a drunken Senator from California named McDougall who when not drunk may not be invincibly offensive, he said: really now and so it's you Sir! Let me have a good look at you, well I am quite glad to meet you, ah well now. I guess you are quite notorious you know, you'll excuse me because I had my dinner and so on the eternal nonsense about Republicans, Democrats, himself and the war. Blair and Fox came in while we were speaking, for Dahlgren seems to be greatly looked up to by all the members of the Cabinet.

I dont think the soldiers have been at all acted upon by the abuse of the papers. They dont look unfriendly and they are too fine fellows to do so on acc[oun]t of honest opinions. Johnson & I agreed we never saw finer if such fine material for an army as in the regiments we saw at evening parade & drilling in all directions. Got back only at 7.30 Bertadano Spanish Legation waiting for us. Dined very soberly. Met 15 Mas[sachusetts] Reg[imen]t marching off to sound of their own voices—a very great quantity of baggage. The old woman we saw driving all round the camps—a regular old patriot. Found a letter on table asking me to see McClellan at 9 p.m.

1. Stephen Decatur (1779–1820), U.S. naval officer, active in the Tripolitan War and the War of 1812. He was killed in a duel by a fellow naval officer.

2. Isaac Hull (1773–1843), U.S. naval officer, commander of the *Constitution*, 1810–12.

3. Oliver Hazard Perry (1785–1815), U.S. naval officer and commander of American naval forces on Lake Erie during the War of 1812.

4. Gustavus Vasa Fox, assistant secretary of the navy.

5. Capt. James Harmon Ward, Connecticut-born U.S. naval officer and authority on ordnance and naval tactics. He was killed in action in June 1861 when commanding a flying flotilla at Matthias Point.

6. Adm. Maarten Tromp (1598–1653). In December 1652, during the First Dutch War, he defeated the English admiral Robert Blake off Dungeness near Dover. A popular story at the time, though probably without foundation, was that Tromp fixed a broom to his masthead after the victory, indicating that he would sweep the English from the seas. Tromp never repeated his success and was killed the following August off Terheijde near Scheveningen.

August 26, 1861

Johnson is grumbling at an excursion, received a pass today from the Adjutant General; Major Van Vliet[1] called from McClellan. Found letter from Bernal[2] at Beningers. The day is fine and warm. Went across Long Bridge, troops drawn up in meadows beyond "Tete de Pont". Awful smell from slaughter houses and river. McDowell on the grounds and Clarence Brown; they rode over to talk to me, their attention being attracted by one of the Staff, saying: "There are two Englishmen." Asked Brown how he knew; said, he could not tell, supposed it is the mark of the beast. McDowell and I spoke about the abuse of the Press, he said he did not care what they said of him 'though one paper went so far as to accusing of being drunk and playing cards during the battle, he said he was very much rejoiced to find that I was as much abused as he had been. The President and Seward came on the ground in an open carriage accompanied by McClellan and an escort. Dragoons accoutrements very dirty. A review and marched past. Rode with the General to Arlington introduced to Sherman[3] keen, smart fellow said: I can endorse every word you wrote about the battle. Dined Wadsworth, Keys[4] &c. &c. Table spread under the flap of tents, magnificent water melons of which McDowell can eat his own weight. Much talked about the battle in a temperate modest tone, I had not lost a particle of confidence in you, I don't see why you should M. President. McClellan is stumpy with an ungraceful seat on horseback. The military hate the Press and particularly the Herald with a bitter "rancure". They hope this will end in a strong Government. Rode home with Sherman and Brown who came to dinner, by the Acqueduct; lost my pass. Genl. McDowell came in, whilst I was at dinner. Had a long talk "de omnibus". McD. who now commands only a division, is to be promoted, even the Southern papers admit the modesty of his report. Edge who called this morning, told me about a ridiculous comment in the Chicago Tribune by Dr. Ray[5] a fat elderly man who introduced himself to me near Fairfax Court House, he said he saw nothing of what I saw! I can't help his blindness, fortunately I stated nothing that cannot be corroborated by well known people, for a man has little chance of standing on his private character. There is a sublimely independent article in the Herald of Sunday calling on Seward to demand explanations of Lord Lyons and to turn me out of the country on account of some letters intercepted from Southern people in Mure's bags. I wished Heaven they could succeed in the latter part—no one ever dreams of paying the smallest attention to what the Herald says. Wrote to the Tribune in reference to the 69th and T.F. Meagher. A young man called McIvor Hillstock, waited on me to inquire after some man called Phillips Day "soi disant" correspondent of the Morning Advertiser,[6] he wore the Indian war medal and told me he had been in Toombs Troop[7] and afterwards with the French Volunteers at the Siege of Capua.[8] To bed at 1.30 Brodie of course.

1. Maj. Stewart Van Vliet of Vermont was chief quartermaster of the Army of the Potomac. He was appointed brigadier general of volunteers in September 1861.

2. Frederick W. Bernal, British consul in Baltimore from 1861 to 1867.

3. Brig. Gen. William Tecumseh Sherman of Ohio was assigned a brigade command in McClellan's reorganization of the Army of the Potomac on 4 August 1861. He subsequently commanded Federal forces in the West.

4. Brig. Gen. Erasmus Darwin Keyes of Massachusetts. A career officer, he left the army in 1864 and moved to San Francisco where he became a successful entrepreneur.

5. Dr. Charles H. Ray, editor of the *Chicago Tribune*.

6. Samuel Phillips Day, correspondent of the *Morning Advertiser* and *Morning Herald* and author of *Down South: Or an Englishman's Experiences at the Seat of the American War* (1862).

7. Capt. Henry Tombs commanded the 2nd troop of the 1st brigade of horse artillery in the Indian Mutiny of 1857. He was knighted in 1868 and subsequently rose to the rank of major general.

8. On 2 November 1860 Bourbon troops loyal to Francis II surrendered to Piedmontese forces at Capua, fifteen miles north of Naples.

August 27, 1861

A most fearful day of mug & fever, seedy as could be. I hear McDowell says it was water melon. Why the deuce did he let me eat it then. Johnson came over very lovely in starred cravat & white cross lined

delicate suit. Monson d[itt]o There is a most atrocious & amusingly blackguard article in the Herald. 2 indeed & also copy from the fat ass of Chicago Tribune. We allude to quite different things, places &c. Of course I shall do as my Lord does, take no notice of them at all. This would be best I have no doubt. My Lord & I are both roundly abused in the same article & accused of want of good faith &c. It is strange that respectable people can read such trash. Called upon by son of Sir D. McGregor[1] & by one L'Amy.[2] Dined with Johnson & Sheffield. The former was more than usually bakadoorish—is a little cracked I think, pompous as a peacock & yet such a good fine fellow au fond. We nearly quarreled however last night. He was angry so was I. Talked with Sheffield of Munich Count Arcote, Mde. Quatresons &c. fishing. I retired comparatively early with Monson & got to bed actually before 12 o'clock—read some of Bulwer's "What Will He Do With It".[3] I was too unwell to do anything for the fever. Took plenty of portwine & quinine by way of cure. Little black boy grinning like a tom cat all day because of his teeth being out. I am beginning to believe in the possibility of peace being declared in a year or two. The naval operations must be very grievous to Secesh. Try my best from liking the men I can not like the cause & yet am accused of aiding it. There is a melancholy fact in the great Republic tumbling to pieces. Assuredly it was a great work. But it was of man—not of God. All its greatness & the ideas of its life was of man—the principle of veneration did not live in it. There was nothing even in the Washington worship to save it. God & the Queen!
Sent off short letter by Capt. Moore for Persia to Times.

1. Sir Duncan McGregor, British soldier, who served from 1838 to 1858 as inspector general of constabulary forces in Ireland.

2. A Scottish soldier, formerly associated with the Central Illinois Railroad.

3. Edward Bulwer-Lytton, first Baron Lytton, novelist and former secretary of state for the colonies, published *What Will He Do with It* in 1858, the book first having been serialized in *Blackwood's Magazine*.

August 28, 1861
Raining. Did not get up till 9 a.m. but felt much better. No lettres of consequences. An alarm of fighting last night—not true I shd. suppose. Breakfasted, big enormous gudgin. What a belly & size & eye! Bought chesnut for 140 drs. Warranted sound, the swelling of hock will grow no larger he swears—recommends bandages for the legs.

Paid 18/25 cents for carriage of gig. James sulky about purchase of horse. Brown horse sold. Govt. buys up everything. Herrisse write from 11.30 to 2 p.m. Lord Adolphus Vane[1] called, did not see him. So also of others. Wrote from 2.30 till 3.30 in diary. Try & do some every day. Then drove out with Johnson to various people leaving cards, hot day, among others Dolly Vane whom I found in front bed room of third storied house, & asked to dinner which he accepted affably, asked some dishes from Gautiers wh. were not bad. Brodie, Johnson who was magnificent & Dol Vane formed the party & we went heavily into drink. In ye eve[nin]g there was a tremendous gathering, Wise, Edge who has no property of wise & Wise who sharp enough has no edge, Clarence Brown, dear little Olmsted, Vizetelly, & Barros—altogether a very wild hurly burly after dinner smoke & all sorts, song, once Dolly nearly cried over his own bit of sentiment. He argued like a good un & told some very quaint bits about his reception in the hotel here, how the men seeing his name in the book persisted in taking no notice. Then society lapsed into song & Johnson sang & Dolfus nearly busted into tears at some bit of his own pathus. Altogether it was a strange riotous sort of night & was prolonged till owl's first post. Vane looks clear & collected. Olmsted & horrid Hedge tackled him on American politics. How foolish the Yankees are sometimes. It is believed I sent my Bulls Run to the Times to Charleston first!

1. Lord Adolphus Frederick William Vane-Tempest was Conservative M.P. for Durham North from 1854 until his death in 1864.

August 29, 1861

We all dined with Lord Lyons, Haworth just ret[urne]d from New York, Stoeckl, Haworth, Brodie, Monson &c. Old Stoeckl would not have anything but complete smash of the whole concern U.S. & C.S.A. together. Dolly Vane is not asked because it appears he is in disrepute a little & Monson who was a friend of Lady Susan[1] does not give him a very good character.

1. Lady Susan Vane-Tempest, only daughter of the fifth Duke of Newcastle, married Lord Adolphus in 1860.

August 30, 1861

In the morning I am so wearied I can not get up nor can I get up an appetite either & so I lie abed & work out dreams into realities. This morning little Black John with teeth wide open comes & says Mde. Jost say she have got um fish & there was placed on ye table a large creature, spasm of whale perchance & awful to admire. I am of opinion decidedly that the old woman is une espionne & has wallowed up to her neck in moral & physical dirt. Old Jost has all the Swiss hardness. Ye Gods how hard that is—bullies thirsty soldiers, squeezes out gold from all he touches—no children, little fat evil breathed niece. The mind refuses to recognize the fact that a man can be so much abused & yet so safe to all intents as I am here tho' it is owing to my great seclusion only appearing on horseback that I am so exempt from insult. Dr. Black by the by sent me a very kind letter to McClellan who indeed as Dr. George may not be quite amenable to the same kindly sentiments as he was before he did his trick in Western Virginia & aspires to be commander, as thy King Caesar. Thou shalt be King hereafter. He is among small men large. Seward is big among manikins. Johnson took my letter to The Times for the steamer tomorrow. I dont think much of it. The Duke¹ was so very much hurried he cd. not come over to see me. In the afternoon Olmsted called on me & we went together with Haworth to see Camp of 18th Reg[imen]t. This was curious enough. Mass[achusetts] men who never saw a tent before. Where am I to put my hammock said the fellow. This is not so bad as might be. A "bogus" entry.

1. Robert Philippe Eugene Albert Ferdinand d'Orléans, Duc de Chartres and grandson of Louis Napoleon, who together with his older brother, the Comte de Paris, had been banished from France by Napoleon III. They were to serve as aides to General McClellan during the Peninsula campaign of 1862.

August 31, 1861

There came in this morning a little note from Wise or Los Gringos to ask me to dinner. Our little friend is really smart clever quick & does not perhaps tell more fibs than needs be for imaginations sake. He swears Cassell published a book of his Capt. [Brand] Pirate by Lt. Wise Royal Navy & he has to remonstrate with him thereon.¹ I am amused with the ready way in which Lippincott² threw over the idea of the letter when he found that all his notions were wrong altho' I dont doubt but according to the law of contracts I could have made him adhere to his proposal. He brags & tells lies enough to be a Bull's Runner. There is now an end of this month wh. take it all in all has I presume exposed me to as much obloquy & danger as man was ever in, at least of such sort as I have been exposed to. Ray has been dangerous but is now nothing because I can at any moment crush him out—put dirt on his head & prove him a mean malicious liar. Of course I never for a moment fancied I could please U.S. or C.S.A. Dahlgren s[ai]d this eve[nin]g Foote[3] was first man who ever battered down 6 ft. granite with his shells—China. Naval men will insist on believing these things. D.'s faith in his guns is very great, perhaps well founded, but it is a tremendous & vast experiment. We had much interesting talk on such professional topics & I was pleased greatly with the tone of the sailors. Webster & son of the Great Daniel[4] who was witty dry clever quaintish & cultivated & I liked him much in consequence, like all Americans however he retired without a goodbye which always makes me feel constrained. I dined with Wise who had Col. Webster, Capt. Foote, Capt. Davis[5] & later Dahlgren with whom I walked home. He is a charming & first rate fellow. Good under all rapports. We had a fine banquet very jolly evening good wine & tout à quoi peut vouloir. And to bed late.

1. John Cassell, London publisher, particularly of popular periodicals for the advancement of the working classes. Wise's *Captain Brand of the schooner "Centipede," a pirate of eminence in the West Indies* was in fact published in London in 1860 by Trübner & Co.

2. Joshua Ballinger Lippincott, Philadelphia publisher. The company J. B. Lippincott and Co. was originally founded in 1836.

3. Capt. Andrew Hull Foote, son of a Connecticut senator and commander of the U.S.S. *Portsmouth* in China from 1856 to 1858. In 1861–62 he commanded naval operations on the upper Mississippi, including the capture of Forts Henry and Donelson. He was promoted to rear admiral in the spring of 1862 and died the following year.

4. Col. Daniel Fletcher Webster, eldest son of the Whig statesman. In March 1861 he organized the 12th Massachusetts Infantry and was killed at the Second Battle of Bull Run in August 1862.

5. Capt. Charles Henry Davis, Union naval officer, who entered the service in 1823. He was chief of staff and fleet officer in the expedition to Port Royal, South Carolina, and was promoted to rear admiral in February 1863.

September 1, 1861

I was not nearly so lively as I ought to be today & cd. not even get up in time for a ride. This saints day & day of Grace to St. Partridge will be no day of saint or grace or mercy to me. There is a calm in my mind about all things American but I am by no means at all calm about things at home. The N.Y. H[erald] of Saturday is delicious. The most intensely blackguard penny sheet of the Seven Dials would be pure attic to it salt & all. Herrisse came in & I sat down & wrestled over the papers with him in the spirit. He tells me that there are slaves in this city but they used to carry them over once every year formerly to Virginia as a slave state in order as it were to renew their servitude. I dictated a letter to Sumner by way of reply to Dr. Ray & Herald. I doubt whether I should send it or not. Herrisse is quite useless as an amanuensis despite his very great & thoro' acquaintance with English. He wants the accent. About 4 p.m. I went out for a ride right away to the Chain bridge & back, sun rather too powerful to be pleasant. It was in all ab[ou]t 9 or 10 miles & I came back quite hot enough. The negresses were wonderfully fine in their Sunday clothes. Little M. Herrisse dined with me poor little man. Wise announced to me the success of the Hatteras exped[itio]n[1] adding that he would give me the papers as soon as there was a chance. Butler is in town & I ought to go & see him. It is very strange how men are victimized here by vanity & mobs. Butler was obliged to make a speech & the drunken beast McDougall did the same & hung on to him. This is too bad. There is a good deal to be done yet ere Sir George Brown[2] wd. come out to please a mob in England & make a speech beside a drunken Senator or M[ember of] P[arliament]. Sheffield & H[aworth] I think came in.

1. On 27 August a combined army-naval expeditionary force of seven ships and nine hundred troops under the command of Brig. Gen. Benjamin F. Butler began a successful assault against Confederate emplacements at Hatteras Inlet on the North Carolina coast. The Confederates surrendered two days later.

2. Sir George Brown, British soldier and commander of the Light Division in the Crimea. Wounded at Sebastopol, in 1861 he was commander in chief in Ireland.

September 2, 1861

Papers this morning contain acc[oun]ts of great success at Hatteras. Sat down to letter wh. was very unsatisfactory whilst I was so sick & could not eat a morsel. Informed Delane & Morris I should not write by Boston in future—unless on rare occasions. Edge little beast came in this morning to show me a caricature of myself by way of being agreable in wh. I am represented looking thro' a large glass & drinking London stout. L'Amy came in & arranged to dine with me on Tuesday & to come over this evening to see McClellan with whom he was formerly [illeg.] when the General was Chief of the Illinois Central, whereupon he displayed consummate energy & got affairs into working order very rapidly. I must say it is very pleasant to hear such good acc[oun]ts of him for I would rather the North shd. be the victor than the South. After I had sent off my letter I wrote some little. Went out for a time. Poor old Scott is now a mere pageant & is scarcely heeded by any one here. They are all for the young men. The officers who pass him in the street do not salute him. It is hard to save a republic, hard indeed! Lay down on bed regularly tired & done up & was awoke by Wise who was full of letters about ye affair at Hatteras wh. is described as a glorious victory. I made a mistake as to the stories.

Prof. Way[1] & Wise dined with me. Way was drunk I think when he came & confessed to cocktails. At 9 L'Amy called & I went to McClellans—parlous officers smoking Van Vliet & Col. Marcy.[2] Sent up Black's note when Genl. was in & were rec[eive]d by him in his bed room. A short stout young man, dark haired, clear blue eyes, rather a Napoleon head, smokes & chews, dark moustache close hair, dark complexion—very kind, our talk was of all sorts of things in war. S[ai]d he only knew Black as a child. Spoke of Volunteers as military men do—inquired kindly of Beauregard his old comrade, promised me all kind of facility. Returned & staid up rather late. Letter to The Times Brixton sent off by Capt. Moore left at Embassy.

1. Way was an English electric light experimenter. On 23 September he organized a demonstration of his apparatus for the president, sending flashed signals a distance of thirteen miles from Fort Washington to the White House.

2. Col. Randolph Barnes Marcy of Massachusetts was Gen. George B. McClellan's father-in-law and an inspector general in the Army of the Potomac on McClellan's staff. He was appointed brigadier general of volunteers on 28 September 1861.

September 3, 1861
Did not rouse up for early ride—felt seedy in fact. After 11 started on sorrel spite of sun & forth I went to Chain bridge because Haworth told me there would be a reconnaissance thence & also a move on

Munson's H[il]l. Such a boiling day. Turning up from canal around bey[on]d Georgetown came upon high plateau miserable huts like Crimea half ruined inhabited by pigs poultry & Irish. The improve-[men]t in air & dress of the women is very remarkable. They begin to aspire after neat feet shoes socks &c. Many such huts, then camps, noone asked for my pass talked with odd sentries very odd on top of barns & such like, heard of Secesh at ye other side but nothing of reconnaissance. Back & to dinner when as it was begun in came L'Amy & Vizetelly from Navy Yard, Haworth boring me vis à vis. The most curious thing I saw was the Pres[iden]t sitting in front of a house near reservoir in his grey suit with some officers. Wise says he is beginning to inquire into ordnance questions & great guns &c. Vizetelly came in during ye evening & told us all passes were revoked. The revolting mucus Edge was also I think upon me. At 11.30 a great move took place after the company had gone. McClellan sent out 2 brigades & batteries &c. to strengthen his right wh. was menaced by increased forces. I heard voices & there was Stoeckl, Riggs et alii in such excitement to know why the move[men]t was taking place. They wd. not believe when I said it was only reconnaissance. I went over to Vizetelly & H. but they were asleep & so I returned to my bed & slept expecting a battle tomorrow. McClellan did not send for me.

September 4, 1861
At 7.30 started with Haworth for Chain Bridge but could not get passes to cross river as Marshals office was not open. My horse behaved in the most beastly way, bucking & jumping so that nothing wd. quiet him. Morning blazing hot & I comparatively miserable & in immense sweat obliged to go over big stones at a gallop to Haworth's immense delight. Rode as far as the aqueduct—heard guns firing—a skirmish near G[rea]t Falls in wh. Feds behaved well. Home changed clothes mass of sweat till 2 or so, took bath, no appetite for b[rea]kfast at all. Vizetelly came in reported fighting. Gave him a note to Cullum who said my pass from Scott ought to be good but wd. not give pass to V. inside lines ref[erre]d him to Porter.[1] All passes whatever suspended & refused, & brother chips are in much agony & abuse Govt. Look out at distant smokes. Drove out Haworth & V. to McClellan's—too busy to see me—sent up my pass & Cullums letter by Hudson[2]

who s[ai]d it would be better if Scott gave a new pass, but as he had taken that course &c. I cd. do so. Evidently no pleasant feeling. Drove on to Navy Yard. Saw Dahlgren.... Hale's rockets[3] talked of. D. has no faith in rockets. Great masses of smoke from woods. Driving back halted at Capitol & peered thro' glasses. Drove on to Georgetown over to reservoir—looked out more. Saw nothing particular. On going to H.'s was told by Charles who was told by Hospital Steward he had seen 90 wounded brought in. 1000 killed & 25 guns taken! &c. Van Vliet had just told me there was nothing whatever. Wise came in after dinner & L'Amy & they said my lecturing would be an immense success [illeg.] a month. I wonder is it so. French reg[imen]t on march & Californians. Home to bed at 11.30.

1. Brig. Gen. Fitz John Porter of New Hampshire. He was one of General McClellan's most loyal subordinates. In January 1863 Porter was courtmartialed and dismissed from the army as a result of his conduct during the Second Bull Run campaign but was later exonerated.

2. Maj. Edward McK. Hudson, aide de camp to Gen. George B. McClellan.

3. Aerial missiles designed by William Hale, a British engineer, in the 1840s and based upon a revolving guidance principle. Hale's rockets were used by the U.S. Army in the Mexican War and again tried during the Civil War but were not generally successful.

September 5, 1861

Did not feel inclined to do anything today—neither to eat nor work nor ride—acted accordingly, & was pleased when L'Amy came in to hear McClellan was not going out. It then turned out to rain like fury & kept at it all day. A mail came in with a few lines from Delaney of Augt. 17 very gloomy. None from dear Bucky. The first mail she has ever missed to me. A note from Monson to ask me to dine with Lord Lyons tomorrow—accepted. Paid Mde. Jost to 29, 192 drs. Cook sick ordered dinner from Marconnier. Wrote to Senator Sumner as to my letter. Paid little Herrisse. He did me no good. Way called electric light to be shewn. Herrisse charged 50 cents per hour. I saw Lincoln walking about in a full suit of black wh. he wears since the missus has come home. My banquet was not satisfactory. In the evening I went in to Haworth who had just ret[urne]d from a visit all day to Genl. Smith[1] spite of rain. Brodie was dining with Sheffield & Barros came in from boring me. He is an awful bore. After a long story from old Haworth I went off to take a walk. Had a stroll towards Penn.

Avenue [...]. There is a general hatred to the Irish I observe among the lower orders. And yet what could they do only for them. I am persuaded they have made America a nation—for the most part at least what it is. Went back to Haworths & found them all sitting as usual in solemn tabaks concilium.

1. Brig. Gen. William Farrar "Baldy" Smith of Vermont, an engineer officer, served on McDowell's staff at Bull Run. He was promoted to major general in July 1862.

To Charles Sumner, September 5, 1861

Washington D.C.

My dear Mr. Sumner,

I have written a few words in reply to certain strictures & contradictions which have appeared in some papers here in reference to my letter describing the flight of the surrogates from Bulls Run, & I now ask your permission to let me send the letter to you for your opinion as to the necessity of publishing it.

I hope you are enjoying your repose. From Lord Lyons down to myself the Britishers here are unwell—& rather more than less. McClellan is working hard, & is doing much good. The enemy must be greatly embarrassed by his inaction which is really hard work drilling & the like & they are feeling their way above & below the Capital for a weak spot. Washington is I feel safe from direct attack, & a turning movement into Maryland is the only thing to be feared. Such an operation would be attended with extreme hazard, but the Confederates must do something. I think if they do attack they will be beaten. The death of Jeff. D. if true will throw the apple of discord into their ranks. They believe in no other man.

Yours with intense respect dear Mr. Sumner,

W.H. Russell.

September 6, 1861

I wrote a very short & very stupid letter to Times, to deenyman & to Delane & sent it off by old Haworth to New York. McClellan & Beauregard are playing a game of Micawber. There is no chance of our side moving—a warm hot day which affects my head & makes me forget that I am neutral & have no right to speak of our side. There was an obligat[io]n on me to throw a piece of paper into the balcony today. Am I maundering. This morning came 2 portraits of my dot, oh so dim & sad & the hands crossed so pensively. Would to God for her dear sake I were a better man. How very very much there is to be grateful for. I fear the children & future more than I can tell you thro' my dear diary, for it is sad to think indeed of the little control I have, & of her weakness poor soul in dealing with a wild child like Alice. At 3 McClellan sent orderly for me to go out & ride at 3.30. I sent word back that I could not I feared as I was writing. Went in after dressing & saluted old Genl. Scott—talked with Cullum a good deal. He says Scott is very kindly, praised Halleck[1] & analyzed Lee,[2] Beauregard, Johnson.[3] I rode out thro' the streets & saw nothing wonderful. At 7 dined with Lord Lyons—Stoeckl, Hurtado,[4] Geoffroy,[5] Carlisle, Brodie, Monson, Sheffield, very good grub, pleasant talk. To Riggs for a time & to McClellans at 11. He rec[eive]d me in his shirt & we had a very long talk in his bed room. He consulted me as to style of his General order respecting Sabbath.[6] Much talk as to strategy. He told me Beauregard had packed up tents & that I might be wanted at any hour. Genl. Burnside[7] a very nice fellow came home with me. L'Amy captured Monson & sat up discussing Bulls Run &c. till 2 a.m.

1. Maj. Gen. Henry Wager Halleck of New York was principally known as a military theorist. In November 1861 he was placed in command of Federal forces in the West, replacing General Fremont, and the following year was appointed by Lincoln as general in chief of Federal armies.

2. Gen. Robert Edward Lee of Virginia. In 1861 he acted as adviser to Pres. Jefferson Davis and from November 1861 to March 1862 was in charge of the South Atlantic coastal defenses, after which he became commander of the Army of Northern Virginia.

3. Gen. Joseph Eggleston Johnston of Virginia was commander of the Confederate army in Virginia.

4. Don Marcelino Hurtado, Granadan minister to the United States.

5. Marc-Antoine Geoffroy, French chargé d'affaires in Washington.

6. McClellan's General Order No. 7, issued on 6 September 1861, sought to encourage "a more perfect respect" for the Sabbath. It ordered that, except in circumstances of military emergency or necessity, all work and "unnecessary movements" be suspended on the Sabbath and that the men should attend divine service after morning inspection.

7. Brig. Gen. Ambrose Everett Burnside of Rhode Island. In early 1862 he organized and led the Federal expedition against the North Carolina coast and in November was appointed reluctant commander of the Army of the Potomac, presiding over the disastrous defeat at Fredericksburg.

September 7, 1861

Giorno e diurno d'horrore![1] Remained in quite a victim to sad thoughts. Whilst the small German girl sang & carolled like a bird over her hard labour in washing down the floors. Such is life. And yet she may be as wicked as Messalina[2] for all I know & may be made more wicked still. It's awful to think of the work the passions do in their own wild way. I read Great Expec[tatio]ns[3] very uneven—good bits. Estella perfectly unnatural. Miss H[aversham] & her life ridiculous. The compeyson in a story all balls & Pip himself a disgusting & foolish creature, as well as very mercenary in spite of a few decent acts. I lay as I say on ye sofa & read. That little excrement Edge came in & went out leaving a bad taste in my mouth & smell ditto. L'Amy next came a good fellow for all his cute Scotchery. Went & got me a pass for the interior lines. The rumour of Jeff Davis' death is not at all believed now—& yet I was told it poz last night by Cullum. There is no dependence on what one hears on any side. Lay in reading & thinking & fretting. L'Amy & Sheffield dined with me & we had a very bad dinner indeed—at the which I was much indignant. Dolly Vane came in & bothered me awfully with his deafness. Wise also. Vizetelly. We had controversy as to whether they wd. attack in front or not. Wise says yes Dolly says "no". They went at 11.30 fire broke out soon afterwards. Bell rang alarm, troops on the tramp &c. &c. The frequency of fires suggests I think treachery am[on]g the blacks. Rec[eive]d letters of Augt. 23 from deenyman who was rather sad I think poor soul when she wrote—also Times & an economist of value.

1. "A truly horrible day!"
2. Messalina (22–48), Roman empress, third wife of Claudius, who was executed for adultery and conspiracy to overthrow her husband.
3. Charles Dickens's novel *Great Expectations*, published in 1861, had first appeared in serial form in *All the Year Round*.

September 8, 1861

At 7 sent out to L'Amy who however was drawing Priam's curtains by the dead of morning to say I wd. not ride out till after breakfast. He came & at 11 we went for a long long ride on a hot day. Up to Arlington—nearly spilt indeed by furious steed very awkward starting—ran with sweat. McDowell no one in, rode on & wd. not be let inside Fort Corcoran because pass was not so worded. Went over Aqueduct bridge Georgetown, & rode out to Chain Bridge & thence on to Smith's H[ea]d Q[uarte]rs in decent house. Whiskey & water,

Poe Engineer,[1] Smith a very fine soldierly looking man with clear blue eye, invited us to ride works with him, did so. On road some mountain howitzers drawn by hand—also 2 Napoleon 112 p[oun]ds a battery Griffins of artillery,[2] a strong earthwork on top of hill. 5000 men at Station. 2 reg[imen]ts in spite of McCl[ellan]s order throwing up a breastwork with vigour. Then we had a pleasant chat. Found Smith an anti abolitionist. Rode back over Chain Bridge, proceeded up to ye heights & so home thro' Georgetown by the Cemetery. I met Lincoln & Mrs. & taking off my hat to their carriage horse shied & nearly threw me again. Dined with Sheffield. I was very much tired pulling at my brute tho' I dont suppose we rode more than 16 miles or 18 any way. My youthful black villain Master John also rode out & hurt his leg. He is a most original character. Ah said he I have better silver & glass than Madame Jost at home. He says he's a staunch Union man & wears a most preposterous tie. I am glad to say I got in at a tolerable hour today to my own bed, but then it is strange I can scarce ever sleep when I do. Is it strange?

1. Capt. Orlando Metcalfe Poe of Ohio was a member of the Corps of Topographical Engineers on General McClellan's staff. He served with distinction as a military engineer both during and after the war.

2. Maj. Charles Griffin of Ohio fought with distinction with the 5th U.S. Artillery at Bull Run. He was promoted to brigadier general of volunteers in June 1862 and in April 1865, now a major general, was one of the commissioners appointed to receive the surrender of the Army of Northern Virginia.

September 9, 1861

There is no use in my keeping horses if I cant ride. I am trying to sell one as well as the waggon. An American officer said to me "I would like to trade with you Sir about that horse...." It is evident that by want of method I kill out my day completely & yet I do get thro' [illeg.] of work also & people wonder when & how I do it. When I came in to Lord L[yon]'s today Dolly came in well got up indeed. He did not recognize me & only bowed stiffly—afterwards springing up apologized very much. It is strange I never imagined he cd. mean any offence. Dolly & Tinker applied to Sec[retary] of State for passes & were refused. No one can be allowed to do so under the Pres[i]d[ent]s proclamation & passes are "It is expected bearer will not enter revolted States." Wise told me there was a muss between Lord Lyons & Seward as to armament of American ship of war on Lake Michigan.[1] Also Seward is uneasy about the Canadian reinforcements. The real difficulty to come however is the San Juan at Vancouvers Island.[2] Nothing will do there Wise says but compromise.

I dined at Lord Lyons where was Dolly very calm & collected—agreable at dinner—also one little fat man called Tinker going South & the attachés & Johnson who was grand indeed. Pleasant conversat[io]n. Lord L. speaking of Roebuck[3] s[ai]d "oh some such duchess has got hold of him most probably. That is really the danger of outsiders in diplomacy. They fall so readily into the hands of the Court." He is right I think. We went to McClellans but he was not in. Ret[urne]d to Johnson. Sat for a time & then to bed. I wrote a few lines for the steamer—no great shakes.

1. Lord Lyons had drawn Seward's attention to the presence of the 685-ton U.S.S. *Michigan*, whose tonnage greatly exceeded the limits for Great Lakes armaments drawn up under the Rush-Bagot Agreement of 1817. The secretary of state, in fact, surprisingly agreed to consider the case, helped no doubt by the fact that the United States had wanted to remove the ship for use against the South but had been prevented from doing so by its inability to negotiate the Welland Canal.

2. The San Juan dispute began with the occupation in July 1860 by American general William S. Harney of San Juan Island near Vancouver, which was claimed by both Britain and the United States. The U.S. government disavowed Harney's action, but the issue of sovereignty remained unresolved and was not finally settled until 1872.

3. John Arthur Roebuck, M.P. for Sheffield, leading British Liberal politician and Queen's Council. Roebuck was the leading Parliamentary advocate of Confederate recognition.

September 10, 1861
Dolly Vane bad me good by, promised to write if he got South. A day of druggering. Send off a letter to the Times per "Asia" tomorrow New York. Am exceedingly seedy so indeed—unable to ride even. Still I pounded away at some sort of letter or other. Wrote a few lines to Deenyman, my father & Delane. I must give over. The Americans are very angry because I am not a great philosopher & dont admire their Republic in wh. opinion & life are not safe. Williams[1] maintained today after dinner that the slaves would fight ag[ains]t abolitionists. Gordon[2] maintained that slavery was the root of all ye evil of republic. The others condemned for the same reason universal suffrage & it alone. It is evident that mob law & rule revolts the well educated & those who pride themselves on ancestry & that ye contest will always be going on between the oligarchy & the pollarchy & the result will be disruption sooner or later. Republics want the weight of the crown

to keep down the struggling factions. Men's opinions here are not strongly attached to the Union tho' they are devoted to America. And well they may be. A great Empire indeed. At 6 went over to friend Russell[3] a very nice fellow, thin & precise & clear—252 I St.—Wise, Capt. Davis, Col. Wright A.D.C., Col. Gordon Mass. Banks[4] column, very nice fierce Northerner, our friend Williams a.d.c. McClellan. Dinner good—splended Madeira of fabulous age. Wise chatted away & we spoke of boot & plunder &c. told stories "Excrement Sir. Sacrament he————its' dogs &c." It was very late indeed when we started to go home & to my amaze for I was tired came Williams with me to talk Secesh & stirred once more grog till 2 nearly. Gordon asked me to go out to Dodsville to see Genl. Banks, "a remarkable man". Williams will command at Bladensburgh.

I gave Dolly Vane letter to Bunch Baltimore.

1. Maj. Lawrence Williams, 6th U.S. Cavalry.

2. Col. George Henry Gordon of the 2nd Massachusetts Regiment. He was promoted to brigadier general of volunteers in June 1862.

3. Maj. W. W. Russell, U.S. Marine Corps, and aide to Gen. George B. McClellan.

4. Maj. Gen. Nathaniel Prentiss Banks, leading Massachusetts Republican and former speaker of the House of Representatives.

To Charles Sumner, September 10, 1861

Washington D.C.

My dear Mr. Sumner,

I have had 12 copies of the enclosed letter[1] printed but not one has as yet left my possession but this which I now send you. Will you be good enough to read it & let me know what you think of it as a document in refutation of charges against me & of the propriety or necessity of making it public. There is of course no desire on my part to drag you into my quarrel & in case you are of opinion that I should make the letter public or that you desired to do so your name my dear Sir might be left out if you pleased altho' it is the chief ornament of the letter.

We are waiting here. McClellan is doing his best to get his troops into order. Hard work.

Yours very truly & always,

W.H. Russell

1. The printed letter to Charles Sumner, dated Washington, 31 August 1861, contained a detailed defense of Russell's actions on 21 July and of his report to *The Times*

describing the Federal retreat from Bull Run. A copy of the letter can be found in the Sumner Papers. It is unclear as to why Russell apparently wrote twice on the same day to Sumner on this subject.

To Charles Sumner, September 10, 1861

Washington.

My dear Mr. Sumner,

I have just received your letter & agreeing in all you say I enclose you the document of which I spoke for your private perusal with a request that you will when you read it & let me know your opinion of it, freely & as a friend & criticizing it as tho' an enemy had written it. No one has seen a copy of it but Lord Lyons to whom I sent one this forenoon.

In order to spare your eyes & patience I had the letter printed but after reading it I was struck by the fact that I ought to have had the Chicago letter placed beside it. However stet. If it will do no good there are only six sheets of paper to be put in the fire. If there are infirm in faith perhaps a private view might restore their confidence. I hope you are gathering up strength again—above all hope—in your vacation.

Yours ever my dear Mr. Sumner,

W.H. Russell.

P.S. I'm sorry to hear there is a little wrangle going on about our Canada reinforcements—& about the U.S. armament on Lake Michigan. Our friend W.H.S[eward] is testy again I believe.

September 11, 1861

Not well, no appetite. L'Amy came in & reports all quiet at Munson's hill, breakfasted with me—in came Williams also. One soft voiced round faced good looking young man with moustache introduced himself as Lt. H. Scott formerly of 57th. out of money borrowed £4 of me to go to New York. I am abused today in Republican because I speak well it is said of those who gave me dinners. It was only yesterday I was abused because I spoke ill of those who treated me hospitably. Theres lots of quotat[io]n Sismondi,[1] Guizot[2] &c. but the writer is a corporal, a terrible corporal of artillery Robinson. In the afternoon came reports of artillery & anxious people looking out. I got a carriage & drove out Johnson to Chain Bridge who never stopped an eternal grumble the whole time. As we got down towards river we saw batteries of artillery & old officers riding down after us & next we met 2d. Wisconsin, a very poor looking set of men coming back from the battle. I had asked L'Amy to dine & it was past 7 ere we had our grub. Johnson had a diplomatic dinner of Monson, (Brodie cd. not come) Sheffield who goes tomorrow. I forgot to say the firing was caused by a reconnaissance sent out towards Lewinsville from Smith's Brigade wh. the enemy nearly cut off as they got guns down on their flank & killed 7 US & wounded 12.[3] Poe who rode in with me part of the way was however quite satisfied with his work & s[ai]d the troops behaved well. They cheered like good uns certainly. I find that young Blackguard Scott has been asking Monson for money also. But that looks well as he wd. not have the cheek to ask if he did not intend to pay. Cd. not see McClellan. Vizetelly came over.

1. Jean Simonde de Sismondi (1773–1842), Swiss historian, author of *Nouveau principes d'économie politique* (1819), which attacked laissez-faire liberalism.

2. François Guizot, French historian and statesman. He served as French minister for foreign affairs from 1840 to 1848.

3. On 11 September a Federal reconnaissance force of approximately two thousand men was attacked near Lewinsville, four miles west of the Chain Bridge, by Confederate forces under Col. J. E. B. Stuart. Stuart claimed a major victory, although the Federal troops had already been in the process of withdrawing from Lewinsville when the Confederates attacked.

September 12, 1861

(Month in Josts lodgings at 36 drs up) I find a very great & decided dis. I sat & worked a little but there is not much to say unless one draws on his imaginat[io]n for the view of what is going on elsewhere or goes into terrible deductions. I am satisfied all the party men here are furious with me. Blair is I believe a very dry politician of the worst possible school. Seward is creature of circumstance alters according to the hour a good deal.

Johnson, L'Amy & self walked to Pres[i]d[en]ts garden & saw the great man himself slouching about in a grey suit of shooting stuff. He is not a very swelllooking man for sure. Johnson was very insupportable haw! hawed! everything & asked "whaw is that fallah?" till dinner time tho' we did play like billy goats now & then in the garden. Dined at Lord Lyons where were Stoeckl, Geoffroy, Osten Sacken,[1] Johnson, attachés, Vizetelly. Bell[2] did not come. Excellent dinner— very pleasant talk de omnibus. Unfortunately I went with Vizetelly to L'Amy taking with me a snob one Gundry & Johnson became quite furious when in talking of rails I spoke of him as a swell. He nearly burst. With very many good qualities he is still very unpleasant & by no means safe. Thats the worst of it. To bed rather earlier than usual. My Lord seemed to be adverse to the pub[licatio]n of the letter in question. I mean that to Sumner on the ground of doubtful policy. Johnson goes tomorrow.

1. Baron Carl Robert Romanovich von der Osten Sacken, first secretary of the Russian legation in Washington.
2. Maj. Gen. Sir George Bell, British soldier, veteran of the Peninsular and Crimean wars.

September 13, 1861

News in of Floyd's[1] retreat across the Gauley. It seems more decisive than I made it & Rosencrans[2] nevertheless has had a mauling. I wrote letter & sent it off by Johnson as well as parcel of supplies & fair "Arago" will arrive about end of this month. Going over to Embassy found Brodie busy with dispatches. Johnson walking up & down "Whar is the d——d thing to sail from &c. I'd better go take leave of my Lord." He came up after a few minutes "Short & sweet". I offended the poor fellow by suggesting to him when he s[ai]d he could not find the pier that he cd. ask & this was after I had found it out for him on the Dial. At last the great one departed. General Bell came in & sat for some time—talking de omnibus. It appears McClellan took him away & kept him out till it was long past 9 o'clock & he cd. not get back of course but he telegraphed to Lord Lyons. I saw a notice today that a pet[itio]n was being in signature to Seward ag[ains]t me for "treasonable" misrepresentations.[3] Johnson said ere he left "I will put Tanfield beside me & then I shall have some one who will not spit on me & who does not stink." He is a great original as ever I met in all my long days—curious very. L'Amy dined with me & in ye evening came in General Bell with his orders, he had been dining with Scott (who was taken prisoner he told me at Lundy's Lane)[4] & was much pleased with him. Bell looked beautiful in gold buttons orders blue coat &c. told story of capture of his watch & clothes &c. in Spain & Spanish girls. Vizetelly came in—& some others but I retired to bed & broke up party driving out Barros &c. Brodie I hear went round to Vizetelly & sat up till all hours. Why does not the poor fellow do something to clear himself from debt.

1. Brig. Gen. John Buchanan Floyd of Virginia, former secretary of war under President Buchanan. He was dismissed from command after the Fort Donelson failure in February 1862.

2. Brig. Gen. William Starke Rosecrans of Ohio, Union commander in western Virginia. On 10 September he clashed with Floyd at Carnifex Ferry, forcing the Confederate general to retreat across the Gauley River. Rosecrans suffered casualties of seventeen killed and 141 wounded in the engagement. He later commanded the Army of the Cumberland in the western campaigns of 1862 and 1863.

3. The petition to the secretary of state from a group of Philadelphia citizens condemned Russell's letter of 10 August, in which he critically evaluated the condition of the Federal troops guarding Washington.

4. Winfield Scott's first brigade played a leading role in the Battle of Lundy's Lane on 25 July 1814. Scott was severely wounded in the engagement.

To John T. Delane, September 13, 1861

My dear Delane,

If the remark has been made to me once I heard it fifty times lately. "Why does The Times quote the Herald almost exclusively & give its name in the American news particularly after the language it has used towards you" & I must confess I have not been able to answer the question. By lies incessant attacks to which I cannot reply the paper & its congeners has succeeded in exciting a dangerous feeling against me. They take me as the exponent of Englishmen England & The Times & would like to avenge themselves upon me—tria juncta in uno.[1] As long as a man stays quiet & is with superior officers there is little or no fear of him, but when the field is approached it becomes a different matter & there is little safety from the animosity of those behind his back. Nor indeed along the roads & railways or in hotels would one be safe. I have heard from various people all in the same strain of warning, & the only thing that makes me stick out here is the determination not to show a white feather for these fellows. But that may go too far. Davis writes from New York that it is the bitter "leaders" do the harm & excite the people & that I will be made the scapegoat of people's sins at home. It is quite obvious I think that the North will succeed in reducing the South. There is an iron will in McClellan & he will not move till he is able to do so with an enormous force well drilled & equipped & secure against defeat as far as man can give guarantees. But meantime the North must be amused by something & I doubt if their passions will not be increased to frenzy by hostile comment of their inactivity & want of means to carry on the war so as to render it very unsafe for the men who have the boldness to utter such speeches or are connected with the commentator. Seriously & truly neutrality in tone is the only safeguard for your correspondents here unless they go in body & bones for the Union. *I am going to be lectured upon* at Willards' 17th. by Professor Amasa McCoy[2] & the President is invited to attend. "The Times" is regarded on all sides as a Secession print or as an agent which is doing all it can to break up the Union—as the tool of what is called "Rothschild & the aristocracy", & these delusions are not the less motive power in the minds—& arms—of men almost mad by the horror of their situation. The situation in which I am placed at the moment too when I am as weak as a cat from Potomac fever is anything but agreeable, & I look out for articles in The Times very much as a wounded man looks out for a marauder with a knife in his hand on the battlefield. I don't want to ask you to sacrifice the policy of The Times to me, but I would like you if possible not to sacrifice me (& no end of children & wife—only one mind in spite of your bigamous imputations) to the leaders in "The Times". There is no one at this moment who could come out here & write in the spirit of moderation with safety & like Defoe he would be pelted by both sides. There is no use in trying to persuade them they cannot accomplish their objects. You are at once set down as an enemy & in the fight vae victis.[3]

What then is to be done? I am at a loss I confess. The storm may blow over—now it rages furiously. The fear of insult makes me hold aloof from such men as Seward who is at present very wild with Lord Lyons, & the Pres[i]d[en]t whom I met the other night at McClellan's looked as black as thunder. The last time I spoke to him he s[ai]d "The Times is the most powerful thing in the world, perhaps except the Mississippi" & he of course feels sore if it be turned against him. Our neutrality will no doubt gain us the ill will of both parties & if they patch up their quarrel they may be at us hereafter. Their fighting strength is very considerable in a defensive war & this mania once aroused will make them truly formidable. Dillon who is pulled by wire pullers, & is caucus mongered commercialized & moneymarketed most terribly writes that there is a party at the North now formed wh. will sweep away all the Blacks & then say to the South "Treat". I dont see it. Pray more if it did, the men who have the power in their hands now are the soldiers & I am well satisfied they wd. very soon dispose of that party. The leaders such as McClellan & Fremont wd. never tolerate any compromise that was not won by their arms & they wd. be quite supported in that resolve by their troops & an immense mass of the nation of the North. This is a horrid embroglio in wh. political parties with arms in their hand are raging over the land & producing all the horrors of war without its results.

As I write on I think of that poor old eye of yours on which I am inflicting such a lot of bad m[anu]s[cript]s. Morris today sent me a full catalogue of mishaps—God help us—Poor Bird,[4] & Simpson's[5] leg—(why will men go in busses?) & he does not write in good spirits. He's not a good fellow at complaints about himself but my wife says she fears he is not quite well. As for her poor soul her patience is admirable under most trying circumstances for the anxieties we are in about the children are endless & she has no one to share them with her. Her health is improving but she is still a most severely tried invalid with the most terrible of all diseases nervousness added to her other maladies among which is a most ridiculous attachment to her very undeserving husband. I wish you could—I know you would help me thro' & out of my dilemmas. As the army must go into winter quarters I shall run over for a month to see my family & friends & you "facile princeps"[6] of them all. But if before that on consultation with McClellan & Fremont I find my presence distasteful so that my mission can no longer be continued with advantage to the paper, it will be best for you to consider what steps to take, what advice to give, & to withdraw me altogether if necessary tho' I confess I should not like to give all the rascals in U.S. such a triumph over me & you.

Yours ever & always truly & faithfully,

W.H. Russell.

1. "three joined in one."
2. Amasa McCoy was a popular lecturer from Ballston Spa, New York, who expounded on, among other subjects, mining and the fine arts. His funeral oration on the death of Daniel Webster was widely circulated.
3. "woe to the vanquished."
4. T. O'M. Bird was *The Times*'s correspondent in Vienna during the 1850s.
5. John Palgrave Simpson, *The Times*'s correspondent in Paris.
6. "the acknowledged first."

September 14, 1861

Thank God rec[eive]d a letter of 30th Augt. from Deenyman in wh. there is evident marks of bettering & that horrid accident at Brighton had alarmed me. She sent me heartease pulled by poor little baby. Faustum felix sit.[1] I am to be lectured on it seems by a Professor on 17th. decl[aration] of independence & ye President is invited to attend. Curious little bits turn up in ye papers. Herrisse is going tonight to make an engage[men]t to teach Mrs. Lincoln French. The empressement towards Joinville is said to have been caused by Clotilde[2] having rather snubbed Mrs. L. who is really a motherly good natured grisette en dimanché.[3] I lay wretchedly seedy nearly all day. Unable to eat a morsel sick worn out & fevered at times 'till I was as dry as a bone. The New York papers are trying hard to make something out of the nullity & nothing going on along the lines. The arrests of 22 members of the Maryland Legislature in Baltimore[4] have scarcely produced an effect here so easily do men become habituated to the exercise of the most arbitrary power when in the midst of great political troubles & so rapidly do all constitutional guarantees for liberty disappear in a revolution above all in a republic. I dined with L'Amy who is a regular brick, Vizetelly also there. Just as we were ready for dinner Haworth came in. We were very social. Bell in ye even[in]g, Williams screwed, Kirkland[5] a.d.c. McClellan. "If I thought he'd use his power a day longer than necessary I wd. resign that moment. I believe him incapable &c." Vizetelly quite & utterly boisterous & noisy & h'ess. Monson jolly. L'Amy rather fine eventually. Wise telling grams. Singing—not good. Men never tell a national story no matter of what sort. It is sure to come to grief & produces a dull impression. It was late when I got home & found letters of no consequence & papers to 31st. Augt.

1. "May it turn out well."

2. Princess Clotilde, daughter of King Victor Emmanuel II of Sardinia, was the wife of Prince Napoleon. They were married in 1859 when the Princess was 16 years old.

3. "a working girl in her Sunday best."

4. Between 13 and 16 September 1861, twenty-seven members of the Maryland state legislature were arrested on the orders of Secretary of War Simon Cameron and Gen. George B. McClellan. They were accused of conspiracy and seeking to "free" Maryland from Union control. Some were released almost immediately after taking the oath of allegiance; others remained in custody, the last being freed in November 1862. Other prominent Maryland officials were also detained, including the mayor of Baltimore, George W. Browne.

5. Capt. Joseph Kirkland, aide de camp to Gen. George B. McClellan.

To [unknown], September 14, 1861

Washington. *Private & intended to be so.*

Sir,

The sincerity of your tone in the letter I have received from you under date of Sept. 12 induces me to trouble you with a reply which was not I believe desired. I have looked over my letter of 10 Augt. & in vain for anything to justify you or others in demanding that my liberty of speech (or of thought) should be restricted. If the same liberty be conceded to a foreigner which is given to a native let me recommend you to look to the headings & statements in the New York papers about the date of the dispatch of my letter, & thus calmly consider which cd. do the greater harm—the agency which existed on the soil & at the moment of danger to inform the enemy of matters which he ought to know, or that which when returning here was more than a month late, & referred to matters gone & passed away. You say I published the plans of the war "with sneers" to the world. I deny the publication or the sneers. There is a vivacity of opinion in the people here wh. hurries them from one faith to another & the belief in the story of the morning is upset by the telegram of the evening. So that when my letters come back they are as unpleasant as the ghost of Banquo at the banquet table—& are regarded as strange delusive intruders. But as long as I stay here I must do my duty & state facts as I find them or as they appear to me to be. In the letter I refer to, & which is I suppose the same as that you allude to there is no sneer whatever. Everything I had to say is said out in plain English. It is not for me to explain the why & the wherefore of facts obvious in themselves or to say why the regiments I saw at the time were not equal to the infantry of countries accustomed as you say to war. But had you waited you would have seen perhaps that I am a not untrustworthy observer & that I have noted improvements as they arise. I should have thought that the greater a nation was the greater would be its forbearance. To you it may be the Union against Rebellion. To us it appears the constituted authority of the older form of what was the whole Union against the constituted authority founded on the right of insurrection of a portion of that Union. Of course the North believe they are right. But the South are equally confident. It is strange that one can talk of the nation opposed to internal enemies who sees the people of richest portions of the nation united State by State in a Confederacy as resolute in resisting the North as the North is in carrying on the war for the assertion by force of the Union founded on mutual consent. I am almost inclined to doubt whether you read my letter at all as I go on & compare it with your own, but I consider it necessary to assure you that my communications are dictated by the desire of stating fairly—not all—but the general result of what I see & if I see the fault is in my senses & not in my heart. It would be a poor commentary on the text of the Constitution that the people of America had resorted to the worst excesses & engines of absolute power to prevent my freedom of speech & writing.

Your faithful s[er]v[an]t,

W.H. Russell.

To J.C. Bancroft Davis, September 14, 1861

My dear Davis,

I am very sorry to hear of your cough because this is a bad time of year to have one & I would certainly advise you not to work till you get it under & before winter comes on. Why not try some sea place where the air is soft. I agree with you that the least said in reply to newspaper criticism here the soonest mended, but I was anxious to show "soldiers" that I did not err so much as was supposed to be the case. Enclosed is a letter which I have had printed merely that my friends eyes may be spared. I have sent only 3 copies of it out & wish it to be kept as quiet as possible. Of course it is not intended for publication & is only meant for the eye of those who take an interest in me sufficient to induce them to remember Dr. Ray's letter & the charges made against me & who were of such infirm faith as to think they were true. I send you a letter from Raymond I beg you to return, but the letter to Sumner you may keep if you please. It becomes serious when a man is lectured upon as if he were a wild beast, & when petitions are be[in]g circulated against him by foolish people for treasonable misrepresentations printed by an Englishman in an English newspaper, reprinted here without his consent by Americans. I think Delane is a little out in his tone but it is not he who is in office now. I apprehend Dasent[1] is back. The fact is no people stand criticism in misfortune—none so badly as U.S. which has all the faults of vigorous youth & brooks no check nor control.

Pray let the saddle remain in N.Y. till I send for it. I may never make a campaign on it for I have no desire to be made the victim of a sharpshooter a tergo[2] & at the same time vitiate the policies of my insurance in England. I wish to God McClellan wd. move & win a battle & then I could show that I have no partisan feeling in the matter at all. But there is no chance of it. He is quite right. He won't stir for some weeks yet. I wonder will Beauregard at all anticipate him. I am bent on going to the West to change air &c. If I'm disposed of en route it will be but a barren offering on the Altar of Liberty of a victim of Liberty of speech & writing.

Yours always,
W.H. Russell.

1. George Webbe Dasent, assistant editor of *The Times* and brother-in-law of the editor, John Thadeus Delane.
2. "in the back."

September 15, 1861
A very hot day. Herrisse came after b[rea]kfast & worked at papers. Prof. Way called & spoke of experiments last night as success. The Sunday paper here has of course its wee run a muck at me Lord help them....

To G.W. Dasent, September 15, 1861

My dear doctor,

Welcome back from the geysers & hunners the salmon & runes or ruins of Iceland—I hope rejuvenate & full of lore & ballads & ancient story. As I presume J.T.D. is released for a little & has carried off his poor eye to rest in green fields & blue sky, I send you a few lines to beg that you will treat me gently as may be or rather that you will not forget that there is a material guarantee at this side of the Atlantic in the hands of John Bull for the good behaviour of The Times which could lose much of its value if it were exposed to the peculiar processes of reasoning by which convictions are changed in the land of liberty. Dont for a moment imagine I am at all anxious that you should muzzle the thunder on my account. All I fear is vinegar. They are in such a sore irritable state here that a drop of acid plays the devil & makes them leap like dervishes. I wrote to Delane by last mail saying how often I had heard people express surprise that the N.Y. Herald was so frequently quoted by The Times—as that most infamous paper was thus made prominent in the eyes of Europe, & was enabled to boast as it does that "The Times" is forced to quote it whenever it wants any information. The fact is that its information is frequently false & when it is true the other papers are about as well informed. It is now doing its best to embroil the two countries, & its game is to denounce "The Times" as a secession paper &c. Their mendacity as journalists is equal to their infamy as men. Looking ahead they know what enormous popularity they wd. attain if in a union of both ad hoc they got up a war in England, besides wh. I really believe they are secretly Southern or in the pay of the Richmond Govt. Out Heroding Herod as they do is always suspicious. There is only too much ground for irritation against us in the way in which the Englishmen here express their desire to see the Union broken up—& if it be true that the Sumter was allowed to coal at Trinidad[1] there will be a most jolly shindy. Just imagine the Herald persisting in saying I sent my Bull Run letter to Bunch our Consul at Charleston before it went to London. Our consuls are nearly to a man Secesh—Molyneux at Savannah tremendous, Bunch Charleston rather d[itt]o thoro' good Britisher, Magee Mobile moderate Secesh, Mure New Orleans Secesh rather than otherwise, Bernal Baltimore furious Secesh. Of the North I dont know enough to speak. Pardon this long yarn. McClellan will not stir till he is ready to move. We are in the midst of a reign of terror without knowing it.

     Yours very truly,
        W.H. Russell.

1. The 500-ton cruiser C.S.S. *Sumter*, commanded by Raphael Semmes, was the first warship in the Confederate navy. Blockaded near New Orleans for over two months after the outbreak of war, it made a dramatic escape at the end of June 1861 and became one of the South's most effective raiders during the first year of the conflict.

FOUR

All Quiet Along
the Potomac

To J.C. Bancroft Davis, September 16, 1861

Washington.

My dear Davis,

Which steamer do you write by? I find it is out of the question for me to send letters by all, & so it would be as well if you could divide the mails between us. Can you tell me what there is in my letter dated 10th. August which seems to make people so angry. There is nothing doing or likely to be done here, & I am going away for a week or so to the West to see something of Pa.

Yours v[er]y truly always in the hope that you will soon get rid
of your cough,
W.H. Russell.

I beg of you to treat me as a friend as far as criticism is concerned & to give me the benefit of your advice & censure as to my letters whenever you think fit.

September 16, 1861 [Baltimore]

Eutaw House Baltimore. This ye anniversary of my marriage 1846!

September 18, 1861

To breakfast, drank milk, eat bread & off at 7.45 for train of 8.15. Grass grows in many streets of Baltimore—it is in fact decaying except in ye haunts of commerce partibus infidelium.[1] Our train bells its way thro'...

1. "in the regions of the infidel."

To J.C. Bancroft Davis, September 25, 1861

Sherman House, Chicago.

My dear Davis,

I am on my way to Washington & would therefore feel obliged by your ordering the saddlery case to be sent to me to Washington. I am sick & seedy & sore but I am going back to my vomit (literally) at Washington for fear that an attack may take place tho' I don't think any is likely to occur till there is another desperate outcry from the people on one side or the other for an advance. Things to my mind in a military sense do not look well. There is really no inclination that I can see for the war on the part of the American native born population *here* altho' the Irish & German populations are fighting con amore & pro dolore[1] (viz 11 per mensem)—I speak of those masses who form the rank & file of the armies. Because there can be no doubt of the readiness of native born Americans to take commissions as officers or of the town populations to become privates if they have no particular business to detain them at home. I speak again of Illinois & Wisconsin which I have seen in parts for the last few days. One of my farmer friends said to me—"When they come here for their war taxes we'll chuck them into the slews." But of course one swallow does not make a summer nor one wild duck a winter either. I for one should deeply deplore any permanent severance of the Union & I have no doubt the North if properly handled & directed must prevail in beating down the Southern opposition. But what will come then. Not a Union such as existed before, but an armed Confederation holding a portion of its territory by a military occupation. There is indeed I believe much of good in this war to the American people for it will purify the air, divert them from a universal hunt after place & contracts & dollars & elevate the whole moral sentiment of the great race which has such a glorious land & generous impulses, but which pardon me for saying it required a little humbling—as much as ever John Bull did—& that is saying a great deal. If Missouri goes, Fremont's operations will be rendered very difficult & I for one don't envy him that sail down the big river into Secessia if Kentucky & Missouri are inimical. Iowa must resort to drafting & of the 500,000 men voted by Congress not one half are as yet ready & you know how bad enlistment for the regulars is in the large cities. Can you tell me anything about the pet[itio]ns against me for "treasonable" expressions. Surely my letter of Augt. 10 was most harmless. Write to me about this if you have time to spare. How are you in health? Better I hope.

 Yours always truly,
  W.H. Russell.

1. "with love" and "for sorrow."

September 29, 1861 [Dwight, Illinois]
Raining all day, fine fleecy clouded morning.

September 30, 1861
Great day of excitement. L'Amy & Walker went out shooting. I prepared for the beak, special engine—Col. Foster churning up his grand oration, & Morgan[1] crusher. Started by 8 p.m. train for Cleveland, Ohio—train crowded no sleeping cars, no food, rough time of it.

1. A citizen of Dwight, Illinois, who had sworn out a complaint against Russell charging illegal hunting on the Sabbath.

October 1, 1861 [Cleveland]
Cleveland in the morning dirty looking place on hillocks over great lake. At 3.30 or so reached Pittsburg just in time to be late, drove to Monongahela Hotel.
At 12 o'clock at night drove to station for train, met L'Amy & went on with him sleeping double in the car & lucky to procure a place.

October 2, 1861
Such misery & dirt. The car from Harrisburg was surely the filthiest sight ever witnessed—floor one sea of yellow green spits with apple peel, grapes &c. floating ab[ou]t in them. Our breakfast consisted of grapes cheese & gingerbread.
Left Baltimore after dinner at Eutaw House at 3.30.
Arrived at Washington before 6 p.m. Jost's very finely decorated.

To Charles Sumner, October 2, 1861

Washington.

My dear Mr. Sumner,

Thanks for your paper with Mr. Everett's[1] very fair tu quoque in it. I do not approve of the tone of many papers in G[rea]t B[ritai]n in reference to American matters, but do not forget I pray you that in reality it is Brightism[2] & republicanism at home which most of those remarks are meant to smite. America is the shield under which the blow is dealt just as I am selected (to compare x with ——y) as a sort of convenient exponent of the Times & John Bull generally when a bit of brick is to be thrown or an arrow fired. I wish you would write me a line as to the Ray letter—mind that I don't intend to publish it, but that I ask because I would like to show it to two or three men if you thought it was ad rem.[3] I have been to Chicago & find that the Ray has no sting there & as far as I am concerned I would let the justicatif piece lie in my drawer tho' since I wrote to you I had two extraordinary & unexpected corroborations of the truth verbum ad verbum from two witnesses. It is the first time my veracity has ever been challenged in the fiercest controversy—& it is best others should believe the contradiction, not that I am hurt. I have adopted a course somewhat opposed to my views of self respect. The phrase "the bubble burst" was used before the retreat on Washington from B[ull] R[un] & in the H[ouse of] C[ommons] by a foolish young Tory member who was cried down at once. We don't compare little England in 1745 & the sudden success of a Highland raid[4] with the efforts of the Great Republic. Again the panic itself was not so much to be wondered at as its causelessness. Believe me teamsters or civilians had nothing to do with it, the panic came from the front to the rear not vice versa. It was the political results combined with the bragging & offensive tone & threats of the N.Y. press which made it a peg to hang dirty clothes on. If after Wagram Napoleon had retreated in disorder & never stirred for months what would Europe have said of him & his troops.[5] May I ask you as to my moral Bull's Run at the hands of W.H.S[eward], if I deserved it. He says he never read my letter & thus accepts all the accusers charges ag[ains]t me as true.

Yours my dear Sir very tr[u]ly always,

W.H. Russell.

1. Edward Everett, renowned Massachusetts conservative politician and orator. He

was American minister to Great Britain from 1841 to 1845 and U.S. secretary of state, 1852–53.

2. John Bright, leading British radical politician and admirer of American democracy.

3. "to the point."

4. Prince Charles Edward's abortive invasion of England in November and December 1745. The Highland rebellion was finally crushed the following April at Culloden.

5. On 5–6 July 1809 the French army under Napoleon defeated the Austrians under Archduke Charles.

October 3, 1861

Navy move. All the world laughing about the pump & wooden guns at Munson's Hill.[1] The enemy muzzling into nothing. I & L'Amy paid visit to McClellan but he was out & I only saw Van Vliet who was civil & pleasant & of a clear blue eyed smiling countenance. Hudson a.d.c. is a very fine handsome type of man as one wd. see anywhere. It appears as if Beauregard had completely befooled & bamboozled the Federalists & indeed where he has drawn his troops to no one can say. This is a sort of war in wh. trickiness & strategem will do a very great deal of service for the troops are not by any means to be handled with much celerity & the man who gets the start in carrying out his design will secure an immense advantage & will give great trouble to his antagonists. As yet Beauregard seems most crafty & reticent. I wonder if McC. is all they think. I begin to detect traces of weakness & of loss of command of small details wh. a Genl. should have. I dined with Lord Lyons where I met one Buchanan an offensive creature rather, long nosed rough mannered red bearded rat eyed, said to correspond with Morn[in]g Post. L'Amy also there. We adjourned to my rooms, Clarke of Riggs & Co., Anderson,[2] Warre, Brodie, Vizetelly came in, & songs were sang, Haworth being perfectly astonishing with a curious old phallic relic of some obscure & forgotten hunting table. And so the wassail went & Vizetelly got into fine voice & woke up sentries in distant Arlington. These symposia are very great aids to drive away melancholy but with them also goes work labour reflection. Everyone is however astonished at my power of work they say. And yet I am passing on & leaving so little behind me! Except children.

1. When Confederate forces withdrew from Munson's Hill overlooking the Federal lines near Washington at the end of September 1861, it was discovered that their bat-

teries were in fact two large stovepipes and so-called Quaker guns, i.e., logs painted black to resemble cannons.

2. Henry Percy Anderson, temporary attaché at the British legation.

To J.C. Bancroft Davis, October 3, 1861

Washington D.C.

My dear Davis,

I returned here last night from the West where I had a pleasant tour barring the action of a nasty individual who raked up an obsolete statute against me & had me arrested on the prairie for shooting on a Sunday when I had gone out in consequence of the entreaties & assurances of my companions that it was the custom of the place— aforesaid guardian of public morals being also one living in adultery with another man's wife, separated from his own, & a frequent Sunday sportsman. I was fined 7 drs. but the people were so much annoyed they offered to pay the money in Court.

I hope you are quite well & free from your cough. When I last wrote I begged you to have the case of saddlery & the canteen forwarded to me here. If you have not done so perhaps you will take care of them till Capt. Haworth sends for them on Saturday unless you can send them on speedily some other way for a move may take place at any moment. Let me hear from you. I think things will brighten up for the North. I wish too the press at the other side would reflect that in dealing blows at Cobden[1] & Bright & Chartism[2] under the shield of U.S.—for that is their real game—they are exciting much ill feeling here & that I am the scape goat very often of the same thing.

Yours always truly,
W.H. Russell.

1. Richard Cobden, English radical politician, colleague of John Bright and, like him, a strong supporter of American democracy. He was member of Parliament for Stockport.

2. Radical English movement for political reform, based upon the People's Charter of 1838.

October 4, 1861

Sam Ward was on to me 'ere I was up.... I wrote a despatch & sent it for Haworth who left in the train today at 2 for New York & cd. not come over to see me before leaving as he had letters to do. It was agreed that after oysters L'Amy, Warre, Brodie should drive out, but I found after all it was I who wd. have to pay for the carriage. However it may be cheap to the Times for tho' the carriage may not be a vehicle of information it affords us a means of learning what is going on when an emergency arises by throwing us in contact with men who understanding one to be a man of honour will not hesitate to trust him with honourable secrets & so on. Rot & utter absurdity & balderdash. Pretty drive, good oysters I said, drove out to Egbert Viele's command & found Maj. Genl. in his caboose very snug with an awful strong minded femina[1] of great vigour & ugliness who walked into me at once uncommon. But Egbert was very jolly. He has 4500 & is going off to Annapolis, whence he expects to do a good many great things in battle. I dined with friend L'Amy at Tollemaches, Anderson the only other present. I spoke severely to Charles concerning the bad conduct of the man Dawson who refused to let me have ye statement he volunteered to make. Sam Ward came in but was not in his usual force tho' he did "Stand the Clock ag[ains]t the Wall." He dined with Seward who said that I had neglected him—never been near him for two months. I must explain to Mr. Sec[retar]y how that is. Seward must be aware that in writing his despatch he laid himself open to many charges of being quite infra dig.[2] I am below the level of a State paper. This at once stamps the status of a correspondent even the greatest such as may arise in time to come. No I must go forth & leave if I wish to be. I have lived in stirring times.

1. Viele's wife, Teresa Griffin Viele. They were married in 1850 and divorced in 1872. She was the author of *Following the Drum: A Glimpse of a Frontier Wife* (1858).

2. Russell is referring to the secretary of state's response to the Philadelphia petition. See *The War of the Rebellion: A Compilation of the Official Records of the Union and Confederate Armies*, 128 vols. (Washington, D.C., 1881–1902), ser. 2, vol. 2:74.

October 5, 1861

A day of intense heat, oppressive muggy. Who shd. come in but Foster[1] of the well known Crimean hut all the way from British Columbia. Mde. Jost refuses dinner & I am preparing to depart. Mr. Phillips Day heated wild eyed mean & ill kempt correspond[en]t Herald visited me under difficulties. He had been taken to Provost's & asked to give up Genl. Scott's pass & alarmed &c. he did so—is going home. House called. Drove out with Foster, L'Amy visited Monson. Sent "Diary in India"[2] to General Scott. Wrote civil private letter to McClellan requesting a pass to visit all ye lines. I spoke of my past experience of my position & assured him of my honourable discretion & this I sent under cover to him by Van Vliet. Jost is rebellious. A grand dinner in ye evening—present Foster, Irvine, Warre, Vizetelly, L'Amy, Anderson, Russell. It was ordered from Marconnier—a soup, a fish, a dish of cutlets, two foul or chickens & a fine plum pudding. Ah me it was but a sorry affair. There came in the nice smart odd witted young Sec[retar]y of ye Pres[i]d[en]t[3] also Wise who came in with some relation of some great man just to look at us I suppose.... For a great wonder no singing—I may say indeed to my great delight. The Pres[i]d[en]ts Sec[retar]y is rather young. We are told the Pres[i]d[en]t goes about running from one to another & dragging off his ministry. Sam Ward went off today & would not stay to dine with us. He is on some very quaint & curious old game is old Samuel. He was much pleased at an expression in Morris' letter relative to the exposé a pièce justicatif wh. I enclosed Morris from Ward some time ago. I fear he does not always tell the truth does he?

1. Col. George Foster Foster was a former British army officer who settled in Esquimault, British Columbia, during the late 1850s. He was elected to the Legislative Assembly in January 1860. Foster Island in Queen Charlotte Sound is named after him.

2. Russell's *My Diary in India* had been published in London the previous year by Routledge, Warne, and Routledge.

3. John Milton Hay was appointed Lincoln's assistant private secretary in early 1861. He would later achieve fame as a writer, historian, and, from 1898 until his death in 1905, U.S. secretary of state.

October 6, 1861

This 19th. after Trinity, alas! alas! I am found to be in bedrooms. Oh how I long for some certain sure faith. I believe in God the Father everlasting & him bounteous maker of Heaven & Earth. And then I stop & shudder & doubt. Who shall know? Give me the eyes of faith & the heart of hope & the living life for repentance of God all Good. I was writing part of ye day & talking the rest of it to Foster who came in & exposed the nakedness of our Govt. in British Columbia. Foster proposed to buy some land in lots for me at Vancouver to be paid for as I could & to be taken by him if not approved of & I consented. He swears he will do this thing. What a fine thing if little deenyman & Alberta[1] had nice little bits of property secured for them. Hold fast to this thing be sure & forget not. A short drive to Georgetown with

Foster, in a fly & we returned from a glimpse of the shores of Virginia in a hot atmosphere. I dined at Marconnier with Foster & was not badly served but the price was ridiculous & stumps hard with me. Went in to Lord Lyons with Foster & introduced him. Stoeckl came in & was in great form questioning everything. I am sorry I missed my friend Col. Lebedorff. I hear he dranked. Subsequently home where was a tabaks concilium attended by Brothers Warre, Foster, Monson, his cousin, L'Amy. Brodie was discussed. It is only too obvious that he has eloped with Mrs. Pope. Stoeckl told me Lebedorff had inquired after me very warmly & wished to see me. My old friend of the Invalide Russe, Poor Swabey & his caricature of our meeting in Crimea, & the curious days off old Fort, when de Lacy Evans[2] commanded in the good City of London Jack Cargill master.[3] What I wonder of his son? How the memory wanders on & spins threads from hive to hive.

1. Russell's second daughter, born in 1853.
2. Sir George Delacy Evans, general of the British army and veteran of Waterloo and the Crimea. He was Liberal M.P. for Westminster from 1833 to 1841 and from 1846 to 1865.
3. Capt. Jack Cargill of Aberdeen, master of the steamship *City of London* that served as a supply carrier in the Crimea.

October 7, 1861
The heat today is quite intolerable, muggy & nasty & very disagreeable, shirt sticking to my back. I had not any desire to eat, not the least. I was sick & already all the advantage of my trip seems going. This is too bad. I must prepare for an arduous campaign. Morris says avoid all danger. Lord how funny. Why I am living in an air of danger & only the goodness of Providence saves me. But I feel I have a sort of public duty after all. I am a little apt now & then to think I am indeed what I was called by the City Chamberlain long ago "the unaccredited ambassador of the people". To my country I must then give the task of due support & consolation if aught happens me in the discharge of this trying duty! It rained thundered & blew furiously. The lightening was very magnificent. In a lull I run over 20 minutes before dinner & grappled with the papers—at dinner Larken, Foster, attachés as usual—not L'Amy—why I wonder. L[or]d L[yons] is rather pleased I failed to liberate my minors from the cruelties of the U.S. army. The press is becoming very amusing in its contempt for "civilians" and "politicians". The flashing of ye lightening illumi-

nated ye drawing rooms & in came Foster wet & dingy—remained for some time talking. Mercier it appears is much exercised about ye Orleans princes.[1] Ye Duke & the Count are rather with McD[owell] than with the McClellan. After dinner we adjourned to the halls of dazzling light & remained there for some time. Lord L. seemed to think it likely the Bermuda[2] had got out of Savannah. There is not a word on wh. anyone can rely now in the papers wh. is a proof that in times of peril a press like that of the U.S. can be kept in order not from patriotism but from pure pressure above all.

1. Louis Philippe Albert d'Orléans, Comte de Paris, his brother Robert, Duc de Chartres, and their uncle, François Ferdinand Philippe Louis Marie d'Orléans, Prince de Joinville. The Prince de Joinville was the son of the deposed French ruler, Louis Philippe.

2. The Confederate iron steamer *Bermuda*, outfitted by Fraser, Trenholm and Co., the South's financial agents in Liverpool, and carrying war supplies, successfully reached Savannah in September 1861, thus calling into question the effectiveness of the Federal blockade. The British failure to detain the ship before its sailing was regarded as an act of gross negligence by the American government.

October 8, 1861
Spitting rain—no appetite for b[rea]kfast at all. Guns & horse going past to be viewed by Genl. Waterproof neck mufflers &c... Foster came in & bade good by previous to his going by "Persia"—promised me set of shirt studs buttons & links to be ready at Storr and Mortimers[1] on arriving in London. To write to him at Oriental Hanover Square. Sent off my letter by him to Judkins Persia—item sent off letters by Moore for England to dear Mary. Oh my soul what sorrow at times is that wh. is upon me about you. McClellan has not replied to my letter concerning the pass wh. I think not very civil but I think he is a non writer & non committal man. There is a whole mass ragged or bran new clad men passing but their uniforms are ill made & badly put on. After storm of last night it is better weather. Missouri names things & places are quite beyond human understanding. Price[2] has gone South it is reported. Fremont is going West, there is no chance of his overtaking the rebels. I dined at L'Amy & was so seedy I sent for Dr. Miller feverish cold I think chest stuffed—nasty sensation. Larken, Warre &c. came in. Brodie no doubt has eloped with Mrs. Pope or has she eloped with him—a horrible nasty woman as ever I saw. Brodie is hopelessly done for now—nothing can

save him I think. A judge behaved well today in a matter of habeas corpus ag[ains]t Genl. Graham for refusing to deliver a minor.[3] This will test the question to a certain extent. I heard a man say today "Wall—if I can see that Russell I'll tell him I think him honest but pray jewdiced." There is a bit in a Washington paper about me & a horse sale which shows I am honest & I am praised because I am not a rogue.

1. Leading London jewelers.
2. Brig. Gen. Sterling Price, former governor of Missouri, had retreated south into Arkansas after capturing the Union garrison at Lexington on 20 September.
3. Jeremiah Lyons of the 23rd Pennsylvania Regiment had been brought before Assistant Judge William H. Merrick on writ of habeas corpus and was adjudged to be a minor and released. His commanding officer, Brig. Gen. Charles K. Graham, had detained Lyons again, however, and Merrick had ordered the general to appear before him to explain why he should not be cited for contempt of court. On his appearance Graham had pleaded the exemption of the military from the action of the courts in such matters, but Lyons was again produced and again released.

October 9, 1861
Such a change in the day bitter cold comparatively, gloomy & muggy. Took stables at 7 drs. month from this day. McClellan went out today from Lewinsville with 10,000 men, but ye many are not to be seen in any direction. It is not likely there will be a fight. I sat in writing— looking over accounts such like. Lesley Chief Clerk War Dept.[1] visited me very civil & s[ai]d he "Come & see Mrs. Lesley. She is a very pretty & agreable young lady & will prove nice society." Strange sort of thing for a man to say. He has been an editor & correspond[en]t also. N.P. Willis called. He s[ai]d artfully "as McClellan tells you everything I had a mind to follow you when I heard you had gone Westward." He told me he was co[rrespondent] of M[orning] Chronicle from abroad for some time. I dined on my poor restaurant fare, gloomily, hungrily sickingly. Miller called & talked ridiculous politics, much exercised because Beaureg[ar]d has not entered Wash[ingto]n. Says Colonel Worderly at Josts "I'll be back at 4 here" "Well now Col. you can't thats a fact!" "Why so Sir?" "Cos taint to be done. Hell & thunder do ye think you can fly. Its over 5 mile & its now 3.30...." Immense trains of ammun[itio]n & grub passing to & fro—a German reg[imen]t, cavalry men not riding furiously as before. McClellan to be over with ye Pres[i]d[en]t tonight. Went over to L'Amy after dinner & there

were Monson, Warre, the stalwart Larken, Vizetelly, Anderson....
Converse till a late hour. Irvine is I am sure beginning to suspect
that we are pulling his leg. I signed cheques & p[ai]d money lots of
money today—Jost among others. Cold a little better but still I have
much oppression about the chest & want of nice copious breathing.
Did not get to bed till late.

Lesley told me Govt. had decided to recruit no more minors.

1. James Lesley, Jr., chief clerk in the War Department. He subsequently became
U.S. consul in Lyons.

October 10, 1861

A bitter nasty cold drizzling day as ever was. I did sit down & write
for some time & had a little review of Genl. McClellan but did not do
much with his acc[oun]t of Crimean War.[1] He requires a little rubbing
down for his remarks *are* cheeky. He rides out about 9 every day &
comes home late at night after a very extended tour examining into
all sorts of things & making himself known to the Army. He draws
away as much as possible from the civilian world & I was rather
amused the other night in calling on him to find ye orderly closing the
door. "General's gone to bed said he & can see no one. He sent that
message to the President who came here to see him 10 minutes ago."
I dined with L'Amy & Anderson & Irvine. Mure came in during the
evening from New Orleans 23 days—detained in various places—a
good account of Confed[eracy]. There are enormous forces at work.

1. In April 1855 Capt. George B. McClellan was a member of the board of officers
sent to observe the European military system. Although arriving too late to witness
most of the military action in the Crimea, McClellan was able to make a detailed study
of the siege of Sebastopol. His report (Senate Executive Document No. 1, 35th Congress, Special Session) contained a particular recommendation for the use of a new
cavalry saddle based on the Hungarian model. The recommendation was subsequently
adopted.

October 11, 1861

Fine weather. Mure came to breakfast very much washed out poor
fellow. He tells me I am hated at New Orleans beyond all mention
especially by Forstall et les autres. Baring[1] will share the divine rage.
He says he defended me. But the outcry is loud. How much more
angrier wd. they have been had I dined at their houses, the poor

doctor has published a letter—fear of his neck of course. Jackson Mississippi is not a place for larks. Looked for lodgings, found none, had a talk with Lesley, Monson concerning minors—saw stable. Star quotes parts of letters wh. read foolishly now. Met Hudson fine young man, rather cold, Schweitzer[2] d[itt]o a.d.c.'s McClellan. Called on McClellan—not in. Went to ye skittle ground.

Haworth took my letter per Roskill Capt. for The Times.

1. Thomas Baring, dominant partner in the Anglo-American merchant banking firm of Baring Bros.

2. Lt. Col. N. B. Schweitzer, 1st U.S. Cavalry and aide de camp to Gen. George B. McClellan.

October 12, 1861
Russell, Duncan, L'Amy & I drove to Alexandria....

October 13, 1861
Strong wind bright & cold. After breakfast Duncan, L'Amy & I rode over to Arlington.

Upton's.[1] Lunch. Wadsworth. Observatory.

Duncan came in during evening.

1. Upton's House hotel, near Munson's Hill.

October 14, 1861
Sat in my chamber & wrote. Butler Duncan came in & after went out on horseback. A row in street bayonet is drawn on patrol by soldier. No news except of two defeats of Federals. Repulse of Rosencrans,[1] & rumoured capture of Vogdes at St. Rosa of Billy Wilson's Zouaves guns spiking &c.[2] Butler Duncan's ride to Long Bridge successful & then he packed away & went off to New York.

Dined with Wise.

1. During the first week in October, illness and detachments in Rosecrans's army necessitated its withdrawal to camps near Gauley Bridge instead of attacking the combined Confederate forces now under the command of Gen. Robert E. Lee.

2. On 9 October Confederate forces under Gen. R. H. Anderson attacked the camp of Col. William Wilson's 6th New York (Zouave) Regiment on Santa Rosa Island four miles from Fort Pickens. Among those captured was Maj. (later Brigadier General) Israel Vogdes of the 1st Artillery.

To John T. Delane, October 14, 1861

Washington D.C.

My dear Delane,

Morris & you wish me to remain here if there is no danger & to see the end of the war I suppose if there is no risk. It is impossible to express one's opinions freely or to be on a battle field in America without risk & danger & the literary assassinations previously are but the preparations for the execution. I am a pachyderm as to myself, but not as to others & tho' I know you & Morris would not say it if anything were to happen the kind world would certainly observe "He was really a very thoughtless wicked & unnatural fellow to lose his life & expose himself after repeated warnings to leave the country" &c. &c. such as are usually said—& their trite reflections as to wife & children. I have so often to allude to my family ties that I fear you think it's a sort of cheval de bataille of mine but God knows it is not & whilst I am out here on account of them to a great extent I am anxious to do my duty to them as well as I can by living for them, & trying to provide for them. My wife is now in such a state of health that she is not able to bear the responsibility of the management of two growing boys & two girls almost as difficult to manage. If then I remain it will be at the risk of exposure against the consequences of which I rely on your friendship to shield me & mine. As a man I should like to remain & see what is to be seen of this extraordinary spectacle if it did not consume a lifetime but as W.H.R. husband, father, & ex-Ed[ito]r of the "Army & Navy Gazette" there are hosts of opposing considerations which ought to be in some way encountered & overbalanced. In a country such as this an insult, a row, a drunken sailor—an act of ruffianism may expose me to assassination if the one be resented, or the others encountered. The Americans know well that so long as I am here they have one who knows a little of military matters & can not be humbugged by all their inflated nonsense, & the press & the politicians would desire nothing better than to hunt me out of this country but it is strange how little influence they have had except on the very lowest of their demagogue ridden populace. I meet with the utmost civility from Army & Navy officers in spite of the frantic adjurations of the Press to them to cut me. The Pres[i]d[en]t is cold indeed but he says it is because I represent The Times which has shown such a bitter enmity to U.S. & has tried to injure its credit by falsehoods &c. &c. Seward complained to a friend of mine that I have never gone to see him for nearly two months! This after his letter! McClellan who at first was very polite has become quite invisible & is evidently afraid to raise an outcry by showing me any attentions as he did at first, finding that they were publicly noticed but he is not discourteous by any means & I think I would have no difficulty in being permitted to accompany one of the Generals say McDowell whom I like very much in case the army takes the field. All this good feeling of the officers is however exhibited under a certain sort of restraint, & there is a smack of dislike towards the Volunteers in it all as well as a spirit of defiance towards their own press which they cordially detest & abominate. Could it not be possible to arrange for me to go home for a month when active operations must probably be terminated for some weeks. My wife's letters to me are most affecting for she is patient, & yet has such good reason to complain. I am not in the least degree I assure you irritated by the fair criticisms of the press, but I am rather anxious to apply my pedal to the podicular extremities of the Gordon Bennetts here. I will write to you again in reference to the matter & in ye meantime I shall hold on as well as I can.

When does Beerwhiskey[1] make his bow in our awful presence? If he could get into the army of Secessia he would do a good stroke of service—& he would also be of great use in Missouri & in lots of places where it would not be safe for *me* to go. What I am afraid of is that it will soon not be safe for any one connected with the paper & avowed as such to appear among the wild lines of the North west & West. The shout ag[ains]t "The Times" is savage & even such men as Butler Duncan are as fierce ag[ains]t it as the blackest Republicans. I rode with him all round the lines yesterday having introduced him to McDowell who came along with us attended by his staff, & he is now returning to New York satisfied that Wash[ingto]n is safe & that they are getting value for their money. N.Y. would give 500 millions now as readily as she would have given 5 millions three months ago. The articles on American credit have riled them all enormously.

I must confess to you in confidence that our consuls do lay themselves open to the charges of favouring Secessia by words & deeds. It is not possible for men to resist the influence of the genius loci & such men as Molyneux, Magee & Lind[2] are therefore more or less thoro' Southerners, but Bunch (not Bunce) & Mure are really neutrals &

tho' the former is a little lively & indiscreet he is most able, indefati-
gable & thoro'ly British & Mure is as thoro'ghly Scotch & therefore
cool cautious shrewd & useful. They as well as Bernal however are all
hated because they looking on the quarrel as Consuls with fees &c.
thereupon dependent deprecate the attempt to coerce the South in
the belief that if the South were let go there wd. be no quarrel at all.
Mure is attacked on both sides & the New Orleans papers demand
that he shall be sent away by their Govt. whilst Mr. Seward informs
L[or]d Lyons he may be compelled to withdraw his exequatur. Very
pleasant fellows! And yet they are with all their faults a prodigiously
fine people & I can not help admiring many things about them tho' I
am now unwilling to say so lest it should be supposed I did so from
cause. It is their cursed press. I say so not because it has abused me
but because I really believe it is a curse conducted as it is which ren-
ders the country so obnoxious & going further back we may say it is
the politicians who work the press for their ends who are the fons et
origo malorum.[3]

I can see no hope of the South continuing this contest if the North
leaves the matter to its leaders in the field & at sea. Dolly Vane
has gone back a rabid Secesher but he never saw the army across
the Potomac & had no means of comparing them with Beauregards
troops. However he "a'nt of much account". I am quite satisfied if New
Orleans be taken before the taxes come in for collection it is all up
with the South for the people will fall away from the leaders—& it
is curious comment on all their boasting that Davis has really not
got 130,000 men in front of Richmond. How are you now? All right I
hope—with all my heart & soul. Will you send me a carte de visite for
my little memo. book & let me see. You shall be placed not far from
my wife & children I can assure you & the company won't be noisy
at any rate. I have lots of things to say to you but I know you have
no time to read long letters. I live in a lodging over a public house.
Everything very clear & rather nasty. I am equipping myself for a
campaign. I have got a nice cart or ambulance, saddlery &c., but no
tent as yet & no horses as it is very difficult to procure a quadruped
to carry me at less than half the national debt! If I cannot hook on
to McDowell I shall be in a fix. As to going out by myself in an independent corps catering & moving my own traps &c. it would never
answer. Consider what I have said in the early part of my letter & let
me have your aid & assistance on the matter. There is an intention to

push on gradually towards Vienna & Fairfax & I think the Leesburg force will fall back & the enemy will stand if at all in their old quarters before Manassas or if strong enough may make a fight before it. If driven back they will fall back on Richmond wh. is very strong by nature. They shd. be attacked from James River I am quite certain. They have no idea now I think of trying to get into Maryland. Kind regards to all friends. Where is my brother petrel Eber?[4] He would be delighted here—such lots of position to study. I have been seedy but since I am fine for shooting on Sunday I am much better.

　　Yours my dear Delane as ever & always most truly,
　　W.H. Russell.

1. Russell's nickname for Col. Corvin de Wierbitsky, who had agreed to write occasional letters on the American war for *The Times*.
2. Arthur T. Lynn, British consul in Galveston since 1850.
3. "the root and source of evil."
4. Ferdinand Eber, a refugee from the Hungarian rebellion of 1848, was one of Printing House Square's most distinguished foreign correspondents. He served with Russell in the Crimea.

To Charles Sumner, October 14, 1861

My dear Mr. Sumner,
　　In the interval between my last letters I returned from a short trip in Maryland, & then went away to the West for the purpose of seeing the prairie, killing the chickens thereof & as it turned out of contributing to the education of the youth of Illinois—& now I have your letters to hand & hasten to assure you that I feel the force with my fullest of your reasons for asking me not to strengthen my little edifice by the corner stone of your name. I found at Chicago that the Ray had no sting there & I have resolved to take no notice whatever of the letter or article he concocted unless I have an opportunity of revising my letters in England for a more solid form. It appears the people of Chicago are greatly amused at the worthy doctor because he by his own showing led the flight to Washington & then leaving his horse in the streets where it was found three days afterwards never drew breath 'till he found himself safe by the borders of Michigan—so says rumour in the land of the prophet. I have taken a lesson from Mr. Seward's letter & have resolved to look on myself strictly in the light of an Englishman writing for the English public whose

incubations shd. not be reproduced here if they are offensive altho'
I shall not on that account be less conscientious or less earnest in
my attempts to find out & tell the truth according to the light that is
in me.

You ask me what news there is—& I suppose you refer to military
matters. Well so far as I can see the position of affairs has improved
for Northern interests. The army is gradually expanding into Virginia & the enemy are slowly falling back before it. An advance to
Vienna can not be long deferred & in that case I expect the Confederates at Leesburg will retire. Another advance will bring the front
of the army nearly to its old position before Centreville but in much
better form in very greater force & in all ways better prepared for a
battle. If Beauregard resists the aggressive & expanding process at
Manassas there must be a repetition of the conflict on nearly the old
ground but on a much more extended scale & with the great increase
in numbers of men & above all with his preponderance in artillery
McClellan ought to be able to overcome all the obstacles of the enemy
& to overlap & beat them in spite of their advantages in position—
for I believe they are inferior in number & in guns & in all but perhaps the craft of their leaders & the animosity of their men. There is
still to a European an awful lack of real discipline in this army & the
country is so difficult that no general can control or oversee the movements of the enormous mass once it is set in motion. The bat[talio]ns
must get into the woods & be lost like rabbits in the warren. I am not
sure of the result if the C.S.A. be nearly equal.

There are many little questions of controversy between the State
Dept. & my Lord just now consuls in trouble exequaturs in jeopardy
explanations asked for & the like. Some of the consuls have been indiscreet—the genius loci has been too strong for their neutrality &
the neutral tint is of all others the most difficult for a man to dye into
himself in such a contest. You are astonished or grieved that we in
England do not exhibit greater sympathy with the United States in
its hour of trial. I believe there is a large profound & general sympathy for the institutions which are endangered & for the principles
at stake in the contest, but the Government of the United States has
at all times been so irritating & aggressive in its tone & demeanour
towards the Govt. of Great Britain that I am not surprised at the men
in power remembering now how we were treated during the Russian
war, at St. Juan & elsewhere—at the enlistment troubles.[1] I am not
astonished at their resentment when they see a portion of the most

widely circulated papers in the States menacing England with the loss of Canada & losing no occasion of making the most monstrous charges & accusations ag[ains]t Englishmen. There would perhaps be an overwhelming sentiment of popular sympathy with the North in this conflict if they were fighting for freedom but the pretence that this is an anti slavery war cannot be sustained for a moment & is sedulously disavowed by the Govt. itself. The words of [torn] opinion nationale may be more genial & consoling & generous than the tone of our press but it must be remembered that sympathy without acts is a cheap way of gaining favour—that Plon plon may not be averse to a little liberalism in order to vex mon cousin[2] who is determined to show no favour or affection to the North & that the acts of France have been "more neutral" than our own. Besides in England we are threatened by Americanization which to our islands would be anarchy & ruin, & the troubles in America afford our politicians & writers easy means of dealing deadly blows at Brightism which is often attacked under the guise of the war & the troubles in America. The most irritating articles are often meant for home opinion and Washington is often attacked that Manchester may be beaten to the dust. The war will at all events free us & perhaps the U.S. from the sway of the Cotton King here but I confess I would be glad to see him dethroned in England for ever. It is not safe for any country to be dependent on the staple of a manufacture for its peace & prosperity. I must not bore you any more. We all jog on here much as usual. McClellan has a tremendous responsibility & tries to rise up to bear it. Dear old Genl. Scott is a little refractory now & then & the President, who by the by smiles on me no more, is terribly in the way "wanting to know you know" in the various departments. The lettres de cachet are not used in such abundance & there are some feeble mutterings about "Habeas Corpus". The affairs at Cornico & at St. Rosa are not creditable & sound like surprises & from the far West comes no note of action or triumph. If Fremont put Cameron under arrest it would be a very quaint proceeding—bringing the matter to an issue.[3]

Yours very truly dear Mr. Sumner always,

W.H. Russell.

1. British recruiting in North America during the Crimean War led to a diplomatic crisis between Great Britain and the United States and the dismissal in May 1856 of the British minister, John Crampton.

2. The French emperor, Napoleon III, Prince Napoleon's cousin.

3. Secretary of War Cameron had gone to Missouri with an order, to be used at his discretion, signed by the president for General Fremont's removal as head of the Department of the West. At a meeting between the two men on 14 October in Tipton, Cameron agreed to withhold the order until his return to Washington in order to give the general time to prove himself. The reprieve was short-lived, however, and Fremont was forced to relinquish command on 2 November.

October 15, 1861

I dined with old L'Amy solus. Afterwards came in Vizetelly who drank himself into the melodious monster period. Sir James Ferguson[1] also Bourke barrister[2] from Secesh who arrived from Secesh today also came in after dinner at Lord Lyons. They are going home strong Southerners I perceive. These men dont see the future. If they think to popularize a slave empire in Engl[an]d they are mistaken. Warre also came in Brodie who dined up stairs & was severely attacked by L'Amy & promised reformat[io]n, & then Kirkland & young Capt. ——— & then a great sing song of course till past 2. Ferguson & Bourke went earlier, Mure also vamoosed early. I am satisfied more than ever from what I hear ye South must go notwithstanding her great energy. They speak of ununiformed reg[imen]ts of men clothed by ye women & things of the kind. The animosity is terrible.

1. Sir James Ferguson was Conservative M.P. for Ayrshire. Between August and October 1861 he undertook a tour of Canada and the United States, including a visit to the South.

2. Robert Bourke was the son of the Earl of Mayo, a barrister and a future Conservative M.P. He later became governor of Madras. He became Baron Connemara in 1887.

October 16, 1861

After breakfast I rode over by ferry at 10.30 to the Heights of Arlington & there found McDowell & his wife[1] in front of tent—little child playing, talking French.
I dined with L'Amy & Anderson & the only others were [illeg.] Sir Ferguson & Bourke who came in late having been out riding towards ye front—& were not dressed.

1. The former Helen Burden of Troy, New York. The couple were married in 1849.

October 17, 1861
Old Josty posty grumbled & said no when I spoke of dinner.
Colonel Foster, Anderson, L'Amy, Vizetelly, Waller & self dined at
Josts, James brought a striped bass very fine. Soup.

October 18, 1861
I was very seedy with a raking cough all day. Brodie's affair was
arranged by L'Amy cashing his bill for 300 & paying Daumet who
was furious 'ere he wd. let the clothes go. We are (5) to pay shares if
B. does not meet ye bill. Lord Lyons pays passage &c. Everyone at
Legation rejoices at his departure poor devil. He was given in charge
to Waller with ye bags & sent off smoking his cigarette. I gave him
a letter to Delane. We sat down to lunch as my Lord was out with
Seward. I ret[urne]d wrote letters, visited by Mure. Was just able
to drag myself to bowling saloon & played with Warre & Vizetelly.
Met Marcy, McClellan's father in law on my way & fancied he either
cut or did not see me. I dined with L'Amy, Anderson, Col. Foster,
Vizetelly & was dull enough. We are much amused by de Beaumont[1]
the little Frenchman of the Legation who is average pour le sport &
big [illeg.] of the sort. Wrote to Quain to O'Dowd[2] & Oxenford[3] for
a Miss Coombs[4] who is going from N.Y. to play at ye Haymarket &
for whom Sam Ward is much interested, pretty virtuous & clever.
Weather exceedingly warm and disgustingly muggy. Hot as a June
day. In Tribune appears an acc[oun]t of Mure's difficulty, indefati-
gable fellows—also in Herald another attack on Ferguson who is
s[ai]d openly to hear dispatches &c. Wise came in & was full of talk
& fun & footer. U.S. wants big guns very much. There can be no
doubt of that. I am asked by de Beaumont if I am not going away
because it is so reported in N.Y. papers. Is not that says some one a
reason for believing he is going to stay with us for ever. There is an
immense difficulty before me in the way of marching with this army
if the Pres[i]d[en]t or McClellan disapproves of it & it is my intention
to repair to Seward tomorrow & to Cameron & to take the lion by the
horns, as an American orator in the West said. I got to bed earlier
than usual. Tant mieux. A note from Quain saying the last specimen
was *nearly* quite free from albumen. Thank God for it. Her letter was
far more cheerful than usual & she has been reading "What Will He
Do With It" & is uneasy because Bulwer is not of opinion that men

called Willy prosper.[5] Letter to The Times by City of Glasgow. Lord Lyons drove out with Seward over ye camps.

1. Louis Frédéric de La Bonninière de Beaumont, secretary to the French ambassador in Washington since December 1860.
2. James Cornelius O'Dowd, Russell's close friend and assistant editor of the *Army and Navy Gazette*.
3. John Oxenford, long-serving drama critic of *The Times*.
4. Miss Julia Coombs made her first British appearance at the Haymarket Theater on 4 January 1862 as "Neighbor Constance" in the comedy *Love Chase*. The critic of *The Times* (6 January 1862) praised her appearance but found her performance to be too devoid of passion, reflective, he wrote, of the current "tendency towards underacting" among many American stage artists.
5. Much of the narrative in Lytton's novel concerns the sad story of a crippled old man, William or "Willy" Waife.

October 19, 1861
In a letter today Seward demolishes Lord Lyons in a dispatch as to the arrest of two British subjects. It is published by S. to be a set off to the Sea coast circular wh. has played diabolus.[1] I missed saying a word of it in correspondence. I must write tonight at length. Went out driving called on Lesley War office who told me to make applicat[io]n to Cameron who was away.
Colonel Foster dined with me solus cum solo.

1. On 10 October Secretary of State Seward issued a circular letter to the governors of the seaboard and lake states advising the implementation of new defense measures. The advice was reinforced by a second circular letter issued on the 14th.

To J.C. Bancroft Davis, October 19, 1861

My dear Davis,
    As Fremont has been diverted from the M[ississip]pi by Price so I think the naval exped[itio]n will be obliged to attack the rebel batteries on the Potomac whatever the original design may be. It would be most embarrassing to close up the river, & could inconvenience the army & city incredibly. I think Manassas will be again the scene of action whenever "the young Napoleon" gets ready for action unless indeed he succeeds in getting round the left flank where he is gradually feeling his way. Beauregard is concentrating on his right so as to be ready for any river movement or descent in both senses. Its all

stuff I think about ye Rappahannock. I am very glad indeed to hear you are so much better tho' you have to all appearance transferred your cold to me in a most cruel way.

Write soon to yours truly,

W.H. Russell.

Seward has picked up in his second letter I think. The first can only be explained on the ground that he is determined to resort to his favourite panacea of making the severed States reunite by a war with England.

October 20, 1861

A lovely morn[in]g. Distressed by dreams in my sleep, at 10 drove out to Chain Bridge with

October 21, 1861

Never stirred out all day, wrote to Morris, Delane, Quain, Mrs. Williams, Mary, Alice, Alberta, &c. Cavendish Taylor came in before dinner & we dined together. Afterwards came in Warre, one Tuson & Prentice, Vizetelly very drunk, Anderson, L'Amy, Wise, Colonel Foster, M. Barros. Pleasant for a poor fellow trying to write.

October 22, 1861

A day of rain. I wrote away for the mail till 2. News of a fight as it is called near Leesburg between advance of Stone's across the river yesterday morning wh. was repulsed, then they were reinforced & Banks moved up—& up to 2 today they were left in possession of river.[1] Loss is Baker[2] killed Pres[i]d[en]t in great distress. Mrs. Lincoln wd. see no one, wished body taken to White House but upholsterers interfered. Cogswell[3] also killed & another Colonel lost an arm. House of "Tribune" came in booted & waterproofed proposing to go out to fight but I do not think I ought to impose myself on any officers tent, & I will not take the field till I can do it in due form.... I was rather bored, & Lambkin was cross & curious. Off I went to ride with Anderson in furious rain.

L'Amy carried my letter for "The Times" to the Legation per Asia.

1. On 21 October Brig. Gen. Charles P. Stone, having advanced with part of his division across the Potomac toward Leesburg, was ambushed at Ball's Bluff by Con-

federate forces under Brig. Gen. Nathan G. Evans. Over nine hundred Federal troops were killed, wounded, or captured in the engagement, which led directly to the establishment of the congressional Committee on the Conduct of the War and to Stone's own arrest and imprisonment for six months in February 1862.

2. Col. Edward Dickinson Baker, former Illinois lawyer and congressman and Republican senator from Oregon, 1860–61. He was a close friend of the Lincolns.

3. Col. Milton Cogswell of the 42nd New York Infantry ("Tammany Regiment").

October 23, 1861

Muggy morning C[avendish] T[aylor] came in & permeated the room in his nervous way—baby Tuson & Prentice also hailed to breakfast. James came in at 10 having been told zehn uhre by Karl. This is troublous speaking in the Frank Germayne tongue. There is not a word additional of the fight in the upper Virginia. Cd. not get my boots & as ye others were wet could not go out to ride out to fight. Two men one a colonel the other something else killed falling from horses yesterday. James having hunted Warre for boots sent me impertinent message wh. nearly made me dismiss him. Went out & saw Wise at Navy Dept. No answer received yet, to my letter, from Cameron, fluried to Bradys[1] met Dr. Miller who told me with eyes full of joy & jaws full of quid that Stone was killed, Rhode Island Battery taken &c.

1. Mathew B. Brady of New York, celebrated Civil War era photographer.

October 26, 1861

Terrible anniversary. Birthday of my last born. Dear Mary's trial & commencement of our great sufferings 1860. Set out for Review with Lamy—riding my new purchase or old new one. Fine day crossed ferry many citizens going over. Distant salute. Found Fitz John Porter's division 12 reg[imen]ts 16 guns a few squadrons cavalry. McClellan & a fine staff—on the ground—also Mr. Bealy N.Y. his daughter & Miss Gerolt Prussian Ministers daughter[1]—Kennedy & daughters &c. &c. Day grey & mild. Had a long talk with Barry Ch[ie]f of Artillery. He is doing his best to reduce calibres. McDowell & I also conversed as to rations for soldiers, & issue of spirits wh. I favour & to wh. he is flatly opposed. Review not bad, ladies mounted on horseback &c. I was in great pain with my foot wh. swelled in ye boot & I rode back full split as hard as I could gallop. That horrid Indian feeling in my foot. In ye evening dined with Lord Lyons where we had nice little party & were very pleasant. Some of ye regiments were not of first rate style in any way. They have no idea of being well set up, & delight in lovelocks & long open coats no straps turned up boots. The principle of obedience is not in the men. Thus in order to stop furious riding sentries must be placed at ye street corners for the men would not care a lump about the orders. How little I thought this day twelvemonth of the awful trial my darling was to be subjected to. Dont let us speak a word of others. Oh well I remember—the drive to Lady Alfred Churchill,[2] little Farre[3]—the birth all night—the night when I came home to hear she was ill—the growing fear—darkness—the tender words—I die happy. There is something in all this terrible in the anniversary & here am I now—oh so far away—career altered.

1. Baron Friedrich Von Gerolt, Prussian minister to the United States.
2. Harriet Louisa Hester, third daughter of the fourth Baron Calthorpe and wife of Lord Alfred Spencer Churchill, son of the Duke of Marlborough and M.P. for Woodstock.
3. Arthur Farre, leading London obstetrician to royalty and fashionable society. He was professor of obstetric medicine at Kings College Hospital.

November 2, 1861

A tremendous day of storm & rain—gail ominous for exped[itio]n. Can it be there is no blessing on Federals till they really make war on slavery.... But then that wd. argue that ye South wh. is slavery is to triumph. I am low & cast down exceeding. Think of home—sin too. Papers received. Thumb much swol[le]n. Letter rec[eive]d in time for City of Baltimore for The Times per teleg[ra]m. I wrote over to Sheffield & Anderson to put them off. My Lord & Monson dined at Seward's. Warre at Legation & Ambrose his man was very anxious we should dine with Warre who is not permitted however to ask anyone without my Lord's permission. It is astonishing how much my thumb is mending tho' I fancy I must have had a small concussion of the brain. I think so. Mure wd. not be put off & insisted on coming to dinner wh. consisted of soup chops & steak à l'anglaise. Afterwards poor Sheffield & Anderson who had been driven out by my cruelty to dine at Gautier's turned up & then Wise of course who spoke of the storm & said he was satisfied it had blown past the place where the fleet wd. be but he wd. not tell us anything of the destination. He had asked me to dinner at his house to meet Everett but at last Everett & Kennedy turned out sick & Wise was called away so I should have been solus. Everett is I think trying to be made Special Mediator to some European Court either Russia or Belgium to effect an intervention & I am sure an intervention will be played for by some knowing cards but the South will have everything its own way unless the North is able to strike a great blow by this naval expedition. I think of the troubles of this terrible time last year God forgive me. Kyrie eleison.

November 3, 1861
A day fine & fair after the great gale but in ye evening ye clouds gathered again—cold & raw. Herrisse came at 11 & I dictated till 2. Tolerably well—hand better. I was up at 8.30, breakfasted at 9. Felt rather full of pains & aches. Had visitors various from diverse parts. I am rather glad to hear Bill Seward mentioned to several persons he had received my wild ducks & among others to Mr. Everett. The curious man who wrote to praise the Washington police for the gentlemanly way in wh. they took up pigs is at his work once more & is full of the praises of the sweetness of Mrs. Lincoln &c. I hear that disgusting fellow Wikoff is master of ye situation at ye White House. Mrs. L's meanness is beyond belief. A man came in with stories about her. The Scotch Gardener under last Govt. is now by her influence Lt. in U.S. army & is detached to W[hite] House to superintend ye cooking.[1] The servants are foisted on U.S. as "labourers on ye grounds" but are paid servants wages somebody pocketing ye difference. She beat down a poor widow for worsted from 20 to 14 cents after immense chaffing. She has the devils temper & made Abe surrender & appoint one of the men (Wood) as Com[missione]r of Public B[ui]ld[in]gs[2] by shutting herself in her room. Afterwards she sent Wood to the right about because he wd. not put down expense of Plon plon's dinner to public acc[oun]t as manure money for House. Mure came over & dined with & bad it was indeed to see ye bold buccaneer at his pranks. Foster came also. And we had much talk & little dinner because of course nothing was to be had of a Sunday. Lord how the time is rolling on. It is to me but a few days since I was in ye full rush of the War. We talked of Inkerman[3] tonight too—a great acc[oun]t of the personal incidents of the fight to little Wise who asked many questions & seemed interested in knowing all that could be known or told by me. He does not give much in return.

1. John Watt, the White House gardener, was the subject of intense rumor and controversy both before and after his dismissal in February 1862. The allegations mainly concerned the White House accounts and the leaking of the president's annual message in 1861.

2. William S. Wood served as commissioner of public buildings, but his appointment was not confirmed by the Senate. His relationship with Mrs. Lincoln was briefly the subject of Washington gossip.

3. The Battle of Inkerman was fought on 5 November 1854 during the siege of Sebastopol and resulted in a Russian failure to break through the British lines. Russian losses were estimated at over twelve thousand.

November 4, 1861

Hand becoming better. Republican contains some "writing" poetry by Pres[i]d[en]ts son whom Ed. calls "Little Willie Lincoln"[1] on Baker's death. Had difficulty in preparing for my banquet of wh. ye principle ingredients were ducks wh. cookey declared were bad but were quite good. Drew for $300 on J.G. King. Cannot find copy of last acc[oun]t & will be hard put to make up ye present therefore. Mde. Jost sent up her bill for month in wh. was charge for 5 drs. for boy since 23d. Oct! & gas God knows how much—refused to pay docked off 10 dollars & sent her a cheque wh. she would not take not no how. I wrote to G. King, Chandler & Hathaway in re my horse—curious. I am writing this on Wednesday & I cant remember what occurred at all. Sent out & got fish at market & started my chariot in new harness. All at dinner went wrong—oysters everything & I blew up the people savagely. Mde. Jost came up with my check s[ai]d she cd. not take it. I told her I would not give her any more nor will I. There seems a general inclination to admit I was not so very bad as U.S. at first said I was. I must show that I am as I feel truly neutral in this quarrel. If Americans were not so offensive to England we might go on very different terms at present. My statement respecting ye condition of our affairs & danger of war a few months ago will no doubt excite surprize & sensation here.

A banquet, present Warre, Anderson, Kirkland, Sheffield & Colonel Foster. Wise of course came in & we worked him about ye fleet but ye little man is very sec indeed. He begged of me to come & dine with him tomorrow to meet Mr. Everett who is here as one of a secret commission B[isho]p McIlvaine[2] another going to Europe J. Kennedy the third. Anderson sat later than any. Warre went to Legation to write. We wrangled & argued over the Crimean War. Kirkland well said.

The English with free press were best off at the end of the War. The French without it were not at all comparable.

1. William Wallace Lincoln, the Lincolns' second surviving son. He died, aged 11, on 20 February 1862.
2. Charles Pettit McIlvaine, Bishop of Ohio.

November 5, 1861

The old old story, writing tarnation hard. Rec[eive]d a Josty letter de omnibus.... Everett accepted invitation to dinner! But heard of his son's death[1] could not come—& by various causes luckily ye party broken off for I could not get dinner cooked. But McDowell remained & I was set to know what to do till Warre proposed I should ask him & self to Andersons & Sheffields wh. was approved & acted on. Drove about after I had left letter at Legation & had some talk with Stoeckl & Mercier. Saw my Lord also for a time & talked politique in ye street. Afterwards leaving cards at the Galloways saw led horses & French orderly more like ye real thing than anything I have seen. Tried to play skittles—Well Sir. Genl. McDowell came in while I was dressing & we walked over together. His division may be soon actively engaged, he is a little jealous of Blenker[2] & hates ye Garibaldini.[3] If Bulls Run had been a success McD. would be where McC[lellan] is now. Do things go by initial letters? Vizetelly returned from Budd's Ferry.... Told us much of ye wonders of Sickles &c. I warned McD. as to condition roads would be in but he says there is nothing to fear as lumber men can cut ties with ye greatest ease & make ordinary roads as they go along. This may be or not but I doubt it very much. We had some very pleasant talk. He is a very fine fellow. He laughed at ye idea of there being anything of ye Stoic or Spartan type about his dislike or abstinence as regards spirits wine tea & coffee. He is a pure & large water drinker. I dont know he quite understood why our venue was changed for our dinner. The blockade still continues of Alexandria, Washington & Georgetown. I wonder if it be true the rebels have really heavy guns. They throw rifled 68 lb. shell bolts 3 miles into Maryland—but they dont burst. Sickles civil. Vizetelly met a planter who sent me a very kind & pressing invitation to his house—not a bad man to have on one's side I hear.

1. Edward Everett's oldest surviving son, Dr. Edward Brooks Everett, died 5 November 1861 at the age of 31.

2. Brig. Gen. Louis (Ludwig) Blenker was a German émigré who came to the United States in 1848. He left the army in March 1863 and died a few months later.

3. Col. Frederick George D'Utassy of the 39th New York Regiment, known as the "Garibaldi Guards," renowned for its flamboyant attire.

November 6, 1861

Bad weather again. Blowing & queer packing up. Letter from J. Mac-Donald in wh. he promises to look after Jack.[1] Bless him for it. Also short note from Deenyman 22d. date Oct. Towards 2 p.m. increased wind at 4 a gale almost from westward. My packing up caused by a controversy with Madame Jost who sent over ye bill as before-hand complained of. Bill Seward I hear pretends to say 3 months will finish the war if the Naval Exped[itio]n succeeds—nous verrons—mais nous ne verrons pas ça.[2] He is uneasy. Everett & McIlwaine & Kennedy were to have gone to Europe to counteract Slidell & Mason.[3] But somehow or other the mission was broken off, & now there is talk of Thurlow Weed & Bishop Hughes.[4] What ye latter can do it is beyond me to say. Can he be going to excite a Catholic sentiment for U.S. which in its toleration is anything but Roman? Thurlow is a very crafty old fellow but he will be of small weight among the pol-ished politicians of France or England. There is an opinion that ye Emperor of the French is very much opposed to ye North but I am at a loss to see on what grounds it rests. The journals flatter & praise him & France at the top of their heart & he can scarcely care for the refugees such as P[rince] de Joinville & the Orleanist princes. I seek in vain for a solution. It is quite certain Plon plon went back with ye idea that ye South would hold its own. I am still confident ye North must win—nothing can help it if she uses her naval forces & the men money placed at her disposal with ordinary skill & a little patience. McClellan is tottering to his fall I ween if he remains inactive. I slept at my new quarters 17th. St. Karls occupying L'Amy's bed & making myself as snug as I could. I must admit that I would be more com-fortable at Mde. Jost's than anywhere else but that I cannot submit to bare faced imposition & robbery. I told her so indeed. See what a loss the avarice of ye woman causes her.

1. Russell's second son, John, born 1854, who was at boarding school.

2. "we shall see—but we shall not see that."

3. James Murray Mason, former senator from Virginia and leading southern Demo-crat. In 1861 he was appointed Confederate diplomatic commissioner to Great Britain.

4. John Joseph Hughes had been archbishop of New York since 1851. During the Civil War he acted as unofficial emissary for the Union in Europe.

November 7, 1861

A lovely day take it all in all. I am sure there is no great exaggeration of ye beauty of this Indian Summer, été de St. Martin when it does come. L'Amy intends I hear to stay in New York altogether—as long as he has attractions there anyhow. Put ye horse to & Haworth drove out to Bladensburg found out trap must have 30 yards or so to turn in—not very pleasant. It was intended for "on to Richmond" I can only suppose & no return. Country looks beautiful. Roads very bad after rain & storm, trees stript of leaves. Stopped at public at Bladensburg which is a small forsaken wooden village, & had a filthy cocktail whilst Haworth ate some bread. And so home. Bridges even here are guarded. The depot extends itself right into the city now. Dined at Lord Lyons & dined middling well—don't think much of the new cook. Afterwards had pleasant chat, & Warre, Anderson & I went off to Ball given by 6th. Cavalry in ye Poor House. A nest of small whitewashed rooms long passages, dancing not possible for more than 2 or 3 couple at a time. Many supper tables spread & great consumption of drinks—whiskey hock champagne hot terrapin soup cold pie &c. Introduced to sundry & various ladies—& had to drink with prodigious load of people. Duke de Chartres there, speaks French English—latter properly spelt but very badly pronounced. He is a slight youth tall slightly stooped & thin legged with a blue eye light hair, pleasant expression but rather feeble projecting & hanging under lip, dressed as officer Captain U.S.A. He said his brother & uncle would be very glad to see me—& talked about Ireland &c. very chattily. He was dragged & pulled about to drink by all sorts of people who called him Chartres or Capt. Chartres quite affably. He laughed & took it all well. Officers civil to me except that one man a Capt. Arnold[1] was inclined to be quarrelsome apropos of Bulls Run but Colonel interfered & took up matter. In our cups I fear. Got home at 4.30 a.m.! & so to bed. Drunkies at ye end predominated.

1. Capt. Abraham K. Arnold, 6th U.S. Cavalry.

November 8, 1861

Very seedy & no wonder indeed for last night or this morn[in]g was enough to kill diabolus ipse.[1] Heard of Haworth being in, went down & had late breakfast & as we were discussing it in came Stoeckl with an invitation to call on him & a general thirst for news. I am announced among the Lions at the ball. God help us—quaint & curious surely. Stoeckl thinks the North in a very bad way. But are the South not much worse herr Baron! An attempt of a very abortive character made to impose a horse on me by James—only $300. Rec[eive]d letters from dear old Soul & from Peter—likewise papers. Must mind Haworth who has a very keen eye for ye main chance as ever I met. Witness lunch at my luds &c. &c. I have conversation with Anderson who declares I have done all that was right & becoming in reference to the row last night & says strongly I must take no more notice of it. I find I am not able to write 10 lines together in consequence of great nervousness & so I give up attempt to make news. I drove Haworth in my trap to railway station—& then took a turn by various places. Taylor goes to Eur[ope] tomorrow in Arago. Happy man be his dole! Mure dines with us.... There is still nothing from ye Exped[itio]n except ye glorious news which is no news at all. I am quite sick of the folly of these things. The puerile talk about our pretty certain to give them a good whipping. Price running at one time—at another advancing in enormous force & so on. I am sorry I could not write something today but I really was so sick & seedy it was quite out of my power to do so.

  1. "the devil himself."

To J.C. Bancroft Davis, November 8, 1861

My dear Davis,

  Glad to see your hand again. The causa belli was the tone of W.H.S[eward] in reference to belligerent rights & certain acts of our consuls Bunch &c.[1]—of the latter he demanded the immediate withdrawal, or the refusal of his continuance of his exequatur would ensue, because he had in compliance with instructions opened communication with the Confederate Govt. at Richmond in reference to ye treaty of Paris. Our Govt. backed him up & diplomatic relations were all but over with fulminations of war in the air when S. cooled. I don't at all approve entre nous of the articles ag[ains]t Capt. Paris & Capt. Chartres, tho' if you had seen the latter at a ball last Thursday dragged about by every fellow to "take a drink" sloshing whiskey, would republican tho' you be have felt that he was in danger of degradation. You are quite right in saying it is not the fault of the people of the North if they dont win—it will be in the nature of things & in the means themselves. I see a storm brewing. If this naval expedition is a failure things will be complicated immensely. I look upon the attack upon Columbus[2] as another defeat & the news from Beaufort so far is very far from being favourable. McClellan evidently does not trust his troops enough to induce him to make a forward move just now. He will be forced to do it & in this fight the odds are heavily against the attacking party. Balls Bluff will encourage them to hold in to Leesburg, & an advance from Vienna would be most dangerous. The new move of the Confederates I cant make out at all.[3] They can't mean Maryland—if they do they are beaten—it is either a ruse or they are afraid of their right flank & rear towards Norfolk.

Yours very truly,

W.H. Russell

P.S. Regards to Mr. Bancroft pray & respects to Mrs. Davis who is I hope quite well.

1. The American government's irritation at British consular activities in the Confederate States finally came to a head at the end of October when Secretary of State Seward revoked the exequatur of Robert Bunch, the consul in Charleston.

2. On 7 November Federal forces under Brig. Gen. Ulysses S. Grant attacked Belmont, Missouri, on the Mississippi River opposite Columbus, Kentucky. The fierce engagement resulted in both sides losing over six hundred men, with Grant being forced to retreat to Cairo.

3. In his letter to *The Times* dated 25 October (published on 12 November), Russell noted rumors of Confederate landings in Maryland. He reported that the man-of-war *George Page* had been seen the previous day between Evansport and Budd's Ferry with decks loaded with troops.

November 9, 1861

I went in to Josts & wrote an immense amount of letters. I am not a man of reflection. If I were how different would be my position, how deplorable my frame of mind. Whilst I am expected to be jocose enlightened wise witty well informed & unflagging in spirits & resources here are dark horrors of memory & present gloom pressing around me. My wife imploring me to come back—dues pressing & all my affairs in one great muddle as well as can be. I see no chance of extrication unless by ye slow process of paying off debts at ye rate of a few hundreds say £600 per annum. Well that would do something if Mary were content & happy—how terrible the disease—ye poison of uric acid appears to be—the whole brain is shaken ye system becomes one vast repertoire of various disorders & ye mind dwells on morbid images. Sympathy & such like wh. in the heart of woman become such powerful agents. I am asked to a banquet by 6th. Cavalry U.S. at ye Poor House back of ye Capitol on Thursday night. I see he asked me & V[izetelly] by couples as a general rule. All right. Mure dined with me as I was solus & talked of New Orleans & all sorts of things. His friend Maury[1] is not likely to be of much avail in carrying letters as he is arrested I hear at ye State Dept. In ye eve[nin]g Anderson brought in Wilmot[2] from Lord Lyons & we had much talk of Dahlgren & Armstrong guns.[3] He swears ye Times is responsible for ye Armstrong gun. Wise very civil to him & ye buccaneer in fine force. Blackwell is also here with wife & daughter. Dahlgren is strongly of opinion that breech load[in]g is a failure—& that Armstrong has done ye most that can be. Sellers' foundary[4] at Philadelphia is well worth seeing I am told. I went home & slept at Josts. Warre made vain attempt to get in to Vizetellys. I secured my retreat very artfully, as Warre wd. have sat up ad ultimas horos.[5]

1. M. F. Maury of New Orleans, a British subject, was arrested in Cleveland on 7 November 1861. He was released in February 1862.

2. Col. Frederick Maron Eardley Wilmot, Royal Artillery, was the second son of Sir John Eardly Eardly-Wilmot.

3. Cannon developed by Sir William Armstrong, British industrialist and engineer and founder of the Elswick ordnance works. Armstrong pioneered the use of wrought iron in cannon manufacture. In 1859 he produced a new rifled breech-loading version that was successfully employed against the Taku Forts in China the following year. Armstrong's breech-loading system was slow to find favor in Great Britain, however. Armstrong was knighted in 1859 and also appointed engineer in chief of Rifled Ordnance.

4. William Sellers was a pioneer Philadelphia machine tool designer. After the Civil War he achieved widespread recognition in both Europe and America for his engineering achievements.

5. "to the final hour."

November 10, 1861

A dirty little boy shouting "extra Chronicle Charleston taken!" The news merely is that a landing has been effected in 2 places & that ye troops are marching inland.[1] Beaufort C[ourt] H[ouse] s[ai]d to have Stars & Stripes on it. Doubtful. This was whilst Mure & I were walking down ye Avenue where at corner of 13 St. we had good look at political prisoners, confined in corner house. One of ye guards came to Mure with letter & s[ai]d he felt for Maury who is confined here because he did business in his state. These state feelings very strong. Day rather fine & cold, bright now & then fine orange sunset over Capital. Breakfasted at Karl's. Colonel Emory[2] called. Master of workhouse who was very drunk at ball s[ai]d "How very pleasant no one drunk!" Met General Van Vliet—also Schweitzer.

McClellan & his wife[3] are awfully in love with each other. He is distrait rather. Lord Lyons taking exercise on horse also attracted attention, & Tanfield ye magnificent. First thing this morning received a card from Lord Lyons for the Tuesday. Grand dinner— hurroo! Wrote many letters at Madame Josts & had only one small walk before dinner with the buccaneer. There dined with us Williams 6th. U.S. Cavalry slightly inebriate & pleasant till he became quite blind. He left his orderly outside till all was blue 5 hours about— also Vizetelly—item very nice fellow. Kirkland came in during ye evening & so of course did Wise who proposed steamed oysters to Vizetelly—rather noisy night owing to Williams. Shef[fiel]d went & worked at Chanc[ellory].[4] Poor Anderson told me of his woeful. And so to bed. General Scott sailed yesterday in Arago delighted to get away from these people. Mure tells me Maury was arrested in State Depart[ment] where he went to look for a trunk ordered to be delivered up to him by Bill Seward. I suspect the man is an ass if not a Secesher, & I pity no Britisher who joins either & is burnt.

1. On 7 November a combined Union army-navy force under Flag Officer Samuel Du Point successfully captured Port Royal, South Carolina, thereby effectively gaining control of the southern coast from Savannah to Charleston. A small detachment was sent to occupy Beaufort on the 10th.

2. Col. William Hemsley Emory, a Mexican War veteran and noted military surveyor. He was appointed brigadier general of volunteers in March 1862.

3. Ellen Mary Marcy McClellan, the daughter of Gen. Randolph B. Marcy. They were married in 1860.

4. The offices in the British legation.

November 11, 1861

A day ventose gloomy clouded. We breakfast with Karl & cometh papers & so on. Write after b[rea]kfast & send off very meagre letter to Times by Boston mail wh. also takes some for P. Burrowes, Mary, father &c. Waller is here also, & Haworth comes tomorrow. Wrote & sent off a very queer & unsatisfactory letter I fear. Had a walk & a game of skittles with Sheffield pained my hand rather. As we were sitting down to dinner the Buccaneer hailed us & we asked him in. He came accordingly & we had jocund Beaune & had wild carouses for him. A very picturesque torchlight procession blue green red orange fires & profusion of fireworks from Blenker camp across ye river in honour of McClellan. I drove out & called on Lesley—nice house, packing up for Nice. He told me ye return of troops called out would be more than 600,000 & more than 600 pieces of field artillery & 16,000 cavalry. His sister in law a nice sensible American girl. Thence to Riggs where we found (Stoeckl & I came back from ye drive) some friends & had high talk of politics. New York Times praises my letters in high terms. Riggs & Stoeckl think ye South can hold their own—they dont want corn wheat shoes leather or food of any kind & Georgia makes cloth &c. Riggs thinks when ye Congress come to discuss ye question of whether ye war be against slavery or not there will be a split. He also opines that ye people wont pay ye taxes. Also only ye state taxes are very high [...]. Ye South set out on ye principle of not paying. Ye North set out with ye principle of paying all things. Fremont had left a debt of 7 million of dollars behind him at St. Louis alone. Riggs thinks Chase doesnt know his exp[en]d[iture]. Stoeckl & I argued all ye ladies out of ye room—& he kept it up outside his house till 1.30. Had difficulty in getting in. Cd. not do it unless by severe ringing & rousing out Karl at last.

November 12, 1861

Glorious day of Indian Summer. Bel giorno! No news of any greater interest from the South. What has become of ye Exped[itio]n? After breakfast visited Mure, & saw landlady & lodgings. Saw Vizetelly & Waller. We are invited to ye Lords all of us—ate oysters, played skittles or bowls, met Fox Sec[retar]y of Navy & Hay Pres[iden]ts Sec[retar]y told me of success at Beaufort. Fox read ye dispatches for me on Penn[sylvania] Ave. Hair cutters shop always niggers why. It's a great business with them always. Dinner at 7 Chase, Major Palmer U.S. Top Engin[eer][1] (foolishly) mild but very nice. Warre's hair surrendered & parted down, Prof. Henry & daughter, Col. Emory & wife, Mr. Kennedy & daughter, Sheffield, Anderson, Monson, Vizetelly, Mure who was most affable, Col. Wilmot, the sideboard with plate very pretty & the liv[in]g room showed to immense advantage—dinner excellent on the whole one mistake a mayonnaise aux homards. After dinner had a long talk with Chase who is sanguine I think that war cannot last long—he thinks this beginning of success & Nelson's victory must begin to tell very soon. He also says expenses are enormous & that they must be remodelled, a strong govt. the result of the struggle. Naval operations would have begun before but the members of ye Cabinet have with exception of Seward perhaps never been at sea & know nothing of it. He is a very keen clear headed man & seems to see his way by the eye of faith. He has never disguised his idea that ye South might have been let go without danger of ultimate rupture. He is proud of his success in finance—justly so I think but the expenses do frighten him. Wierbitsky called today by the by & said a good deal de omnibus. He has written he tells me one letter to the Times as to his impressions &c. We all went home after legation dinner & got to bed about 12.45 leaving Anderson & Waller conversing My Lord very lively.

1. Maj. William R. Palmer, U.S. Topographical Engineers. He died in June 1862 "of disease caused by exposure in discharge of duty," according to the official report.

November 13, 1861

A lovely morn of Indian summer. A visit from O'Hagan—gave him letters &c. My poor friend Green arrested so is Lowe[1] both of Savannah. As both are secesh I should not be surprized if they laid themselves open to some just punish[men]t much as I regret it. Mrs. Lowe[2]— Seward told me—was liberated here. It is strange that the Union should be supported by German savages who plunder & destroy as if they were living in the day of Agricola[3] whilst the English were ye great smugglers. I reminded him U.S. was ye flag wh. smuggled during Russian War. "Yes but then s[ai]d he that was a legitimate contest between two great nations. I admit tho' I lament the fact that sympathy in this country was with Russia during ye war." Raymond attributed it to ye Irish & anti Englishry of ye Irish—but it was admitted by all. McDowell says there is no people in the world about whose criticism ye U.S. care except ye English & towards them a morbid sensitiveness does exist wh. can scarcely be accounted for except on ground of immense fondness for approbation & respect for British opinion. Seward says he & L[or]d Lyons have now agreed not to kick up rows about British subjects. When arrested for offences ag[ains]t U.S. they will be in case of any diplomatic interference treated as objects of indict[men]t instead of being sent to Fort Lafayette[4] & they will be in a much worse position than if they were merely confined & let out for a short time. Seward complained of Greeley's hitting out at him for arbitrary arrests. The press soon comes round here & Greeley is silent now. O'Hagan dined with me & Anderson & Sheffield & we had a great deal to talk de omnibus. O'H. is a shrewd sensible man. He greatly prefers U.S. to Canada he says except for ye scenery. I fear with all our brag some cold shades does cast over us on this continent. To my astonishment learned Mure had gone off at 7 this p.m. without bidding good by. Went across & slept at Josts. Made over my rooms to a Mr. & Mrs. Weldon. [...]

1. Andrew Low, a prominent British-born Savannah merchant, was arrested in Cincinnati with his wife on their return from England, where he claimed to have been on private business. After the intercession of William Evarts and Lord Lyons among others, he was released in February 1862 and allowed to return to the South on condition that he either give himself up after three months or provide a prisoner exchange.

2. Mrs. John Low was arrested with her brother Charles Green in Detroit on 3 November but was released ten days later on a pledge of good conduct.

3. Gnaeus Julius Agricola (37–93), Roman statesman, soldier, and governor of Britain from 77 to 87.

4. Union prison in New York harbor where those suspected of disloyalty were detained after Lincoln's suspension of the writ of habeas corpus.

November 14, 1861
Rec[eive]d invitation to family dinner with Seward at 6 o'c[loc]k this eve[nin]g. Day rather fine but became overcast & not at all like the Indian summer. Breakfasted at Karl's & p[ai]d ye bill for week very large $26.30. Mure having gone engaged his rooms at $50 per men[sem] including fire & gas. Paid Mde. Jost also up to 14th 36 drs. Rode out a new horse for trial to 6th. Cavalry Camp. Found Emory in

also Genl. Stoneman[1] & was introduced to Capt. Pleasanton.[2] We sat in front of Emorys tent talked of riding in California of bush ranging, lassooing bulls & horses saddles &c. A man came in "to take George to Pittsburg", he was dead—formerly they were carried free. Saw ye reg[imen]t out for drill parade—rather dirty & unkempt in all respects. Williams came in rackety as usual. A Mr. Davidson Montreal Bank[3] introduced to me. O'Hagan left. Rode back & to Sewards raining like fury found there silent son F.W., Raymond & Mr. Sec[retar]y in morning clothes. S. very civil—dinner bad, wine poisonous. After while playing a rubber upstairs in came Pres[i]d[en]t, talked freely & broke jokes & told old stories—new to me. "Here" said Seward "are the two Times—if we only get them to do what we want all wd. go well." Oh s[ai]d L. "if the Times go for us the other Times will follow." Seward said when he went across after Bulls Run only one man was doing anything to get men to defend works & that was Sherman & if the enemy had come on said he they wd. all have fled across ye river— this anecdote of 69th. at Corcoran on Tuesday—complaining because Sherman s[ai]d he wd. shoot one of their officers. "And so, said Sherman I will by G—— if he doesn't do what I tell him." Seward's notions of courage. "I" said he "displayed more than those who were soldiers." He said after Baltimore he went north to see if what Teakle Wallis[4] & others told him that ye people wd. carry his head on their pikes was true & he found at Auburn how the case really stood. Arrests were ordered whilst we were at dinner by Seward to his son. He spoke on British subjects & smuggling.

1. Brig. Gen. George Stoneman of New York was the Army of the Potomac's chief of cavalry. He later became governor of California.

2. Capt. Alfred Pleasonton of the 2nd U.S. Cavalry. As a major general, he replaced General Stoneman in June 1863 and commanded the Federal cavalry at the Battle of Brandy Station.

3. David Davidson was general manager of the Bank of Montreal from 1855 until 1863, when he resigned to take up an appointment as manager of the Bank of Scotland. He had emigrated from Great Britain to Canada in 1843.

4. Severn Teakle Wallis, leading Baltimore lawyer who, although opposing secession, sympathized with the Confederacy. He was imprisoned for fourteen months during the Civil War.

November 15, 1861
A day rude cold & raw. Breakfasted at Karl's. My horse jockey friend
John Miller called, & I had to take ye beast at $225. Every one says
it is cheap as horses go. "He says says he John that's the best horse
I seed this many a day. Yes says I, & its one as I want for Sir John
Russell if ever there was a man a suited for a horse or a horse a
suited for a man." Haworth went off, but as I had nothing to write
about I did not trouble The Times at all. My recollections of ye evening last not agreable. It seems that there is difficulty now about
granting passes because of par[agraph] in paper that Secesh officer had got round with pass to Alexandria. Rode out in afternoon,
streets disgraceful, full of mud holes & all sorts of dirt. Ordered wine
from Binninger who has lost much gelt in this fight from ye South.
At dinner Count! & Colonel! Corvin de Wierbitsky, Mrs. Evans of
England, Genl. McDowell, Raymond of Times, Wise, self. Wise very
funny about venerable goose wh. he said was albatross. Pro consul
did not come in but Sir F. Johnston,[1] Chaplin, Ossowatamie Brown,[2]
Warre, Weldon, & afterwards Anderson & Sheffield who filled great
beakers of [illeg.] & dashed his mucous membrane. McDowell is to
have ye arrange[men]t of ye grand review of 50,000 *odd* men 120 guns
& cavalry attach[e]d. There is much confidence excited by victory at
Beaufort. Corvin who insists on talking terrible English told us of his
defence of Radstadt. There is immense confidence in American mind
as to exemption from all ye dangers which threaten other people.
Treatment by ye Captain Morris of Pensacola of Engineer Sickles[3]
of wh. I wrote to ye "Times". Prince de Joinville is quite delighted
with Nelson's being a sailor. I hear Barlow is in town, very curious
he never called on me. I don't understand ye fact also old Duncan is
in town. I was to have gone over to see Seward today at 10 o'clock but
I excused myself on some ground or other as I had so much business
to do. McClellan is going to review 7 divisions about 50000 in all.
McDowells, Heinztlemans,[4] Blenkers, McCalls,[5] Porters.

1. Sir Frederick John William Johnstone, son of the West Indies proprietor and
Conservative M.P. Sir Frederick George Johnstone. He later served as Conservative
M.P. for Weymouth, 1874–85.
2. Probably John Brown, Jr., eldest son of the abolitionist martyr.
3. The U.S. steam sloop *Pensacola* had for some weeks been lying in the Potomac,
unable to move on account of faulty engines. Sickles, the engine designer, who had
aroused considerable resentment because of the large sums of money he had received

from the Navy Department, was detained on board the *Pensacola* by its captain until such time as the fault was repaired.

4. Brig. Gen. Samuel Peter Heintzelman of Pennsylvania, a Mexican War veteran who commanded the 3rd Corps of the Army of the Potomac in the Peninsula campaign.

5. Brig. Gen. George Archibald McCall of Pennsylvania. He was captured and paroled during the Peninsula campaign but resigned from the army in March 1863.

FIVE

The *Trent* Affair

November 16, 1861

Fine sunny day, wind high & strong, leaves falling fast. Report
that Federal pickets are attacked at Beaufort. After b[rea]kfast one
deput[atio]n headed by Evans 3 small hairy Britishers. Second depu-
t[atio]n headed by Walford[1] to me unknown. Revd. Wm. Banister,[2]
son of old Ferula of Alton, & 2 others passes also. Walford my supposed substitute tells me he repudiated very strongly ye notion. A
cold raw day. As I was going over to Lord Lyons I met Mercier
wrapped in his cloak who told me ye extraordinary news that ye U.S.
vessel of war San Jacinto stopped ye Trent in ye Bahamas[3] & took
Mason, Slidell, Eustis & McClernand.[4] Extraordinary excitement in
ye Chancellory. Warre, Anderson, Sheffield very demure as if nothing
had happened deep young diplomatic rogues. It seems at first blush
as if there could be no way of getting out of the affair at all. Went
down to bowling saloon & found the evening papers quite full of the
affair. The tone is ridiculous enough as it assumes nothing unusual
or out of the way was committed. Mercier was in evident exultation.
Stoeckl & all ye ministers called on Lord Lyons with full expressions
of sympathy in ye extraordinary business but no one gave official
counsel. The State Dept. has as yet said nothing of ye matter at all.
There will be great irritation in England I am certain but all here
say Palmerston[5] is a rank coward in spite of blustering. I dined at
Karls as appears from dis bill—in ye evening came in Wise &c. W.
thinks that an apology & surrender of poor Wilkes[6] to vengeance
by dismissing him will be enough but under no case will Slidell &
Mason be given up. He insists on it too that the American squad[ro]n

captured more slaves in one year than we did in five. Already men begin to argue & become excit[e]d over these points. Kirkland who is a clear studious thoughtful honest little fellow is evidently perplexed & knows not what to be at. The arguments for the arrest have not yet been thought of. Wise says Wilkes acted on his own hook as he was coming home from ye African Coast, & intimates that he did it to cut a dash & make a sensation being a bold & daring man. It was his house McClellan resided.

1. Edward Walford, writer of obituaries for *The Times* and a well-known compiler of biographical dictionaries.

2. Rev. William Banister was vicar of St. James Mount, Liverpool, since 1840.

3. On 8 November 1861 the British steamship *Trent*, en route from Havana to St. Thomas, was stopped in the Bahamas Channel by the U.S.S. *San Jacinto*. A boarding party removed the two Confederate commissioners, James M. Mason and John Slidell, together with their families and secretaries, who were then taken to Boston.

4. Russell means James E. Macfarland of Virginia, James M. Mason's secretary of legation.

5. Henry John Temple, third Viscount Palmerston, British prime minister from 1855 to 1858 and from 1859 to 1865.

6. Capt. Charles Wilkes, New York–born naval officer and explorer, who commanded the U.S.S. *San Jacinto*.

November 17, 1861

Up at 8 & off on new horse to 6th. Cavalry outside ye capital, raw bitter cold morning. Anderson came also. The reg[imen]t already on ye ground. Williams carnevalling on point in white kid gloves & the Colonel green & stiff in front, a march past at slow trot & half gallop, mens caps off others slashing horses with swords to make them go. A rough unkempt lot enough but well mounted. Back to Col's. tent where nigger mixed cocktails & hot punch. Oh Lord how cold it was. Back to town with Emory, Kirkland, Williams &c. I breakfasted in my own rooms & sat down to write & read. Went in next door & saw Williams asleep on ye sofa evidently done up. Sunday Chronicle has a mild sort of article justifying ye arrest & there is a great search for precedents of all kinds. Thank God my letters from home are much better than they used to be & my soul seems now fairly on her way to full recovery. Oh Lord make me truly thankful. How great my sins How infinite thy goodness. My financial position is little if at all improved, but I must only work it out as well as I can & it is indeed delightful to hear such good news of my dear boys & of all ye children.

May I be spared to be a better man & a good father. In ye afternoon rode out for a short time but ye day was not at all tempting. I went home & dressed as if going to a banquet! As I had no invitation out & had not ordered dinner I was obligated to search for it. No place open, Gautier closed oyster restaurants closed, only bars filled with rough men open till at last I spied a place where near Willards I had a really decent meal oysters in variety &c. On walls Dion Bouciquote or Boucicault[1] as he calls himself & his wife Agnes.[2] In ye later part went to Riggs where were family talking of going to Europe, a nasty German yankee painter named Leitse[3] & Madame Astaburagua wife of Chilean Minister.[4] I argued fiercely against ye German who evidently hates England in diable. Such a scene. Williams & Kram[5] towards midnight got very drunk & W. shoved Anderson at ye window & sent it out with a smash into street where horses were tied up wh. were so frightened they at once dashed away. Williams swore they were stolen but bridle was found in street. Great scene. Warre & A. tried to stone ye house & I drenched them with cold water.

1. Dion Boucicault, originally Boursiquot, Dublin-born playwright. He and Russell were fellow scholars at Dr. Geoghegan's School in Dublin.

2. Boucicault's second wife, Agnes Robertson, was a former actress. They were married in 1853.

3. Emanuel Leutze, Württemberg-born painter, was famous for his large historical canvases, including *Washington Crossing the Delaware*.

4. The wife of F. L. Asta Buruaga, Chilean chargé d'affaires in Washington from 1860 to 1867.

5. Capt. George C. Cram, 6th U.S. Cavalry.

November 18, 1861

Up early, went over to State Dept. before 10. Saw F. Seward who told me his parent had caught cold at Annapolis & could not stir out. Went & conversed affably with Riggs who takes serious view of affairs as well he may. Saw old Corcoran, much distressed about his son in law Eustis, whom I met at New Orleans & who is now in a "dungeon" at Boston which will kill him. Went to new H[ea]d Q[uarte]rs, saw little Kirkland, Irwin[1] & Mason,[2] introduced to Genl. Williams[3] who gave me pass & was civil. McClellan had been just inside & seems very busy in his new Dept. Much anxiety evinced to know what I think of the case in all quarters. Saw Lord Lyons who was greatly perplexed apparently & unable to make it out at all. He was quite out of sorts

uneasy & perplexed. The orders are that ye Legation are not to speak
of it. I visited the Sanitary Commission, dear little O[lmsted] had
gone out to b[rea]kfast. In ye streets I met Duke of Chartres who considers it a very grave affair. I went to Navy Dept. also & found Wise &
Dahlgren there & had more talk about ye seizure. They are evidently
not easy in their minds but National Intelligencer has an article full
of argument & precedents furnished by State Dept. wh. reassures
them not a little & furnishes them with pegs to hang their hats upon.
Dahlgren swears eternal vengeance. I went in found Prince de Joinville who rec[eive]d me very graciously & talked kindly over Crimea
& India. Ye latter campaign he admires immensely. He is very well
bred & very deaf, looks bilious & melancholy, regards ye seizure as
quite unjustifiable & as a most untoward & unhappy event. I dined
with Anderson where were also Mrs. Sheffield.[4] Wise, Dahlgren came
in. Ye latter is very bitter ag[ains]t us on ye ground that they must
give up ye prisoners—he is in favour of a vow of eternal hostility to
England if she desires to save her honour. Thus men's passions blind
them & wars are made for it is obvious that it would not be possible
to permit political offenders to be taken from our mail boats, under
any circumstances sailing from one neutral port to another tho' the
acceptation of that principle would prove most advantageous to us in
all respect.

1. Capt. Richard B. Irwin, aide de camp to Gen. George B. McClellan.

2. Capt. William P. Mason, Jr., aide de camp to Gen. George B. McClellan.

3. Brig. Gen. Seth Williams of Maine was adjutant general of the Army of the
Potomac.

4. According to *Burke's Peerage, Baronetage and Knightage*, George Sheffield died
unmarried in 1898.

November 19, 1861

I tried to do my writing for the Times but I feel I seldom or never
had a more difficult task to perform. It is very probable my letters
may be the first detailed acc[oun]t of ye arrest of Mason & Slidell in
England & as everything depends on the way in wh. ye news is broken I feel a very great responsibility. God help us. My responsibility
is unattended by that wh. makes men bear it willingly. I have neither
position place profit nor honour but still looking at ye Times as something more than private property—a mere newspaper—to the best

of my ability I use my position to promote ye honour or interests of my country. These men like Lord Lyons who have not a little of my real influence think they do me honour by asking me now & then to a scratch dinner—a collection of the polloi or the trial of a cook. At Corcorans where I dined after sending off my letter were Lisboa of Brazil,[1] Astaburagua Chile, Geoffroy, Weldons &c. &c. Mrs. Weldon sang exquisitely. Corcoran has got ye Greek slave a handsome house well furnished, a fine gallery with bad pictures—[illeg.] at least. Baron Grabow[2] is a rum fellow. I must not forget that Baron & Baroness Gerolt were also present & their pretty daughters, very pretty I think but not very wise looking. Why should they be? Gerolt in talking to me said that nothing could justify arrest of Mason & Slidell & he is a man of well known sympathies for the United Union. Played bowls with Weldon for some time beating him generally. I dined at Corcorans & was late owing to Weldons misinforming me, the others dined with Williams at Gautiers where I was asked & expected also. Here am I around ministers & diplomatists unable to find out anything as to actual views they entertain respecting The Times because I think they are afraid to answer them generally. Hermann[3] came in brought by Waller & performed strange tricks to our immense astonishment. Very clever indeed. He has a quick intelligent eye & an arm of immense muscular power.

1. Miguel de Lisbon, Brazilian minister to the U.S.
2. Baron Grabow, secretary to the Prussian legation.
3. Alexander Herrmann, famous Jewish magician, who performed all over Europe.

November 20, 1861
Day of ye review. Brilliant cavaliers Anderson, Sheffield, Warre, Williams & Vizetelly assembled at ye corner at 10. V. on L'Amy's horse a great sight dismounted for a white screw from ye stables. At Long Bugle there was a [illeg.] & the Proconsul tumbled off & holding up ye stirrup leather wh. had come out said look 'ere, 'ere it's broken, no wonder I fell hoff. He had great brass spurs which went into ye poor creature & his breaches tucked into boots. Crossed the ferry on Lord Lyons' pass hard canter Munson's hill. Met Mercier in gig, saw Hermann & Gorging Bennett's hideous son.[1] Great number of people out at Munson's Hill...& masses of troops in masses of col-

umns. Stopped by drunken dragoons who would not let me pass, but Williams got me thro' at last. Had hamper from Gautiers—all contribute to expense. Bad salute paid as Mac. & very large staff rode round President & Seward & French princes. Concentrated round Mde. Hurtado's carriage where hamper was & saw ye troops march past—70 regiments, 17 batteries, 7 cav[alry] reg[imen]ts. That awful creature Wikoff there, was talked to by dirty little man who passed himself off or tried to do so as an officer. The day fine & sight very picturesque, had great fun with drunkies of various kinds. Met Corvin, Duke of Chartres & others. Had a rattling good ride over the Long Bridge home carried very well indeed by my horse which is first rate in all ways. Met ill looking artist of Frank Leslie's sporting paper.[2] Lord Lyons gave a very grand banquet to which I was not asked. I entertained ye "outside" English Vizetelly, Waller, Dr. Morrell[3] at dinner & in ye evening the other men came in—brought in by our conversation as to horses in which Vizetelly was delicious. Olmsted, Kirkland came in also & we had a grand talk. Olmsted is very uneasy about there being no cavalry & in effect there are not. Kirkland states there were 55,000 in the field. I am inclined to think including gunners & horsemen he was nearly right. Coming home there was an alarm to Morrell &c. caused by artillery opening fire from back.

   1. James Gordon Bennett, Jr., son of the newspaper proprietor, was serving as a 3rd lieutenant in the U.S. revenue service. He took over editorship of the *New York Herald* in 1867.
   2. The best known of the *Frank Leslie's Sporting Paper*'s artists during the Civil War was Henri Lovie.
   3. Possibly Dr. G. K. Morrell, curate of Moulsford, Berkshire.

November 21, 1861
Beautiful Indian summer's day. Sun hot & weather warm. Up early & at 9 was at Willard's with Warre, Monson intent on seeing Hermann do his tricks—the gold in the eggs was well done I suspect by contrivance & an accomplice. The twisting of the chickens neck funny because it excited ye wrath of ye man & ye fright of ye woman who sold them. Went to Gautiers to breakfast with Hermann, Warre, Monson, Anderson & self & he told us of his first wife Osillag & of his present who is a beauty reserved for himself alone. He met Meagher of the Sword on his way & I suspect talked of me. I returned & wrote & arranged papers as well as I could. Hermann made us feel [illeg.] to

fall down with laughter when with great gravity he talked about his orders given to him as an artiste & laid down ye law on ye subject of decorations generally. Anderson well observed that it was enough to make one sure England was right in securing respect for her orders by restrictions of the most serious character. Went into Riggs & had some talk with him & sent him an order for 300 drs. on James G. Kings Sons as I had overdrawn my account by 116 drs. Walked out with Warre afterwards & called on Mrs. Weldon where I found Monson. Madame Jost wrinkled her eyes when she saw me. One lady more trouble than 6 gents. "Where a gent[lema]n wants more wine a lady wants a hot bath" quoth she to Warres great amusement. I dined at Andersons where were Mrs. Weldon, Mr. Mrs. Sheffield, Mr. Count Corvin. We went to Hermann's but were late & the Wizard was exceedingly angry. When we came back found Kirkland, Mason &c. there & had a smallish carouse. It was very difficult to hear all the bad English of Corvin who may be a count who does not look a bit like a gentleman. There is no language I feel the want of so much as German particularly here where the element is so common. Seward says the Irish are not near as numerous as the Germans in the Army. I think he is wrong if those of immediate descent. Went to Riggs in ye evening....

November 22, 1861
A lovely day. A day of struggle to get off my letter. Haworth came in & broke a window. He has dismissed Waller from his service poor devil.... The American papers are now in the full cry that it is all right & that nothing can be done. A bad conclusion I think or England will indeed be low in the scale of nations. Had great difficulty in getting thro' with my letter as I was nervous fussy & uncollected. My wits too got all loose & astray but at last at 4 I was ready & gave the parcel to Haworth at the Legation. The Times I see pitches into Lord Lyons severely for his dispatch to Seward. Well said Shiny Villum whenever I get a good thing *like the Lyons dispatch* I send it to the papers. There is an immense deal of conceit about ye little man. Clay new attaché[1] has arrived & Jenner is coming back also. It appears that Meagher expresses very friendly feelings towards me & wishes that we should meet. This is a most difficult matter. I have been looking thro' my mind & find I like Meagher personally tho' I detest

his politics & that I can scarce see my way from separating the one from the other—the man from the politician. To be brought to terms of peace by Hermann wd. be a magic trick. I dined at Chez Gautier where I find Hermann, Waller, & L'Amy. Went to the Theatre, whole corps diplomatique. Mrs. Lincoln in an awful bonnet facing us & Wikoff in attendance. Wicks very good consort. Afterwards to Hurtados with Weldons where were Mde. Mercier[2] little sport Geoffroi &c. & thence to Andersons where L'Amy, & Monson & Anderson & Sheffield & Waller avec, became tired & got home to bed at 12.45 unusually only on acc[oun]t I think of poor Warre being laid up with a cold very severely. Found an invitation from General McClellan's brother[3] asking me to go & witness Hermann's jugglery.

1. Ernest Clay, temporary attaché at the British legation from October 1861. The son of an M.P., he had previously served in Paris. From November 1862 to August 1863, he served as private secretary to Lord Lyons.

2. Cecile-Elisabeth Philibert Benoit de Lostende, daughter of a French baron, married Henri Mercier in 1856. He later assumed the title of his wife's family after the death of his father-in-law.

3. Capt. Arthur McClellan, younger brother and aide de camp to Gen. George B. McClellan.

November 23, 1861

A darkening morning wh. melted into a lovely day. L'Amy et alii came in & Mr. & Mrs. Weldon later in the day. Went down to Riggs & drew $35, paid bill for James & breakfast of 8/4. Left cards at Corcorans, & wrote to Capt. McClellan to thank him for the General's invitation & left cards also. Saw them at ye Legation where the poor pirate was ye subject of merriment in cartoon & talk. Then I started off solus on a ride meeting Williams unshaved en route. Forgot to mention that in Chancellerie was Ernest Clay who gave me a letter from dear old Maitland Dashwood,[1] a lively grim young old un of the world. Roads very deep & heavy. Out by French ministers to Chain bridge & home by Aqueduct reservoirs. Camps guarded at night & oh Lord if it is not dangerous to go near sentries. Dined with L'Amy solus at Karls, as ye others were at ye Legation dining with my Lord. The Times has a fierce article ag[ains]t his dispatch to Seward & I think it was as I said not a creditable document.[2] Went in & read Wheaton[3] in my room & wrote till 10 1/2 o'clock when I ret[ire]d & found Clay, Anderson &c. in possession. Williams came in, & we sat up till 2.15

or so. This wont do William. Hermann was at Vizetellys so he has put off his notion about making Meagher meet me. At his performance at ye Presidents last night he had a "brilliant throng" as a collection of rowdies is generally styled by Shaw of the Herald.[4] Poor Mrs. Lincoln a more preposterous looking female I never saw. She aped the airs of le monde last night & hid herself behind her gauze curtain peering out now & then only & she was clothed in ye royal ermine whilst ye jail bird Wikoff hovered around in attendance. One night at ye White House she observed Mde. Astaburagua & on being told who she was said "Oh I thought it was Mrs. Mercier." The story of her sending a bouquet to me is all over Washington & much exaggerated.

1. Maitland Dashwood, an old friend of Russell, who regularly loaned the correspondent large sums of money. He died in 1883.

2. Lord Lyons's letter to the secretary of state, dated 14 October, concerned the arrest of British subjects in the United States and their detention in military prisons without habeas corpus. *The Times*'s critical editorial appeared on 6 November 1861.

3. Henry Wheaton (1785–1848), American jurist and diplomat. His best-known and most influential work was *Elements of International Law* (1836).

4. William B. Shaw, Washington correspondent of the *New York Herald*.

November 24, 1861

The New York papers are still at ye Mason & Slidell work. I remained in reading & writing. The early part of the day fine but it at last came on to freeze & snow at 6 o'clock. Lyons R[oyal] N[avy] Racer[1] came in & we had a pleasant talk over old times & the poor dead friends Hugh O'Hagen, fall horse turned mad & street preacher; Rogers married, Prim d[itt]o playing blazes on coast of Bahamas & removed. Poor dear Hugh the times just removed by 7 years from these dates. Had visits from Mr. & Mrs. Weldon on their look out for dinner. How keen she was, really amusing—to save her dollars. I recommended Willards— & on going to Josts found her awaiting fortune. As nothing cd. be done else, she & her spousey tod[d]l[e]d off there & I went with them talking of wifey & children. Hermann came out & made his adieux & so I ret[urne]d home, was much afflicted by little Herrisse who would persecute me with a long visit. The capital presents great calm on Sabbath now, & as the bells toll instead of ringing the whole affair is dismal enough & very depressing, drunkies were tolerably abundant. At dinner L'Amy, Anderson, Sheffield, Clay, Corvin, Russell. Wise, McDowell came in later, item Waller, Warre, Monson. My Lord gives a party tomorrow to ye outsiders to which I cannot go as I have asked ye Weldons & Wise—another to ye diplomats & swells on Tuesday. Ye general talked very nicely de omnibus tho' he evidently had a row with Blenker & his Germans & in point of fact Blenker has resigned I understand. Mac. was saying he had never voted at an election that army officers seldom did so—& spoke of ye cry ag[ains]t military establishments—proposal to do away with West Point &c. Little Sport also appeared & proposed a "tir aux pigeons" or "stipple chase" a many healths to ye bold buccaneer & so to bed. Cold & unpleasant. I dont know what to think of Corvin. He told us of his 6 years imprisonment for his part in ye troubles of 1845. He was confined to Bruchsel after capitulation of Radstadt[2] & would have been shot by the Prussians he says only that he proved he was a subject of Saxony. He says he has 32 years service in army.

1. In his report to *The Times* dated 25 November 1861 (published on 10 December), Russell noted that the *Racer* under Captain Lyons would sail immediately with dispatches for the British consul in Charleston.
2. The surrender of the fortress of Radstadt on 23 June 1849 effectively ended the Baden insurrection against Prussian authority.

November 25, 1861
And so wags the year & the wags thereof wag on & off. I was up not very late & seedily after breakfast sat down to write. It was not easy work plodding on all day. It was cold dark & raw. Wrote & wrote on till 4 with scarce relaxation or stay. Wrote on the view that England can not allow this new principle set down by ye U.S. in reference to right of search & neutrals. Walked out with Weldon left cards on Hurtado &c. I forgot to mention that little Herrisse whom I recommended has received a place in ye Navy Yard under Dahlgren & came yesterday to thank me for it. Went to Chancellery with letter & delivered it to Moore for Asia wh. leaves Boston on Wednesday. Mrs. Weldon & her husband & Wise dined with me & we were very jolly—in ye evening sad enough talking of dear wifey. Mrs. W. & hubby went off to Hurtados where I was asked & I was on ye point of going in when it occurred to me ye invit[atio]n came second hand & so I did not go— returned & talk & so to bed. What a strange little woman very determined very clever very phew out with it artful & artificially natural. There does not now seem to be a chance of an advance from this side. I think they wd. like me to go with some of ye expeditions, but I am

not at all inclined that way at present for I dont feel at all disposed to go running about after ye depart[ment]s & asking for favours tho' in word Wise & such like are very kind. At night as I was in my bed Warre & Anderson made abortive attempts to rouse me. They are terrible nocturnes surely. L'Amy swears ye whole country is going smash. Would it be advisable for us? I think not. Relations are becoming a little less cold, but no one can be sure of a democracy for a moment & they may become quite disgusting in a moment. The worst sign of all is that the Herald—I think ye most infamous journal ever published, has such extensive circulation—for its abuse of England must always keep ye masses more or less excited. Jeff Davis' Message very good.[1]

---

1. Pres. Jefferson Davis's message to the 5th session of the provisional Confederate Congress of 18 November 1861.

November 26, 1861

A fine golden morning—party last night. Re[ceive]d letters of 13. Delane & wife who is frightened by a photograph of mine. D. says that law officers gave it as opinion that U.S. steamer might take Mason & Slidell from R[oyal] M[ail] steamer according to Lord Stowell's decisions![1] Read it to the boys next door. Anderson much vexed. Thence to Monson & read it. He also perplexed, Lyons d[itt]o, begged me to say nothing of it nor did I. Nevertheless popular passion is so clearly indicated in the matter that I believe no precedents or legal opin[ion]s will control the action of the mob. There are it must be remembered immense masses whose bread depends on a solution in addition to the many who are animated by strong hostility to the Union & to the Yankees. I rode out to the Chain bridge & back by the upper road in ye evening—nothing of any consequence to record. My Lord gave a late diplo-dinner party & I gave a small one to which were L'Amy. Poor McDowell is not at all well. His hip is very painful & there is some danger of inflam[matio]n. God forbid. What a terrible thing it would be for the old dear if his division were to be ordered into the field & if he had to make his march in a litter or were not able to move at all. Some men are vexed by fate in a most furious & relentless way—no mercy no forbearance.... In ye afternoon came in a noisy party indeed wh. began to sing. Karl came down nearly mad to our great delight & was ye subject of a chorus immediately. A soldier who asked for a drink was brought upstairs from ye street & availed himself of his opportunities to steal all the clothes which was hanging up in the hall. This is a splendid country, no thieves here either.

1. Sir William Scott, Lord Stowell, was judge of the high court of the admiralty and the most influential interpreter of international and maritime law.

November 27, 1861

A very seedy morning—sickish nervous & the rest of it. Williams came in to carry me off to b[rea]kfast with Kram at Gautiers, but failed dismally. Only two or three of us went—I mean of all who were asked by Kram. It came on to rain & drizzle very much. A great lamentation when it was discovered that ye thirsty soldier had abstracted so much property. For my part it is enough to make me never do a good natured action again as poor dear Rob[er]t Russell[1] used to say. By the by I must write to Persault or he will be offended—darn! How years fly on, se suivent et ne se resemblent pas.[2] I did not pay a visit to any one I cared about today, but still I took out a whole mass of cards & went visiting in a hack. I had an engagement with Geoffroy which I did not keep to look at a whole lot of colibris or humming birds. I dare say Gould[3] would give a good deal to have been in my place. Federalists surprized near Vienna last night.[4] Drove out & left cards at Hurtado, Lisboa, Blondel,[5] Gerolt, Tassara, Kennedy &c. with Weldon & thence to the bowling saloon where we played a few games together. Dined at Lord Lyons where were Clay, Lyons, Warre, Monson. Anderson entertaining the Weldons. In ye evening went in after very slow dinner to Andersons where were Williams 1/2 screwed L'Amy disgusted with ye world &c. But no one was inclined to stay up in my rooms. My Lord did not say much of the question of Slidell & Mason, but he seemed to me to be rather nervous & uneasy. He has received no official communication whatever from Govt. To sleep at 1.15.

1. Russell's cousin, who first introduced him to *The Times.*
2. "succeeding each other but not resembling each other."
3. John Gould, celebrated British ornithologist, author of forty-one volumes and over three thousand papers and memoirs of birds of the world.
4. On 26 November a squadron of the 3rd Pennsylvania Cavalry was attacked on a narrow road between Vienna and Hunter's Mill by Confederate cavalry and suffered thirty casualties.
5. Blondeel von Cuelebrouck, Belgian minister to the United States.

November 28, 1861

Thanksgiving day, celebrated by immense drinking & fighting. Had an interview with a Mr. Schalk[1] who brought me a letter from Count Corvin—for introduction to Wise which I granted. He is a famous man for guns. Sheffield not well, Weldons off, Lyons d[itt]o. Lovely morn[in]g rode out with L'Amy to Smith's brigade over the Chain Bridge—roads very heavy camps dirty & soddened. Smith not in— put in mind of B'klava but McDowell et les autres say "no". Talk of an advance—talk. Great movement of troops however. Coming home met chatty little Lieut. U.S.N[avy] & rode part of way with him—one brother in Black House Va. an unclean gaol in Richmond, mother Washington. Weather changed to rainish & coldish coming back. Shops all closed. Raining heavily in ye afternoon which will take a good deal out of ye martial spirits wh. are marching across the river tonight. Many men drunk & some fighting if I may judge of their eyes & noses. Rode a good bat back. Found Vizetelly sitting with poor boy Sheffield whose brother is dying of syphilis in a tremendous form, God help him. Dined all of us with ye addition of our friend Williams & Vizetelly. I went in to my rooms with & left them all singing & glad I am for they were late & had tittledewink. It was most amusing to see Karl removing the furniture from ye range of Williams as he lay asleep kicking his legs about on ye sofa. There was a most extraordinary apparition at ye window tonight for ye information of Haworth & myself—a woman cooly undressing herself with a light shining full on her & the blinds up....

1. Emil Schalk, writer on military affairs, author of *Summary of the History of War* (1862) and other works on Civil War campaigns.

November 29, 1861

A most extraordinary day, heat almost oppressive, a muggy sickening sort of feel in ye air. I sat down & wrote but had visitors Stoeckl, L'Amy, Haworth &c. Stoeckl came in full of what he had heard at Riggs to the effect that Russell had rec[eive]d information from England that ye law officers of ye crown had, in ye case of ye Nashville transfering her passengers to an English mail, & of the latter being hoarded & deprived of them by a U.S. man of war from ye Britisher,[1] decided it would be justified by Lord Stowell's decisions. I told him ye truth in ye strictest confidence which I hope he will keep.

I learn it was Lord Lyons who told Mercier & Mercier repeated it, & so Riggs got it. I sent L'Amy over to Riggs with D[elane]'s letter to see if it could be made of any use. How I should like to make a little money with honour or without discredit. I could not get into the saddle for a good gallop across country at all in this American's litter today. Vizetelly has been ordered to go South by the I[llustrated] L[ondon] News to sketch on the ground that no one cares for the North in England & that sympathies are with the South. This I hold to be morally & politically wrong for assuredly the South can never be anything but a source of trouble & hostility if independent & the true policy is to let the quarrel run its course in neutrality. I went to Chancellery to post letter per Haworth when suddenly up get Warre, Clay, Sheffield & Anderson & danced "tiddledy wink" in a tremendous outburst. Came on dark & lowering—went to bowling alley & played 2 games very badly. Thence home with the boys & dressed (& sent off letters to dear dot as well as ye Times) & in to dinner where only our lot dined at 7.30. News is in that Savannah is occupied but in reality it is only Tybee light & island which are taken hold of & Pulaski is yet untouched.[2] Wise came in & promised as I was a little angry that I could go with Porter in the next exped[itio]n. Long talk de omnibus—no other visitors & so to bed.

Taylor U.S. 6th. Cavalry[3] talking daytime with L'Amy said ye Republic was a complete failure & the sooner Govt. was changed ye better.

1. It had been widely, but mistakenly, assumed in Great Britain that Mason and Slidell would sail on the Confederate steamer *Nashville* before being transferred to an English ship, thus providing some legitimate basis for an American seizure under international law. The *Nashville* arrived in Southampton on 21 November 1861.

2. Tybee Light House on Big Tybee Island at the mouth of the Savannah River was occupied by Federal forces under the command of Gen. Thomas W. Sherman at the end of November 1861.

3. Capt. Joseph H. Taylor, 6th U.S. Cavalry.

November 30, 1861
Morning broke sunnily & bright—did not get down to breakfast till 10.30. Here I must make hiatus valde deflendus.[1] Rode out with L'Amy in the noon & took Tenally town road. A lovely day tho' roads were rather muddy. Went on & on till we took a turn down to ye left

wh. brought us out over some extraordinary forts they were building on ye top of a hill with the scar open to the enemys side on ye Potomac. Lambkin much exercised thereby. Came back by aqueduct, a most glorious sunset or rather a gorgeous splendrous one ye skies left by the sun behind him a sheet of wondrous orange gold columns & purple fading into delicate crimson hues after wh. out rushes a multitude of stupendous stars—the glitter & intense brightness of some of them beyond any example even in India & I do remember one of some bright ones in these upper Himalayas. It became very cold as we rode back. There were drunkies visible by ye road sides here & there. "The Americans were always famous for earthworks" I want to know who are the Americans quoth Johnson. Pon my soul I ask for information &c. The Pres[i]d[en]t says some wonderful things. For instance that those now alive may see 250 millions in ye Union & that all ye nations of ye world cd. be assembled in 12 square m[iles]. Anderson & ye others dined out & in ye evening repaired to the gilded saloons of Roost Van Limbourg! The Dutch minister.[2] I knew there was going to be an orgy or orgie as Saturday nights usually are. In ye evening in tumbled Vizetelly speechlessly drunk, alas not so but able to talk wh. was worse, supported by House & Brady photographer who was awfully screwed & tried to focus us by shading his eyes & glasses & squinting hideously at the wavering shifting figures. I made attempts to get away but Warre, House & that young Jenner followed me & nearly smashed in my door & dented one panel. I lost my temper, but ret[ire]d & aided in starting Vizetelly &c. The Dutch midshipman brought in by Sheffield became helplessly drunk also. Altogether it was an awful scene & Anderson was angry with Vizetelly & so was I.

1. "a gap much to be regretted."
2. Roost Van Limbourg, Dutch minister to the United States from 1858 to 1867.

December 1, 1861
Horses ordered for 10 & I was ready at that hour having got up at 8 but it was much later when we started leaving L'Amy & Sheffield to follow wh. they did not do by the by. We went out Anderson, Kirkland, Irvine & young McClellan by Chain bridge & aqueduct road to Great Falls. The bridges are not all completed, but it will soon be

ready I think. Where they are not quite finished one must take considerable detours & within 3½ miles of G[rea]t Falls the road turns to ye right & winds thro' woods till the noise is heard & great cliffs peer up over them over the river. The ride interesting but the day was very gloomy & cold & there was no play of colour in the sky. As we passed Fort Defence guns were fired—met only a few labourers in ye ride of 16 miles & some unmistakable seceshers who were grim fowling rifle in hand & answered us very scowlingly & angrily as to the distance. G[rea]t Falls contains a deserted house—a long barn like building & two or three shanties. The head of the aqueduct wh. was in a filthy state & the canal wh. runs to Wash[ingto]n. Soldiers lounging about. Rec[eive]d by a Captain who had a regular brogue & a very irregular face in the dirty barrack like shed, & "had a drink" with him & his orderly. He told us he was under arrest &c. but that he be d——d if he'd stay more than 3 days, because he had refused to serve as Lt. of the Guard he being a Captain. He had shot a man dead a short time ago for disobeying orders, & now my company will follow me anywhere. He was a boot & shoemaker by trade or travelled for a time in that line. Visited ye Falls wh. are really savage & picturesque. Seceshers often come down & have a talk with sentries— one of ye latter drowned a short time ago. Dined at a deal table in a shot marked room & fed us pig & ration beef for wh. we p[ai]d 50 cents each. Send for ye best cigars quoth Enright oh Lord! And the Company pretty rough too. A cold ride home & a long one by ye upper road. Got in at 8 & found McDowell & ye little Dutch midshipman dining. Senator Sumner came in to see me & I rec[eive]d him with one boot off & a bare leg to great amusement as I was forced to pull off my boot after my 35 mile ride—horse bore me well. Irvine ran away when he came, McDowell & he not good f[rien]ds I think. Sumner very anxious as to the course of England, says Seward is very calm indeed now & in a good frame of mind.

December 2, 1861

On visiting Lambkin found Laurence Williams at breakfast & in a good frame of mind. Kirkland came in demurely to look for his gloves. Corvin Count or God knows what visited me to go out to Blenker, but I excused myself & lent him my horse instead to Mr. James great disgust I suppose. Remained in part of time. Cold day writing. Oh my God when I remember this time last year—awful & yet I was saved, saved from the wrath that came upon me—& yet I repent not. Lord forgive & melt & soften the soul within. In ye afternoon Baron Gerolt called on me ye Prussian minister, a clear liberal minded man, & afterwards came Mr. Blondel the Belgian minister a man of greater talent perhaps but rather doctrinaire & not near so liberal. They both agree that England has suffered a serious injury by the Mason & Slidell affair & we had some interesting conversation about it. Blondel s[ai]d when Piraeus French & English fleets lay an U.S. commanded he thinks by Stringham[1] rec[eive]d Persani the Russian's minister & saluted Russian's flag 1854–5 & it was proposed by Barbier de Tinan[2] to seize him then & there but British resisted. Shows U.S. sympathies at all events. Went out afterwards with Lambkin who was drastic rather. Congress opened today at 12. Senate did nothing, in H[ouse of] Representatives resolutions of a brutal kind consigning Slidell Mason to a felon's cell in retaliation for Corcoran &c. were passed & buncombe votes & all sorts of eulogy were passed upon Wilkes who at once becomes a hero "interpreter of international law" &c. &c. One Wainwright came in during ye evening—black yankee with stories to sell. Wise goes on now regularly with his "Leave it all to me, I'll tell you something that will astonish you! You never heard such a thing in your life. I'll let you know when Porter is ready" &c. Dined at Karl's with ye usual party of friends &c. &c. Visited Madame Hurtado where were Geoffroy, de Beaumont, Prado,[3] Warre, Clay & Anderson & thence ret[urne]d to my rooms when all were gone to bed. Sat up chatting with A. for some time & roosted before 1 p.m.

1. Silas Horton Stringham, veteran U.S. naval officer. In 1853–54 he commanded the U.S. Mediterranean squadron.
2. French admiral Barbier de Tinan.
3. Don Mariano del Prado, 1st secretary to the Spanish legation.

December 3, 1861
A bitter cold day, bright sun, water frozen. After breakfast sent for a carriage & drove to Capitol. Message already delivering.[1] Sent in card to Senator Wilson who at once came out & introduced me on ye floor of ye house where Forney[2] was reading ye message. At its conclusion Senate adjourned. The house looked very respectable.

I back to my house & wrote interrupted by visitors, but sent off nevertheless letter to The Times by Capt. Moore from Legation & to dearest Mary by post. Walked back with Clay, Ernest, & then on to bowling saloon where I beat Clay four games. Rec[eive]d an invitation from Simon Cameron Sec[retar]y of War to dinner tomorrow "to meet some members of the press". Accepted. Went in to dinner where was D'Utassy Colonel Garibaldi Legion. Hungarian, served under Bem,[3] taken prisoner at Temesvar, exported to Spielberg. Thro' Count Benisen[4] escaped to Semlin as servant where Fonblanque[5] saved him, went to Kossuth[6] at Shumla, thence to C[onstantino]ple where he was engaged to instruct cavalry. To Ionian Islands where was Sir H. Ward[7] with whom he was Sec[retar]y & Interpreter afterwards with Sir G. Le Marchant[8] of whom he gave bad acc[oun]ts. Has been a fencing & language master in U.S. Raised his reg[imen]t in 17 days supporting himself by his lessons meanwhile is furious ag[ains]t Blenker of whom he makes ridicule & of his antecedents. I doubt if he be not a little mad but he seems in earnest. He has been placed under arrest by Blenker for going out without his pass into town. He swears Blenker sells passes to liquor dealers, sutlers & even cooks for 100 to 20 per mensem. Corvin also came in—after him came Vizetelly with Lt. Edenborough[9] who is an inoffensive sort of snob enow—& with Ned Price ye prize fighter[10] who is a quaint sort of ex pugilist & gave us some notion of his life & of the roughing of it in America with the rowdies. Talked of Heenan,[11] Morrissey[12] &c. Kelly seems a shrewd fellow with a horrid jaw broken nose & sensual mug, a very quick shrewd eye. I am astonished to hear him speak French quite well. I am not so sure if this creature was to the liking of Anderson, but Clay & Warre & he were quite affable. Vizetelly got into his normal & we had the whole roll call of songs ab ovo ad poma.[13] My apples were not cooked till 2.30 & I got away with difficulty leaving them behind me.

1. Abraham Lincoln's first annual message to the 2nd session of the 37th U.S. Congress.

2. John Wien Forney, Philadelphia journalist and politician, was secretary of the Senate.

3. Joseph Bem (1795–1850), politician, soldier, and revolutionary leader, notably in the defense of Transylvania in 1848–49. He died in Turkey in 1850.

4. Alexander Levin, Count von Bennigsen, Russian-born Hanoverian soldier and son of Gen. Levin August, Count von Bennigsen.

5. Thomas de Grenier Fonblanque, British consul general in Servia from 1841 until his death in 1860.

6. Louis Kossuth, Hungarian-born revolutionary leader against Habsburg rule, who was forced into exile in August 1849. He toured the United States in 1851.

7. Sir Henry George Ward (1797–1860), lord high commissioner of the Ionian Islands, 1849–55. He was subsequently governor of Ceylon and Madras.

8. Sir John Gaspard Le Marchant was governor of Malta from 1857 to 1864. He was formerly governor of Newfoundland and Nova Scotia.

9. Lt. Henry Edenborough was detained in Baltimore in August 1862 and held in Castle Thunder. He claimed to be a captain in the East India Royal Navy.

10. Ned Price was a former leading American heavyweight boxer. Among his best-known fights was a three hour, twenty minute draw with the future American champion Joe Coburn.

11. John Carmel Heenan, champion New York boxer known as the "Benicia Boy." In April 1860 he fought a celebrated drawn contest at Farnborough with the English champion Tom Sayers.

12. John Morrissey, born in County Tipperary, Ireland, won the American heavyweight title in 1853. After defeating John C. Heenan in 1858, Morrissey retired and became a successful businessman, serving two terms in the U.S. Congress.

13. "from the eggs to the apples."

December 4, 1861

A frosty morning again but wind still & as day wore on pleasanter air. House came to chat with me de omnibus. The end of Vizetelly's foregathering with Price "Ned" was that he lost 97 or 79 drs. at a gaming house on wh. House observed that the price was cheap & that it was calling him Ned wh. cost so much. Cameron with whom I dine today is Sec[retary] of War & a self made but well made man shrewd & crafty, full of natural talent. He has never been in any part of the world save U.S. but he is well read & informed enough. He has the name of being unscrupulous & a jobber but in reality he needs not to be so as by private contracts & public works in wh. he has been engaged he has made an enormous fortune. He told interesting stories of Mrs. Eaton who broke up Jackson's cabinet & who is now living here a painted old devil. She was a Mary O'Neill a publican's daughter who captivated a member of Congress & at last gained quite an ascendancy over old Jackson.[1] She did Cameron a good turn in early life which he has been able to repay by favours to her grandson recently. Cameron's love for the pleasures of the table is confined to or expended in good brandy & wine. He is rather bawdy in his talk speaks very freely with a sort of openness wh. is attractive & his manners tout vu are wonderfully good & unexceptionable.

I dined with Mr. Cameron 5 p.m. was kept waiting in a cold room whilst he told off deputations. Forney, Wilkinson of Tribune,[2] House, & another. Cameron told me he was a printer in this city at 10 drs. a week & 50 cents an hour for extra work at the case on Sundays & gave me most graphic acc[oun]ts of the state of things in part of States. He is a most shrewd agreeable man, we had pleasant conversat[io]n generally. He says the press rules America. I dont think it does I'm certain it oughtn't. We had good wines—all white no red. After dinner in came deputat[io]n. My eye held by Hannibal Hamblin V[ice] P[resident][3] with Lovejoy,[4] Bingham[5] & other fanatics when there was a big drink & healths drunk. And at last I retired. Went to Andersons with House & off to the Ball of 5th. Cavalry at Kalorama wh. was very good indeed long shed prettily decorated, no end of supper mighty drinks. Some nice women & dancing a great bonfire in the centre of the grounds for the soldiers on duty & drivers to warm by afforded pretty sight. Home at 2.30 or so.

1. The so-called Eaton malaria was one of the first crises of Andrew Jackson's administration after his election in 1828. Margaret (Peggy) Eaton, the wife of Jackson's secretary of war, had formerly been married to John Timberlake, a sailor who committed suicide in 1828, reportedly after hearing of his wife's liaison with John Eaton. The Eatons were subsequently ostracized by Washington society, but the affair became part of a much wider political rivalry between the forces of John C. Calhoun and Martin Van Buren, both of whom sought to succeed Jackson.

2. Samuel Wilkinson was the *New York Tribune*'s principal representative in Washington. He was formerly editor and part owner of the *Albany Evening Journal*.

3. Hannibal Hamlin, former governor, senator, and congressman from Maine, was vice-president of the United States from 1861 to 1865.

4. Owen Lovejoy, Republican abolitionist congressman from Illinois. He was the brother of the martyred editor Elijah P. Lovejoy.

5. John Armor Bingham, Republican congressman from Ohio.

December 5, 1861

A lovely morning & day. I was not up till late & the manager of the Inman line[1] came in as I was at breakfast & talked some time rather detainingly. Afterwards rode over with L'Amy to Arlington where the Ira Harris Cavalry were receiving what one called flags ie. standards from Senator Harris,[2] calling on Cameron en route. Met on ye field Genl. King,[3] McDowell, Col. Davies I.H.C.[4] his Major Kilpatrick,[5] Clarence Brown &c. My friend Chandler on the sorrel, Hethaway & Robinson. Cameron came on the field & afterwards came the Pres[i]d[en]t & his wife in carriage as we were at the

Colonel's tent champagning it—gracious bow from Mrs. L. Chatted with Mrs. McDowell, Mde. de Villanceau &c. & then rode down from camp to meadow where reg[imen]t was drawn up below Arlington House. Then the crowd drew near. Ira Harris made a long & fierce speech in delivering flag no. 1 so that it could not be said Ira furor bravis est⁶ & Colonel Davis made a long & fierce one in reply. Then Mr. Davies presented colour no. 2 in an elaborate speech full of poetry wh. will be sent off to the local & Kilpatrick made a very good reply the only thing wh. was strange as from a soldier being a political disquisition on the causes of the rebellion. The affair was theatrical & being effective "Take this flag then &c. Defend it with &c. We will guard it as &c." Afterwards cavalry went thro' some evolutions one of wh. was seriously interrupted by a fire from the infantry in the rear wh. had ye effect of breaking up the squadron in much admired disorder to the great amusement of the crowd. Waller rode my carter. To dine with Lord Lyons at 7 where were Galt,⁷ Stewart new 1st. attaché,⁸ Lamkins, Vizetelly et polloi. Galt a man of much vigour of intellect I think. Adj[ourne]d to our rooms where Butler Duncan came in & conversation on finance ensued wh. came to this that a general issue of national paper is inevitable with all sorts of dangers & losses looming in ye distance. Duncan evidently not well pleased & very uneasy about monetary position of affairs. Galt pressed him hard in agreement. D. says the North will be split up by victory & then will come the junction of ye Democrats with ye South ag[ains]t the Republicans & a concession to the South more liberal than they could dream of. Hurroo! Hurroo!

1. Liverpool shipping company, founded in 1850 by William Inman and one of Cunard's leading competitors. Its first ship was the *City of Glasgow*, the first transatlantic steamer with a screw propeller and known as the most comfortable emigrant vessel on the North Atlantic run.

2. Ira Harris, prominent New York jurist and Republican senator from 1861 to 1867.

3. Brig. Gen. Rufus King of New York was the organizer of the celebrated Wisconsin "Iron Brigade" regiment. He resigned from the army in 1863 and was appointed U.S. minister to Rome.

4. Col. Henry Eugene Davies of the 2nd New York Cavalry, known as the Harris Light Cavalry in honor of Sen. Ira Harris. He was promoted to brigadier general in 1863.

5. Maj. Hugh Judson Kilpatrick of New Jersey of the 2nd New York Cavalry. He was appointed brigadier general of volunteers in June 1863 and in February 1864 achieved fame for his daring if futile raid to free Union prisoners in Richmond.

6. "Anger is a short madness."

7. Alexander Tilloch Galt, leading Canadian financier and politician. He was a member of the coalition ministry that secured confederation between 1864 and 1867, when he became minister of finance. From 1880 to 1883 he served as the first Canadian high commissioner in London.

8. William Stuart, secretary to the British legation. He deputized for Lord Lyons during the latter's absence from Washington in 1862 and 1863 and later served as British envoy in Greece.

December 6, 1861

Writing my letter as hard as I could & not succeeding in doing much except that I started the theory already ventilated in N.Y. of the paper currency. Riggs says it will produce money & make every one richer & he is a banker & ought to know. There is after all great satisfaction among the representative property men & tories in England with the rupture in America & I confess for one that I agree in thinking this war if it be merely a lesson will be of use tho' I dont go so far as to wish for the utter destruction of so many happy communities. Had there been a possibility in human nature to make laws without faction & interest & to employ popular institutions without intrigue & miserable self seeking the condition of parts of the U.S. does no doubt cause regret that it did not occur here, but the strength of U.S. employed by passion interest intrigue self seeking became dangerous to other nations & therefore there is an utter want of sympathy with them in their time of trouble & England regards the North without fear favour or affection & in spite of liberty rather favours the South. Rode out after sending off my letter to The Times & left cards for self & legations on officers of 5th U.S. Cavalry at Kalorama, an awful rough looking lot as can be. I dined with Mr. Galt Finance Minister of Canada at 5.30 at Willards in private room, present Mr. Ashman,[1] Mr. Seward, Mr. & Mrs. Hibberd of Buffalo[2] pleasant conversat[io]n. Ashman exceedingly like an English gentleman of the best type sagacious pleasant fond of sport, drank over much wine I fear. Dinner very fair & claret excellent, visited the Duncans for a short time & found the ladies I thought very political & fierce—very nice women indeed. I think B[utler] D[uncan] is growing mad—to my mind he has all the air of it so distrait so nervous & uncertain, so unquiet & restless. Mrs. H., Duncan very angry at ye idea of Southerners sending their children abroad & says it is never the case. Mrs. Hibberd is a very nice person also—softly fast. Her husband is a keen little lawyer. Galt came home with me & we had a small party in ye kitchen looking for bread & ate sausage & paté. Warre, Clay, Williams.

1. George Ashmun, former Whig congressman from Massachusetts. He served as chairman of the 1860 Republican convention and in 1861 acted as special agent for the U.S. State Department in Canada.
2. Douglas Hibberd was a Buffalo lawyer.

December 7, 1861

If a fine day to go out & dine with D'Utassy & take Sheffield with me. Woke up with an intolerable flavour of claret & cold punch combined about me & remained wondering why I did it at all. The New York papers have got hold of the imminent advent of the paper currency. Riggs whom I saw this evening says it will really inflate the markets & make all ye people richer so that there ought to be no ground for evil foreboding of any sort. The quarrel between the Col. D'Utassy & Blenker seems smoothing over. This Corvin I confess puzzles me not a little. He has a conspirator's eye & his air or manners is not that of a gentleman I think, but then he comes to us certified by Morris who would never make a mistake on any acc[oun]t surely. Remember if you come to transcribe this passage to dwell on the priest in his captain's uniform & the scene & speeches at the banquet!!! It was rather late when I got off & after passing Long Bridge I found a review had been going on. Met McDowell & Mrs. on horseback on their way from it, also Clarence Roberts.... D'Utassy was in his tent which was very nichy indeed as far as sheltering trees, & a small ramp were concerned. Inspected his stables where our doubtful friend has 20 horses. Lambkin very angry with him. At 3.30 adjourned to a long tent with two tables covered with white cloths & centres of confectionery very nicely & had excellent dinner lunch & wine of sorts. L'Amy, Sheffield & Vizetelly drove out in my trap Warre & Anderson rode out. Horror after dinner an oily chaplain proposed health of guests to which I had to return thanks & then my health wh. was well rec[eive]d d[itt]o d[itt]o. I had to make an oration accordingly. Dinner table curious scene—5 Spaniards 6 Hungars & Poles, 2 Frenchmen, 1 American 8 or 9 Germans of sorts, 4 Italians. I am told they did not march past well. Dined at home at 7 & went out to Willards where I saw ye Duncans & arranged a party for Mt. Vernon at 9 this next Sunday. Visited Riggs on my way home from ye hotel. Saw Packenham[1] who remembers my Mugington the doctor at the Alma,[2] Massey & Marshall also & having visited Galt, Douglas Hibberd, Ashman ret[urne]d to the house & after a short [illeg.] with ye Dutch midshipman, L'Amy, Vizetelly & Sheffield. Retired to my bed at 1.30.

1. Lt. Col. Thomas Henry Packenham, formerly of the 30th Regiment. He was Conservative M.P. for Antrim from 1854 until 1865.

2. The first major battle of the Crimean War. Fought on 20 September 1854, it resulted in victory for the combined French and British forces over the Russians.

December 8, 1861

A che bel tempo![1] Lovely indeed rose late & did not start in 9 boat from this for Alexandria. Lambkin came in rather disconsolate because I was not up & after breakfast were visits from Wallach of the Star[2] a red hot Virginian democrat who was very civil after wh. were visits from M. Colonel de Trobriand 55th N.Y.,[3] with whom Stoeckl jests when he asks him to dinner—because he says how can I give you dinner when you have 200 cooks in your regiment & how can I go to you with my hair in such a state when you have 100 coiffeurs in the ranks? Rode out at 12.30 over Long Bridge to Alexandria over the Long Bridge then & 4 miles out or so on ye way to Mt. Vernon, but cd. not see my party tho' I heard they were on before me. As to the day no words can express its loveliness—it was unpleasantly hot at times. About 3.15 after a halt in wh. I spoke with a brutish Virginian farmer named Barrington by the roadside. Ret[urne]d & got back by 6 o'clock seeing a lovely sunset en route & a dark angry stormy atmosphere & fog rapidly following up the glorious day. Alexandria seems utterly ruinate houses deserted trade defunct. The country is very woody either forest primaeval or second growth—the few houses of farmers by the roadside are of wood whitewashed or painted. Ret[urne]d to dinner where was Col. Schweitzer aide to General McClellan, Williams, Wise, Stewart, Clay came in—& there was a great deal too much of that horrid whiskey to suit my fancy—alas no my stomach whence my head went thence my voice so that I sang all the Irish melodies for old Kram who was melodiously inclined as to listening & always asked for more. He is an amusing fellow—full of humour, his description of the long suffering & faith & perseverance of a British capitalist in a very bad thing was capital, as compared with the dash

of the Yankee & his immediate transfer of the remnants of his effects
to any other thing as soon as there is an inquiry in this.

1. "What lovely weather!"
2. W. D. Wallach, proprietor of the *Washington Evening Star.*
3. Col. Phillippe Regis de Trobriand, 55th New York Regiment (the "Gardes Lafayette"), who came to the United States in 1841. He was promoted to brigadier general
in 1864.

December 9, 1861

A feeble sort of rising in the morning wh. was fine & lovely principally caused by drinking to the health of the bold Buccaneer wh. is
now idiotically established as a war cry.
Wrote somewhat for the Times.
Mr. Chase's report[1] was sent to me with a very kind note from him
expressing his regret that he had not one ready from ye printer &c.

1. Secretary of the Treasury Salmon P. Chase's report to the 2nd session of the 37th
Congress, delivered on 9 December 1861, in which he outlined the various propos-
als for meeting the rapidly increasing expenses of the war. The report was notable
for its recommendation of a national banknote currency secured by the pledge of
federal bonds.

December 10, 1861

Actually broiling hot. Rode out to 3. Avenue visited Seaton.[1] I dined
at Karls &c.
Forney's & what happened. Such a glorious day.

1. William Winston Seaton, veteran Washington journalist and civic leader.

To J.C. Bancroft Davis, December 10, 1861

Washington D.C.

My dear Davis,

I am very sorry indeed to hear of the cause which will give us the
pleasure of your society here, but I hope the prescription will answer
& in that case all will be well minus your bankers account short of
a few dollars. There will be no difficulty about a nag—lots in the
livery stables really serviceable animals for hire, or you can buy one
& keep him at livery. There are some to be hired for 70 dollars or

so per mensem daily fruition for n + 1 hours. The weather here has been supernatural to our notions. Blue bottles buzzing about under the notion that it is summer, & people cramming in ices at the confectioners. Heat absolute heat—today it was nearly broiling. Let me know when you are coming.

Yours ever,

W.H. Russell.

December 11, 1861

Oh so seedy. Anderson came in with news of Karl.
Dined with Butterfield.
Scene with Germans. To bed at 12.30.

December 12, 1861

Before rising in came Brig. Genl.———[1] Anson[2] & Lawley.[3] Towards Congress. Geoffroy. Met Sumner. Mercier.
Dinner at Baron Gerolt. Home. Lawley. Wrote.

1. Acting brigadier general Henry Bohlen of the 75th Pennsylvania Infantry. He was killed at Freeman's Ford, Virginia, in August 1862.

2. Maj. Augustus Henry Anson, army officer and M.P. for Lichfield from 1859 to 1868. He was awarded the Victoria Cross for his conduct at Lucknow.

3. Francis Charles Lawley, a former M.P. and private secretary to William E. Gladstone. In 1862 he became *The Times*'s correspondent in the Confederacy, remaining in the South until March 1865.

December 13, 1861

As Haworth did not come in time L'Amy volunteered to go with dispatches or consented to do so.
I dined at Gautier's very badly & solitarily.

To John T. Delane, December 13, 1861

My dear Delane,

The telegram has just come in & we are rather disappointed there has not been a greater row than took place by latest accounts. But we live in hopes. Lawley has delivered your letter to me & I am glad to find you missed my letters as it will induce you to give me a line now & then. I was on the point of going off to Mexico when I heard there was to be an expedition here & I think now I will wait for it or until I have advices from you. Chase & Seward are civil, President glum. McClellan very angry about the Orleanist princes & also I *think* because I criticized very tenderly some of his short comings. The young 'un is being blowed up to an enormous size. You ask me as to mode of life. It *was* frightful. I lived over a "wine merchant" wholesale & retail—a Swiss named Jost. But his retail business exceeded the more ambitious part of his trade, & customers got drunk by wholesale below, & were always coming up stairs to see "Russell of the Times". They used to come into my bedroom & sit down on me spurs boots & all. For this I paid at the rate of some £40 a month including terrible dinners & feeding generally, but as if that was not enough thy below stairs people of colour used to steal my wine & spirits & sell it on their private account & whenever old Jost wanted an excitement he set himself to devise way & means of making me pay for an "extra". At first I set up with one horse & with a servant recommended by Butler Duncan—you know service is not given in the lodgings here generally. First week he came in & announced he had met with an accident, but it appeared that it was only the inferior part of the centaur's confirmation that had suffered, for on inquiry I learned the horse lay at the corner of the Street with a broken leg— as yet I have baffled the man from whom I took him in attempts to recover compensation on the grounds sworn to by my domestic that he had no particular bone in his leg. I also got from New York an ambulance in which to follow the advance of the army, but as that is not likely to take place at any extravagant speed I have advertized it & the animal which is to draw it for sale & mean only to retain a very good saddle horse up to my weight splendid trotter & actual fencer who will lead me out of another Bull's Run conspirito e forza.[1] Our usual mode of life is after breakfast when it's not post day—oh Lord thyne 3 times a week owing to my trop de zele—to proceed over the Potomac & visit in the camps where the officers are most certainly as hospitable as men well can be. If I dont dine with some of them I return to dinner at 7 in a house adjoining to my own lodgings where Anderson, Sheffield, Clay attachés of H[er] B[rittanic] M[ajesty's] Legation live in commanditi & we pay expenses in common. In the evening all sorts of people drop in. Sometimes we have a General to dine or a friend & there are always stray Britishers to be asked. Now & then we dine out. I have a once a week dinner at the Legation with my Lord who is very hospitable otherwise. The Prussian & the

Russian are very civil also, & they've a number of houses where one can drop in during evening & hear the news if so inclined. Cameron Sec[retary] of War is quite a chummy & Sumner if he was not such a mad blackingman would be also very agreeable. I lodge at 487 17th. St. corner of I near the Legation & have a stable close at hand, so that I can be across the river in a shot if anything is going on. There is more in Lincoln than you would imagine. I'll send you over the photographs by next mail & never fear all I can get for you. I hope you will have a really merry Christmas & a happy New Year. The words are rather sad for me after all. Do be good enough to remember me most kindly to my friends, to all who care for my remembrances. Tom Phinn[2] Mr. Reeve,[3] Barlows best of people, Mr. Milnes,[4] Mr. Lowe.[5] And above all let me be remembered to your good mother[6] & to Miss Delane.[7] I'll send my love to Morris & to others of the household, but you must tell Hardman[8] I'll let my beard grow if he doesn't send me wedding cake. I wish I cd. give him a few hints derived from experience as to his conduct in matrimonial life for he's a chicken in the art compared to me.

> Ever & ever yours,
> W.H. Russell.

1. "with spirit and power."

2. Thomas Phinn, barrister and former M.P. for Bath, was an old friend of John Thadeus Delane. He served as secretary to the admiralty from 1855 to 1858.

3. Henry Reeve, English man of letters and, from 1840 to 1855, chief editorial writer on foreign affairs for *The Times*. He was the first English translator of de Tocqueville's *Democracy in America*.

4. Robert Monckton Milnes, poet and leading Liberal politician. He was M.P. for Pontefract from 1837 to 1862 when he was created Baron Houghton.

5. Robert Lowe, M.P. for Kidderminster and one of the chief editorial writers at Printing House Square. He held a minor ministerial post in Lord Palmerston's government but later served as chancellor of the exchequer and home secretary under William E. Gladstone.

6. Mary Anne Delane, formerly White. Delane's father, William Frederick Augustus, former treasurer at Printing House Square, died in 1857. She died in 1869.

7. Delane's unmarried sister, Georgina. She kept house for the editor after his mother's death in 1869.

8. Frederick Hardman, roving foreign correspondent of *The Times*.

December 14, 1861

Haworth & I had a long walk. Looking for Gudgin fat horse doctor having first visited stables where my poor steeds are in a disgraceful state. Sumner came in & we had a long talk de omnibus in wh. Haworth joined. (I dined solus at Gautier's & very badly. Saw Heap[1] & Porter there yesterday.) I gave a dinner at Green's to Anson & Lawley, Anderson & Sheffield dined also on their own hook. McDowell came in after dinner.

1. Possibly Lt. David P. Heap, Army of the Potomac Engineers Corps.

December 15, 1861
First Anson came in & ate enormous breakfast, after wh. Lawley, next we all Warre, Sheffield, Anderson, Haworth. Anson set out via Chain Bridge just as ye people were coming from church & rode round to Smiths at Smoots House where we found Currie Major[1] & Scrimser[2] a.d.c. who rec[eive]d us at whiskey & water & a smoke & chat. Smith very unwell I regret to say & away. Camps look neater men better, a great deal of horse butting with fir & pine branches. Currie was in our 19th. R[egimen]t & was Brigade Major at Aldershot, wounded at Alma. The house is not at all bad, mirrors in room & terrible portraits on wall. Currie told amusing stories of utter want of subordination, mutiny in refusing to go on guard or on duty &c. Thence rode across country to Butterfields, visited St. John Porter cosey in his tent. He says he used to drink hard.
Olmsted came in to see me. Anson, Lawley & self dined at Harrimacks miserably....

1. Maj. Leonard D. H. Currie, assistant adjutant general to Gen. William F. Smith, Army of the Potomac.
2. Lt. James A. Scrymser of New York, a volunteer aide with Gen. W. F. Smith's division.

December 16, 1861
Lovely day again.
Dined at Karls, Williams and Kram there.
Marquis de Lisboa's evening party cotillon. Walked over with Anderson.

To J.C. Bancroft Davis, December 16, 1861

My dear Davis,
When are you coming? Let me know a day or two beforehand. I dont know where this is all going to end but from the commencement

I feared the worst when I saw that Slidell & Mason were to be detained. I think all Europe will be dead against you. Come up & let us talk it over. I hope sincerely you are getting better. We have lovely weather here. Such fine days. Clear as June & better.

> Yours ever,
> W.H. Russell

December 17, 1861
Such a heavenly day. Late when I got up.
Dined at Sewards. Mrs. Davenport & Geoffroy.

To J.C. Bancroft Davis, December 17, 1861

My dear Davis,
 I dont know anything more than you do except that I think there is a disposition here to back out if they can & give up the men sooner than have a foreign war on their hands. There is not a single diplomat here who sustains them. Even the Prince de Joinville & the Orleanists are dead ag[ains]t the seizure. Lord Lyons has detained the steamer but he has not yet received the instructions from Europe.

> Always yours truly,
> W.H. Russell.

P.S. I'll write more as I hear news according to your request. If relations are broken off with England, which God forbid a N.Y. correspondent could do little enough, but your loss will be greatly felt.[1] I need not say how deeply I regret the cause & I trust you will return quite restored to health & full of power to go on & prosper till you can put pen in the rest & retire from the field.

 1. Bancroft Davis resigned as New York correspondent of *The Times* for reasons of ill health, although his strongly pronorthern correspondence had become increasingly embarrassing for the paper's editors.

December 18, 1861
Rather gloomy but became finer. Sold my elephant horse for $135, a loss of $30 or £5.5s. I dined at Stoeckls. At my desk all day....

December 19, 1861
Writing all day, a most heavenly day indeed.
Lord Lyons told me Seward seemed to keep out of his way.

December 20, 1861
Dawn fine, but gradually clouded over. Were to have gone out riding but in regard to matters of moment taking place excused myself. Long Bridge is not fit for use. Hurroo! Under repair. Beautiful. Saw Lord Lyons at ye Legation, he was friendly & nervous as usual. Said he hoped I would tell him anything I heard as to the President's message to Senate &c. &c. Drove over with L'Amy & Haworth to Senate deposited en route $100 from price of horse at Riggs. Nothing in Senate but speech from [Senator Willey of Virginia] to show South was opposed to democratic institutions [1]—all ye members reading papers or writing & not caring a button for the speaker. Sent in for Sumner who came out & drove home with me. We had a long chat. He told me Seward was down with him at 7 o'clock in the Senate when Lord Lyons called.

1. The speech was given by Sen. Waltman Thomas Willey of Virginia, who had been elected in July to fill the seat vacated by James M. Mason. He argued that secession had been an antidemocratic movement and that Virginia had been forced out of the Union by secret conspiracy.

To John T. Delane, December 20, 1861

Washington D.C.

My dear Delane,
I am trying to find out what has taken place, but at the Legation they are very close, & Seward is not visible. I dined with him the day before the dispatches arrived & he was then in very good humour, & said everything consistent with the honour of U.S. would be done to make England feel U.S. did not mean to hurt her feelings or injure her prestige, but I said that would be difficult so long as the press & public opinion insisted on lauding the seizure as a "bold act" & as one which lowered the pretensions of England. Lord Lyons is a very odd sort of man & not quite the person to deal with this crisis tho' he is most diligent, clear headed & straight viewed. He is nervous & afraid of responsibility—& he has no personal influence in Washington be-

cause he never goes into American society tho' he gives dinners very frequently. For some reason or other I am not so well with him as I used to was & I fancy it is recently since the papers here had such a crow over him about that dispatch to Seward, which came I suspect direct from home, as my Lord writes very good English. There have been some very good articles on the Mason & Slidell affair in reply to the opinions expressed in the English papers & by the law officers whose ground as far as I can judge is neither very broad nor very firm. I believe McClellan is determined not to advance till he has sucked away the greater part of the Confederate army—he says he has only 15,000 men he can rely on, meaning the regulars. There is great discontent in & out of Congress & only the President & the ministry sustain him. He would have to fight or resign. He's a clear headed little fellow can handle troops well, & knows his work such as he finds it thoro'ly. I am sorry to say I have never recovered my lost ground with him so far as I can judge. Ever since the article on the Orleans boys & their associates he has been distant & inaccessible— so I dont go near him at all now a days. With all the other generals I am in very good ease, & with the Ministers also, but there is really very little to be got out of them. Chase sent me the earliest copy of his report but the telegraph beats us all in our attempts to let everything remain in [illeg.] till the mail goes.

As to this war question I wish we were entering upon it with cleaner hands if it comes to blows. There is too much of a legal subtlety in the points raised by the Govt. and it would have been better at once to say Precedent be darned—we won't take political offenders from neutral ships going from one neutral port to another. If U.S. were all right we might pick a quarrel with him on any grounds we pleased. Now his condition will excite sympathy in the rest of the world—perhaps provoke interference, & it certainly may end in a large exhibition of—not pro Union but—anti English feeling in the South. I am preparing to sell off & to make tracks to Canada & perhaps Lord Lyons may allow me to attach myself ad hoc to the Legation till I can get out of the country. This is of course hypothetical—one thing I shall regret that I did not see another great fight, for I am certain McClellan will be forced to give battle, & it would be by no means safe for me to accompany his legions into action with the state of irritation which exists plus Bull's Run even if there is nothing worse than an irritating diplomatic row. The President will send a message to the houses today & I must go down & hear it. The Queen's messenger arrived the night before last but up to yesterday evening I cant hear that anything occurred. They wont tell me a thing about it at the embassy & if my Lord don't like I'm sure I'm not going to ask him. I must only fall back on Mr. Seward who is much less reserved. However you can learn more at the Foreign Office than I can hear in these parts. If there be war I think you will have sharp work in Canada which is the constant aim of the Americans. The defences of New York are very powerful & tho' you may set the sea coast towns in flames as a general rule you will not be able to do more than cripple commerce & open the Southern ports. I am for resisting the outrage & having satisfaction for it without war if possible, but with war if need be tho' I should much regret it. People here are very black & grave, & their feeling will be still more serious if they ascertain that England insists on absolute surrender. Anyhow I am longing for a glimpse of home, & I hope soon to see you all if it be but for a few weeks. I shall write to Morris & Walter[1] & J.C.M[acDonald] by next mail. I am much exercised about these Southern people becoming independent & a slave power & we the authors of it. That touches me nearly. I hope you are well & that "that" eye is as bright & clear as ever.

Yours always truly,
W.H.R.

1. John Walter, the grandson of the paper's founder and its chief proprietor after the death of his father in 1847.

December 21, 1861
Frost last night, a "cold snap" as they call it here. Up rather late, fine clear sunny morning. Cold wind, cavalry review, wont go, news of great victory in Missouri,[1] as news boys say "*another* great Union victory". Went on plodding away at letters. My Lord has several interviews with Seward who gives no sign of what he will do. The surrender is asked for & also reparation—if not ultima ratio. Lord Lyons goes home in that case with all his flock & I with him. But with all their fearful brag & bluster the Yankees will not be such cursed fools as to go to war with us. They are too cute to give us such a chance—no

fear of it. De Beaumont & others called. In afternoon went out & had a walk—round by market crowded with dark servants & purchasers, covered stalls lots of meat—vegetables plenty too.

Dined at Karls, L'Amy, Vizetelly, Sheffield. Anderson dining at Anson's.

1. On 18 December, near Milford, Missouri, Federal forces under Col. Jefferson C. Davis surrounded a Confederate camp capturing 1,300 prisoners, 1,000 stand of arms, and 1,000 horses.

December 22, 1861

A day cold raw grey gloomy—most curious sensation in my back last night could not turn in my bed from pain in loins. Same this morning sent for Dr. Miller lotion & another thing I could not take prescribed for me. Little Sport de Beaumont came for us & we behaved very badly. I could not go—the others wd. not. He was splendidly gotten up & was angry with the Bully buccaneers. After came in Anderson &c., Anson, Lawley. I wrote to Monson for news who came in & told me a great deal. Seward not replied yet, to demand for extradition of Mason & Slidell. War alternative. As my Lord wanted to communicate with Jamaica he resolved to send off Haworth to catch the steamer Cator from New York tomorrow & he therefore does not expect definite reply before Wednesday. House of Tribune came in for news. Black Will departed with a letter for Mary & a lot of cigars & a promise to send me his picture. Behaved badly to de Beaumont.

I dined with Anson, Seymour[1] & Lawley tremendous rain. McDowell came in late.

1. Capt. Conway Frederick Seymour, Queen's foreign service messenger since 1859.

To John T. Delane, December 22, 1861

Washington.

My dear Delane,

I really am in a most utter bewilderment, for I can find out nothing positive tho' everything looks light so far as the tone of the N.Y. papers goes. They have backed down at once, but my Lord is dark & very mysterious. Tonight he is sending off a special messenger to go with dispatches to Kingston for the Admiral & the West India fleet will be put on the qui vive.[1] Now it will be quite necessary for you to obtain letters for me to Admiral Milne[2] & the other good people out here & if possible to let the Admiralty give me a little encouragement. Halifax will not be a very lively place for one's head quarters in case of a row & I confess I am not fit or inclined for a winter's cruise off the U.S. ports, but I will do my best. I am indeed as you know risking much in more ways than one & tho' our friend D.'s letter makes my mind easier by an explicit assurance it does not at all relieve me in other ways & is in fact but a tangible proof of the truth of an idea. I had always in my mind that in the case referred to my old masters would not forget the heritage bequeathed by their servant. At the verge of 40 however a desire to be something for the sake of one's own self & children does spring up in the mind too, & I would go thro' this very cheerfully if I could see at the end of my labours any pied à terre for I can not but recollect how my little bit of ground was knocked from under my feet this time two years when I returned from India. Is there a chance of anything permanent for me which shall not necessitate my kind of scribbling "Wandering Jew" or till health & means of indulging in the cacoethes cease altogether? Do consider for me. I am a helpless poor devil, & would be nigh friendless save for you & one or two more, none so well able to help me as yourself—none more inclined I should think.

There was a rule in an obscure old grammar from which I got my little bad Latin which will I hope justify Hardman's marriage, for it stated that [illeg.] & "interest" require the genitive. I wish the good old man every happiness & success in his overtaking & should like much to be able to see how he goes thro' his preliminary canter at the halter. To my mind marriages are the most indecent affairs possible. There was one here the other day at which some hundreds of the youth of both sexes assembled to inflame their passions by seeing a bride home off to her room upstairs by the groom at 9 o'clock at night & next morning they all called to see how she was & in the evening they called again to see if she could dance or not. I am concerned to think of Hardman escorting a large family at an advanced period of life over battle fields & thro' barricades—a battered old stormy petrel with an infant brood.

In case of the worst I am going to sell off all but one horse. McClellan is I hear going to advance in a fortnight, but if the thing blows over I'll go with Burnside who is to make a dash up the James River— there will be the devil to pay here. From what I see of the coast I really dont think our fleet can do much & land operations of an offensive character wd. be disastrous. F[ort] Monroe would be an awful nut to crack. Washington on the Potomac is a poor thing in armament strong in position. Baltimore would be very tough in a week or two— New York the devil in ditto, of t'others je n'en sais rien. God bless you & us all. I don't think these fellows will give up Mason & Slidell— in which case God bless the world but old Nick will be unchained for some time to come after. Ever & ever yours,

W.H. Russell.

1. "on the alert."
2. Adm. Sir Alexander Milne, in command of the West Indies and North American station since 1860.

December 23, 1861
A violent storm today. Sky black charged with sleet & rain—houses shaking, terrible weather, lasting till night when clouds blew off stars came out & only gusts of wind gave traces of the gale. I wrote but a meagre letter, & sent it off for Boston.

Dined at Karl's—present Lambkin & Shefkin. Anderson dining out cum lupis.[1] Went to my ain room early & in came Olmsted anxious to know if Lord Lyons had a violent passion with Seward as reported. I sent in a note to Monson who s[ai]d there was no foundation for it whatever. Wise came in afterwards. He swears old Scott is coming in to conduct the Canadian campaign which he has studied profoundly, perhaps when he was in prison there. Sat up talking with O. de omnibus till midnight. He declares there is a belief that England wants only a pretext for a quarrel with U.S. We certainly have had no lack of pretexts.

1. "with the wolves."

December 24, 1861
An extraordinary change *indeed* the wind blew it is true but the sky was nearly clear & the frost held its own stiffly. I locked myself in after breakfast & evaded a British officer & also Mr. Beatty. Poor Anderson up till 5 o'clock lost $250 in all to Lawley, Anson & co.— pretty work *indeed*. Sheffield takes it quite to heart good lad. I went forth after a talk with Mr. Johnson of New Orleans a very nice hand-

some clever fellow, to Legation. Warre getting up. Thence to Trollope[1] who suffers from carbuncle, he is a grim one—is well lodged & all that. Walked into town with Lambkin & talked to Gautier &c. &c.... It is mentioned in telegraph report that Prince Albert is dead.[2] I should be sorry indeed if it were so notwithstanding that he is antipathetic to me. It is announced in small type in the telegraphic news. Taking it all in all an unfortunate event—bad for the Queen even if it be Prince Alfred.[3] In ye eve[nin]g had my dinner & hired piano therefore Anderson, Anson, Sheffield, L'Amy, Lawley, Seymour, Warre. In ye evening Anthony Trollope, Johnson.

1. Anthony Trollope, English novelist, who was on a nine-month visit to the United States and Canada. His two-volume account of the visit, *North America*, was published in 1862.

2. Prince Albert of Saxe-Coburg Gotha, the prince consort, died on 14 December 1861.

3. Prince Alfred, Duke of Edinburgh and Saxe-Coburg Gotha, Queen Victoria's second son.

December 25, 1861

Glorious day. People very gay going to church boys firing crackers. Cavalry patrols in street men drunk. I rode out in afternoon horse lame. Mr. Brown is I think a very bad groom.
Dined at Lord Lyons where were L'Amy, Vizetelly & the attached ones good boys.

To J.C. Bancroft Davis, December 25, 1861

Xmas day. May it be happy & followed by many.
My dear Davis,
Up to this date Mr. Seward has not sent in his reply to the personal note handed to him at a friendly but official interview by Lord Lyons on Monday morning nor has he given any intimation of the view he takes of the demand. If Mason & Slidell are not given up war is—I fear—inevitable. You may depend on my letting you know as soon as I hear anything decisive. We are all much depressed by the news of Prince Albert's death & fear the worst for the Queen. I hope you are better with all my heart.
Ever yours truly,
W.H. Russell.

To Charles Sumner, December 25, 1861

Xmas Day. A happy one to you & many of them.
My dear Mr. Sumner,

I hope we may see you sans ceremonie at 7 on Thursday to a quiet dinner & I trust too we shall have a quieter atmosphere & something to encourage appetite & digestion.

The news from England of Prince Albert's death distresses us all very much on the Queen's account & indeed now that he is gone he will be more popular & better spoken. It is not always true that the evil wh. men do lives after them. The good lies oft enterred with their bones.

Yours always truly,
W.H. Russell.

December 26, 1861

A grey cold frosty morning wh. cleared away after a time & the sun came out. Shut out visitors & wrote but visitors came in natheless. General impression that M[ason] & S[lidell] will not be kept, rather unlucky for me. Sumner, Beaumont, Geoffroy dined with me at Karls where were Van Vliet, L'Amy, & Anderson. Irwin, Wise, Johnson, Anson came in during evening. Sumner argued that the Trent affair was at most matter for mediation. There is diversity of opinion as to their surrender or not. Sumner was most unluckily hit over head & ears by me in an accidental remark. Every one saw it at the time but myself.

December 27, 1861

Well & ill, seedy with cold. I wrote away having heard that Mason & Slidell wd. be given up & sent it by Moore for tomorrow. This spoils my prophecies. M. told me dispatch had been given in—awfully long— a secret. While writing Johnson interrupted me. He smells a rat & I went over to Riggs. No positive news. Seemed to think they wd. be given up. Much excitement about it pros & cons in ye city. Riggs laughed at ye idea of keeping them.

The seceshers are down in the mouth as to Mason & Slidell. Corcoran tells me pos[itively] that M. & S. would be given u.p. that they dare not keep them. Dined at Karls, Wise being my guest, L'Amy, Sheffield

&c. Johnson came in told us Mason & Slidell wd. be free—great fun arguing it.

December 28, 1861

Another fine day. "National Intelligencer" contains news that Mason & Slidell are free. Seward, Lyons, Thouvenels,[1] Russell's correspondence. Ill with cold again.

L[or]d Lyons—interview with Seymour &c. Lord L. told me he did not think it would be worth while going to Boston. M. & S. were to be sent on board a U.S. vessel to a U.S. port & there transferred to a British ship. I told him I was going to N.Y. & would go to B. if it were worth while. He is in good spirits as he well may be at ye result. This shd. be transferred to Monday I think.

Seymour sent off to N.Y. with dispatches for admiral.

Dined with Corcoran. Johnson, L'Amy, Warre, Clay, good dinner. Talk over Mason & Slidell. Visited Riggs &c. in ye evening.

1. Antoine Edouard Thouvenel, French minister of foreign affairs.

December 29, 1861

A gray morning turned into a fine smashing day & another witness ag[ains]t the Federals. I wrote for the paper a good deal.

As Johnson is going to New York to see Eustis if he can I resolved to go with him nothing doing here at all.

December 30, 1861

The arrangement as I am told is that Mason & S. &c. are to be carried to some port wh. Lord L[yons] did not name from Fort Warren, & there to be handed over to Britishers.

A great meeting of Buccaneers—splendid assemblage much festivity & song.

December 31, 1861

Left for N.Y. 11 train with Johnson.

SIX

Retreat from America

To Mowbray Morris, January 7, 1862

N.Y. Hotel.

My dear Morris,

Just a few lines to say that I did not answer your last not because I had not much to say in reply to it but because my acts were giving you the most satisfactory response in reference to the main object in my power to afford & the most earnest proof of my desire to meet your wishes. I wish you could come out & see my difficulties in adversum. Now I am on my back little fever—going away, very weakening. I want you to aid me in Willans sudden departure—of his arrival at Halifax I am just informed by a pencil scratch. I dont know what if any arrangements he made with you 'ere leaving, but I request you will pay for me £50 to Dr. Quicke[1] for the boys schooling & £100 to Mr. Freake[2] on acc[oun]t of rent, & deduct it from my salary in such instalments as may be needed. I have much to say when I hear from Willans & fear I must ask for leave of absence any way in the dull season if only for a few weeks. Obstacles increase every moment, & I wrote a sentence to Delane which explains much. I am going to hurl at you next mail all my check books & bank acc[oun]ts up to the end of the last year, & henceforth I shall send you in a monthly acc[oun]t but I got all out of gear in moving by loss of papers &c. & the only way I can devise is to send you counterfoils & checks as I keep cheque book & pay nearly everything except small sums & pocket expenses in cheques. I begin the New Year with about £10 at the wrong side, but I am to be paid $140 for horse this month I hope,

216

& some $120 for sadlery harness not needed now. I have dismissed
my man, hired a black boy at ½ his wages, & put my one horse to
livery. My head is very queer with quinine & as I have written to
Delane, wife & have to write to two or three more forgive & let me off
till next mail. I never had such a disgusting task. God knows its hard
to understand such a people & yet its true that for a people without
a Govt. they do stand an immense deal when they cd. take such easy
methods of gratifying their animosity. I hope you have had some good
runs & that Mrs. Morris[3] & baby are quite well. To the former pray
remember me. I cant flatter myself I make any impression on the
memory of the latter.

 Yours always my dear Morris,
  W.H. Russell.

 1. Thomas Royal Quicke was the proprietor of the Brixton Lodge boarding school
in Brixton Road, London, where Russell's two sons were boarding.

 2. Charles James Freake, a prominent London architect, who in 1868 stood with
Russell as Conservative parliamentary candidate in the constituency of Chelsea.
Neither was elected.

 3. Mowbray Morris's second wife, Emily Delane, youngest sister of *The Times*'s
editor. They were married in 1857.

To Mowbray Morris, January 11, 1862

           N.Y. Hotel, New York.
My dear Morris,
 I have just received your letter of 23 Decr. & am glad I did not act
on my impulse & go to Mexico, as it would have left you in the lurch
owing to Davis's resignation. I am however unable to send you a letter this mail owing to my recent illness which was pretty sharp, & I
was only able to stir out for the first time yesterday. I will however be
able next Wednesday to forward something & then I shall go back to
Washington & await events there in case I can not procure an invitation or permission from Burnside to go with his Exped[itio]n. He is
rather bitter however against me. Davis looks unwell indeed. He will
start I think next week for Europe. My illness was a sort of fever—
everyone in Washington for two months gets something or other of
the sort. It has left me very weak tho' started but a few days. Everyone here is in the dumps—wanting to scratch something or other.
These few lines are to explain why I could not write, not indeed that

there was much to say. But tho' I went out yesterday I was not able
to sit down at the desk on my return.
     Yours my dear Morris most truly always,
          W.H. Russell.

To John T. Delane, January 16, 1862

                                              New York Hotel, N.Y.
My dear Delane,
     Wikoff, you know who he is—I have snubbed & kept him off ever
since I have been here—waited on Stewart yesterday by Bennett's
desire "to ask him as a mutual friend" whether something could not
be done to come to an understanding & patch up the unhappy quarrel
between me & Bennett. I replied that I could not refuse to accept an
apology for a series of gross & unprovoked attacks from the poorest
blackguard in the streets who was anxious to atone for his bad conduct, but that I would not permit any one to approach me on the part
of Mr. Bennett with any other purpose. I had presented him a letter
of introduction on landing & late next day he sent me by Mr. Wikoff a
letter asking me to dine with him in the afternoon which I was compelled to answer in the negative as I was really engaged. I then went
to Washington & immediately without any sort of provocation on my
part a series of attacks was commenced upon me in the Herald which
augmented in virulence falsehood & ruffianism 'till after Bull's Run
they were undisguised incentives to the infuriated people to mob &
murder me & to at all events turn me out of the country. I could give
blow for blow & make my blows be felt where Mr. Bennett's arm could
not reach. He had exhausted all his efforts & I was perfectly indifferent to his assaults, but at the same time was prepared to receive
any expression of regret for his conduct which he might offer. And so
the matter ended, but it is something to have made the blackguard
eat so much dirt—& he would not have opened his mouth for it but
for two reasons. First he found he could not get me out of the country by his threats—secondly he was alarmed at the idea that The
Times would not quote the Herald in future & that thus the European
notoriety on which he prides himself would be injured if not totally
destroyed. I entreated you to adopt the plan long ago—my life on it
he will feel it & you will find it efficaceous. Another thing & I have
done. Ward told me yesterday that a great speculator in the funds &

an enormous millionaire had come to him to ask whether Mr. Russell could not be induced to write more favourable articles for the U.S. so as to influence the Times in its general tone & in that case said he "we could afford to place some hundreds of thousands of dollars at the call of Mr. Russell & his friends." I told Ward that he had better ask his friend to call upon me & make me the proposition directly, but he said that he would only convey the substance of the conversation to me whereupon I said "the gentleman had better communicate directly with the Editor of the Times—the answer he will get from me if he comes will not I fear suit him." Ward further said that "the gentleman" was anxious to know what it would cost to buy all "The Times" shares as to which I referred him to the Solicitor in London & expressed an opinion that it might be done by Mr. Chase when he had raised his $30,000,000 & cd. apply an adequate proportion of it to the object. How far all this was real I know not, but in conclusion I begged Ward *"not to speak to me on such matters again but to direct any one who spoke about them* to go at once to head quarters." You see what cursed scoundrels there are here who believe God himself is venal. I am now nearly well, but there is a sort of weakness & langour over me that I never experienced before. I shall return to Washington next week tho' there is nothing doing there nor in the present state of the roads can an army move a mile. However a hard frost or high winds wd. make them available in 24 hours. If you have no news of "Rinaldo" I fear she is lost—horrible to think of.[1] Bancroft Davis sailed without telling me who is his successor. He is beside himself on the northern side of the question. Butler Duncan d[itt]o d[itt]o. I have your photographs & will send them by next courier. Have you been able to look in at Arran Lodge. I have an English friend with Burnside who promises me an account of the whole affair. I hope my next letters for the paper will be better.

Ever yours as ever,
W.H. Russell.

1. Her Majesty's warship the *Rinaldo* had collected the released Confederate commissioners at Provincetown and was en route to Halifax, Nova Scotia, when it encountered a savage storm that blew the ship south. The *Rinaldo* finally arrived safely in St. Thomas, where Mason and Slidell embarked for England, arriving there on 30 January 1862.

To Mowbray Morris, January 26, 1862

New York Hotel.

My dear Morris,

The only way I can acc[oun]t for my not sending in my acc[oun]ts regularly for the last couple of months is that my mind was in such an uncertain state as to going home or staying, as to fight or no fight that I neglected everything down to my health or up to it as the case may be. I think the best way I can do is to start fair with the new year & to begin from January meantime sending you my cheque books & counterfoils so as to enable you to compare them with the bills which I will forward to you on my return to Washington. Here is an abstract of cheques drawn which I have just had from the bankers.

I am going to see how things are in Canada in defect of their being here anything I can write about to recuperate & to shake off the effects of my fever or whatever it was. I was so much afraid of my wife hearing of it I kept it quite "dark" & made no fuss about it. I wish we weren't so unpopular here, for it is the most difficult thing to stand up in good heart against the cold shoulder. Maybe it will blow over a little time hence. I wish you would let me have a few lines of counsel. I will write to you from my first landing place. Rose[1] & every one advise me to visit Canada now. It was rather well as far as one can see as yet I did not go in the Burnside Exped[itio]n. You may depend on it I will stand by you here *as long as I can* but I have much to say to you.

Always & ever yours, most truly yours dear Morris,
W.H. Russell.

1. Sir John Rose, Canadian lawyer, politician, diplomat, and financier. Rose had organized the Prince of Wales's tour of Canada in 1860 and later succeeded Alexander Galt as finance minister. He subsequently played a leading role in Anglo-American diplomacy.

To John T. Delane, January 27, 1862

My dear Delane,

I am going off this evening for a week or 10 days to the Canadian frontier partly to see how things are going on there, & partly to try if change of air or of life will not stir up my liver or whatever else it is which requires stirring up. I shall go I think on my return either to

Kentucky or back to Washington & if possible get into the field with any army which moves but it is really hazardous to do it & if I am ever in another Bull's Run you may depend on it I never get out of it alive. As to Bushwhacking work I dont go in for it. If I were less unpopular nothing would please me better than to run about over the country in the West & see the work in Missouri &c. but it is a dead load round a man's neck to be feeling always that he is disliked & is liable to insult & outrage. I'm the only English thing they can vent their anger on, & The Times is regarded as so dead against the North that everyone connected with it in the North is exposed to popular anger whilst I am especially obnoxious to it as I am supposed to be the cause of all the ill will of the paper to the Federal Govt. It's hard work playing a neutral game unless you're on neutral ground I can tell you. Do write to me & give me a little advice &c.

Ever yours (in great trouble to catch the train) & always truly,
W.H. Russell.
Kind regards to Mr. Walter. I had a present of apples. Send some to you—spare a few to M[owbray] M[orris].

To John T. Delane, February 11, 1862

Quebec

My dear Delane,

I return to New York on Thursday & thence shall proceed either to Kentucky or to the Coast if any tempting expedition offers. I am holding on here as you see in obedience to your wishes tho' I fear my occupation is gone. However we shall see. If McClellan goes I think I shall get on better with his successor unless it be Harney[1] who is very anti British. I have been received here in the most gratifying way & I have had literally to fly from Toronto & Montreal to avoid public dinners. At last I have had it understood that I cannot accept their marks of good favour & I hope you approve of my doing so in spite of the attempts which are made to induce me to believe that Mr. Russell can eat a dinner which shall not be incorporated with the person of the Times Correspondent. I had a long talk with Gordon[2] about the defences of Canada & he seems to agree with Genl. Scott who told me last June Canada was not defensible along the frontier—that all England cd. do in case of war was to hold certain strong points until she could collect an army & gain such successes in the open field as wd. open the country. Steam on the lakes gives U.S. a most enormous power, & their possession of the islands in the St. Lawrence in case of war wd. prevent our attempts to get up if resolutely held. The scheme of Gordon is very large & so good I doubt if the Govt. will ever approve of it or pay for it. Lysons[3] complains of want of money also. Pray who is your correspondent out here? I tell people I don't know & they wont believe me. Butler Duncan writes very gloomily from N.Y. to me but believes in the future—"greater than ever" a pleasant creed truly. The country about Washington is, as I predicted, beyond the scope of my military operation. Why I should ever indulge in prophecy I dont know. Perhaps its the mantle of Cobden thats on me. I hope whatever happens we'll let France tirer les marrons.[4] It never would do really for us all things considered to assist at the death of our republic in too open or indeed in any way. These States will be peopled by millions where there are now thousands & we must act with some regard to our future relations nor leave it in the power of our enemies to say we destroyed the Anglo-Saxon Republic out of jealousy or any base motive they may impart to us.

Did you cast your eye over the acc[oun]t of Mrs. Lincoln's Ball? Was there ever such snobbery & ridiculous sickening trash? She's like a damned old Irish or Scotch (or English) washerwoman dressed out for a Sunday at Highbury Barn. As a Paddy friend of mine said when he saw her "My God! Where's her apples & pairs?" I haven't seen any Times at all lately while travelling but I'm told none of my letters are in it. Perhaps it was during the period in New York. I do hope my wife was not frightened. Did you see an elegant paragraph in a Sunday paper about my being seen in a maison de joie by two detectives. Pon my word they're a charming set of journalists. If you ask any American how the Herald is to be killed he will tell you by never quoting it, but I can conceive that it may be useful to mention it now & then tho' I unfeignedly regret it. Do write to me & let me hear your views & wishes about myself & Yankee Doodle. I hear this moment that the Emperor has resolved not to interfere at the request of England.[5] If anything can touch the hearts of this Yankee Doodledom surely it must be our conduct in this matter. It remains to be seen what view of it Parl[iamen]t will take tho' I am satisfied that Govt. is right harsh as they may appear to be towards the South. The latter will be very much discouraged & no wonder, but if they give the North another thrashing or two the latter must cry quits for it really has not got the means of going on. The tails of the Kilkenny Cats will be fat compared to them.

    Ever yours,

    W.H.R.

1. Brig. William Selby Harney, a native of Tennessee, was one of the four general officers of the line of the regular army at the beginning of the Civil War. A veteran of the frontier Indian and Mexican wars, he was latterly known for his role in the San Juan affair. He retired in 1863.

2. Col. (later General Sir) John William Gordon, Royal Engineers, who was on a mission to Canada to supervise defense improvements.

3. Col. (later General Sir) Daniel Lysons, deputy adjutant general, who had been sent to Canada to organize the militia.

4. "pull the chestnuts [out of the fire]."

5. In his address to the opening session of the new parliament on 27 January 1862, Napoleon III had limited himself to an expression of hope that the American conflict would soon come to an end, thus temporarily frustrating those who had looked for a more positive statement on the recognition of the Confederate States.

To Mowbray Morris, February 16, 1862

                             Montreal

My dear Morris,

    I avail myself of a quiet halt on my way to my post to say a few words as to my position here. No trains travel on Sundays & I am staying with Rose a great friend of Delanes from whom I receive much kindness & information. I have now been a year in this country all but a few days & I am I fear more & more unpopular each moment I stay here—not personally I do believe & know among those acquainted with me, but politically & nationally. When the press of the United States is unanimous in its assaults it is as de Tocqueville observed long ago perfectly irresistible & no one can stand against it.[1] The fact is not wonderful. The tone of The Times has been regarded with anger & indignation—it is considered by the Federals as intensely antagonistic & embittered & I am looked upon as the main agent in producing that disposition on the part of the paper. Right or wrong there is no arguing the matter away. If you could see what I have had to bear in railway trains & in the streets you would at least give me the credit of no common devotion & endurance—of danger I speak not now—tho' danger there is & will be increasing instead of diminishing. It is really astonishing how I have escaped

hitherto. Mutatis Mutandis.[2] I dont believe an American journalist in
my position would have gone so far had he been placed as I have been
during a civil war in England or in a rebellion in Ireland. I have not
met a man in Canada who has not declared to me he never thought
I should have left the United States alive. God knows if ever I shall
do so. I have in compliance with your wishes remained at my post &
indeed would not have left it as long as it could be said that I had fled
from personal fear by the papers which have so incessantly attacked
me. It was their object it would be their great triumph to drive me
away. The proprietors of The Times removed one source of uneasiness
from my mind whilst I was in great doubts as to the propriety of
my gratifying a personal sentiment in remaining in a position from
which I might be removed in such a manner as would leave a feeble
& anxious wife & five children without any means of support but I
must say I had always considered that in case I fell in the service
The Times would have acted in accordance with its principles & have
looked after those for whom I am working. Cheerfully admitting all
I have gained in that service to which I have devoted some 15 years
of the best part of my life (you will not find fault with me for saying
it) I am sensible that I have done my duty & that I have had my
part of suffering in it also. It is only by this mail I received a letter
from Ferguson of Hanover St.[3] in which he orders me "a horizontal
position" as the only way of diminishing the evils I suffer from that
miserable leg of mine a souvenir of India & you know how useful I
would be in that attitude. Crimean fevers & Indian sunstrokes have
not been the least part of the petites misères of my special duty. I
have incurred the hostility of powerful classes in England who have
never forgiven & never will forgive the course I took during the war
in the Crimea, & I have reason to know that among them was poor
Prince Albert & no doubt the Queen herself. You know that on my
return I declined to turn such popularity as I had acquired to my own
benefit. I refused to accept public dinners on the subscription which
it was proposed to open at Southampton & elsewhere as I have now
refused testimonials & dinners of a public nature in Canada. I have
done so principally because I considered my position as the representative of "The Times" was not one in which I could receive such
marks of favour without in some degree departing from the wishes
of my journal & of my employers & friends on the paper. On my return from the Crimea you know what occurred with regard to the

lectures—which resulted from my want of qualification for the task. But the failure was one of great consequence to me. I had lost my post on The Times nor was my connection with renewed till I went out to India. On coming back there was the unfortunate misunderstanding by my ever dear friend Delane which led to my being placed in a position from which I could not escape without either forfeiting my word & honour or accepting the alternative of leaving "The Times". Then came "the Army & Navy Gazette" which after some trouble got fairly afloat—just as I was getting on in every way—splendid offers from Thackeray from Bradbury & Evans,[4] which would have enabled me to clear off the small incumbrances left by the failure of the lectures came my wife's illness—an enormous expense—utter inability to work incapacity to fulfil any of my engagements. It was with comparative pleasure when I saw my wife's health in such a state that she could be left tho' not with perfect safety I accepted the engagement to go to America for 6 months from you. The terms were liberal but the difference of salary in my favour was not very great when it was considered that for the difference between £1200 and £800 I was separated from home, exposed to many vicissitudes & deprived of any opportunity of adding to my income by writing. That however was my own concern. I was glad to get into the harness & serve under the old banner again tho' for one campaign. But when I overstaid my time difficulties began to arise. The work I had promised to do for which I was to receive most munificent payment which would have placed me in a position of the greatest ease was perforce neglected, & autumn came on me actually without the means of meeting claims which ought to have been met last summer.

I am writing to you my dear Morris as a friend currente calamo.[5] Pray bear with me I'm a huge lump of improvidence & want of forethought I know—so do you. I would to Heaven I had an ounce of your prudence & excellent sense on such matters. But as I was saying I calculated that I would be back in September & then I would go on with my novel[6] already begun for which Bradbury & Evans were to pay me literally enormously (more fools they perhaps) £1,500 when half done, share of profits & all sorts of things, & complete other work which would bring me in at least as much again. When I was compromised so far as to be obliged to remain here by regard for your wishes & my personal character matters became difficult at home but so long as Willans was on the spot he could manage he said provided I could come over for a week or two in the winter tho' he by no means desired me to abandon my post as he thought by doing so I would damage my reputation & above all annoy my friends such as yourself Delane, MacDonald & Mr. Walter at the office. Now that he is away I am in a regular quandary—the word hardly expresses it. I scarcely know what to do. My wife is not much better as a manager than myself & cannot deal with the difficulties which surround her. If I could understand my own affairs I could ask you to act for me as you kindly offered, but I don't see my way to it. It is quite evident that the crisis here is approaching & I cannot now get away. If I could have managed a short visit some time ago I could have arranged matters, but now I must only ask you to do the best you can for me. I think it would be best to allow Mrs. Russell as much as she can require for the house &c. & then to pay any bills she may have promised to meet but I shall wait till I hear from you in reference to that matter. The main question is for me what is to be my future in connection with the paper? It is obvious that Bradbury & Evans have found out "the Army & Navy Gazette" can go on very well without me. In event of my remaining here I ought to know what will become of me at the end of the War which may last longer than any of us could imagine, & in connection with that arise many other questions.

Now here is another matter. By the enclosed letter (*which pray keep & return*) you will see that obstacles will be placed in my way if the army moves. The writer is a capital fellow, but he has become very cold in tone & manner—it used to be "my dear Russell" now "dear Sir"—& all that comes straight from McClellan who never will forgive the attack on the Orleanist Princes & the imputation on his staff that they were not gentlemen. The hint about the *duc* de Joinville is intended for me. If he cant get rations how can I expect them? However in a few days I shall be at Washington & then I shall know more of my prospects. It is more to ease my mind by showing you what things are pressing on me than for any definite object I have written. But I think (if they were required) I might hope to receive some means of meeting the pressure which has been mainly caused by an absence from England beyond the time indicated. I at all events must look forward to a short furlough as soon as events permit of it. As to my interests & my future I leave them with every confidence in the hands of you & Delane. But for my own unpopularity I could have moved much more freely about, but the various expeditionary generals who dread attacks of the press above all things show me a cold shoulder when anything of the kind is hinted at. Burnside consented to take me too late. My expenses in future will not be too great as I have dismissed a very expensive & very dishonest servant & have got into quieter lodgings in Washington. When in the field it will cost me little or nothing compared with my past bills. At the close of the year I paid off the bankers at New York (James G. Kings Sons) by a bill on Coutts for £198 odd which left me about £10 in hand. I drew from them in January or Decr. $300 to put to my credit at Washington with Riggs & Co. to meet checks drawn there by me. The $300 I covered by a bill for £100 on Coutts & since then I paid B. Duncan $150 for waggon, & drew a bill on Coutts for it & for the amount of letters of credit $250 on Canada in this present tour which was necessitated by more causes than one. I send you the acc[oun]ts as nearly as I can lay my hands on them & commence regular monthly statements. Believe me my dear Morris,

Yours always,

W.H. Russell.

1. See Alexis de Tocqueville, *Democracy in America*, ed. Phillips Bradley, 2 vols. (New York, 1945), 1:188–97, for the French observer's indictment of the American press.

2. "With the necessary changes being made."

3. Sir William Ferguson, Scottish-born physician, professor of surgery at Kings College hospital, and the leading conservative surgeon of his time. In 1847 he moved from Piccadilly to Hanover Square.

4. Russell's London publishers.

5. "in full flow."

6. Russell had begun writing a novel after returning from India in 1859. It was finally published in three volumes in 1868 as *The Adventures of Dr. Brady*, after serialization in *Tinsley's Magazine*. The novel achieved a second edition in the same year.

To Mowbray Morris, February 19, 1862

Montreal

My dear Morris,

I have received yours of Jany. 30th this day. Of course I never thought of making it as you say a settled thing to send such orders, but as I have at length explained you my position by last mail you will understand how it was I was obliged by Willans absence & by *my compliance with the requests made to me to exceed the term of my original agreement* to send you those orders, so we need say no more about it if you please. The more that it was a sudden emergency which compelled me to make good Willans promises. I had made Mr. Tuckerman's[1] acquaintance ere I left New York. He was then proceeding to Washington. I shall go there in a short time as soon as I can be sure of being permitted to join in operations free from the risks ag[ains]t which I have been warned. I find that Kirkland's letter to which I referred in my last was omitted. Please to refer to it in re rations &c. & see what he says & when next you write enclose it to me. I am very much gratified by finding that nothing was done at Roanoke. Had I been there & wrote in the sense in which my friend writes I should have been certainly assassinated & I could have written nothing else than the truth. I send what I refer to to Delane. It would not have been possible for me to have been present at the unexpected great success at Donelson[2]—for I never dreamed & don't think of going there. Every one is astonished here at the idea of my going back to U.S. & if you could hear what is said to me you would be satisfied that it requires some confidence in my self & in my judgement to disregard so much advice from outsiders. I hope you are quite well. MacDonald says you are better but you are impossible about yourself & won't give any of your friends credit for caring about you. Nevertheless do believe that I am my dear Morris,

> Yours very truly,
> W.H. Russell.

1. Charles K. Tuckerman was Bancroft Davis's temporary replacement as New York correspondent of *The Times*.
2. Strategically important Confederate fort on the Cumberland River in Tennessee that surrendered to Union forces under Gen. Ulysses S. Grant on 16 February 1862 after a combined army-naval assault lasting three days.

To Edmund [unknown], March 6, 1862

Washington.

My dear Edmund,

Except that Warre & some others are away at Bernal's Baltimore nothing has changed here since I left. I saw Riggs at Tassara's grand hop—well & heavy. Can you tell me the name of a very good sort of fellow who was formerly in the H[er] M[ajesty's] 90th now on Blenker's staff I think, bald on top of head red beard whom I know as well as can be & speak to & yet I cant think of his name. He asks after you. From my visits to the camps I think it very unlikely that any advance can take place for the next four or five days—it certainly ought not to be made, as neither men, horses nor guns could be deployed from the roads. The men are reduced in numbers but are in good spirits & condition. I hear Willans went off suddenly without sending me a line. I don't think the poor old fellow will ever stand Canada.

If you can lay your hand upon it do send me Henrys letter as a pleasant sort of souvenir. It is quite uncertain whether I can get rations or not for cost price or on any terms, & if I don't it will be impossible for me to move with the army in which case I shall lose all chance of setting Bull Run right again either for myself *or* abroad for the large mass of the world which persists in believing me & "The Times" conjointly or severally. Any chance of seeing you? I mean down here of course.

Yours always dear Edmund,
W.H. Russell.

To Mowbray Morris, March 15, 1862

Washington.

My dear Morris,

I send you Marcy's letter just received—pray keep or return it to me. They are determined I hear to throw every impediment in my way. McClellan is never to be seen by me, his staff are all surly & never will forgive us for the attack on the Orleans Princes. They will keep me from the army if they can, but I dont yet despair of dodging them. Stanton[1] has not sent any reply to my letter. To show you how stingy they are I also enclose one of their old passes which they will only give *me* for a week at a time so that if I dont look sharp it may run out at a most unlucky time & get me into a scrape across the river. To others they give papers without date or for a month at a time. All this is most depressing & irritating but it is only natural I fear under all the circumstances for the paper has not been at all friendly to U.S., & they are most unforgiving vain & sensitive. One of the worst results is that the officers I know are fearful of being attacked in the press if they are pointed out for any civility to me. Therefore I never get any intelligence of what is going to be done & secrecy on all points is so well kept I dont hear of any event coming off, & so cannot get a chance of describing it. Stanton is a most fierce Unionist, & in proportion as they attain to success they show their teeth. He is however by no means anti English in the abstract. "The masses of the two countries" he said to me "have common sympathies as well as a common origin." Seward is very cocky.

And now a word more as to expenses. The heavy bills which were sent in shall not be repeated for the simple reason that there will be no necessity for again incurring such expenses. I tried to disarm hostility by inviting pressmen here (& above all at New York in January) to the best dinners I could give them. That work is now over. I asked Raymond (Times), Forney (Sec[retar]y of the Senate, Philadelphia Inquirer), Dana (Tribune), House (Tribune), Greeley, Stewart, Seaton Nat[ional] Intelligencer, Bryant (Post),[2] Daly &c. & the New York Hotel laid it on most frightfully. By looking at the bills you will see I cd. get but very little reductions from my remonstrances. I thought it politic to try the effect of these entertainments, but there has been nothing but a negation of hostility to us & in one of the papers there was an allusion to the "feeding himself into favour" of Forney because he gave me a dinner in return which showed the animus of the press. The result was that I only increased the hostility of those who were not invited. I must now only grin & bear it till my trial is over. It is terrible work being a drift without a companion in this great cauldron of boiling water. Wetherall[3] who has just arrived here went with me to hear Wendell Phillips[4] lecture last night. We had to stand in the back row. Presently it was whispered to an old man in front of Wetherall that "Russell of The Times" was behind him. He jerked his back away from Wetherall's hand as if he had been stung & amused us by continuing to cast the most furious glances at the Colonel all night to my great satisfaction for W. is a six footer & looks fierce you know. I send you a photograph of myself in a pinguified & miserable mood. By the by Bombastes Furioso[5] was a complete success at the Legation & Shiny William as I call Seward complimented me immensely & said I was "as good as Beauregard" "or Fremont" I added. Do you see the words at the bottom of the photograph card? The President was shown a pikter of Mrs. Lincoln by Brady the other day. "No" quoth I "I really cant stand this. I wont have Mrs. Lincoln 'entered by Brady' according to act of Congress or not." I hope you are enjoying good weather & good health. I got a letter today from

Johnson in which he says my wife's health wont be quite perfect till I go back to her.

>Yours ever truly,
>W.H. Russell.

1. Edwin McMaster Stanton of Ohio was appointed secretary of war by Lincoln on 13 January 1862 to replace Simon Cameron. Stanton had been Cameron's chief legal adviser and was a former attorney general in Buchanan's cabinet.

2. William Cullen Bryant, poet and editor of the *New York Evening Post*. Originally a Democrat, by 1861 he was a leading antislavery Republican and strong supporter of Abraham Lincoln.

3. Col. (later Sir) Edward Robert Wetherall, British soldier and veteran of the Canadian rebellion, the Crimea, and the Indian Mutiny. From 1859 he served as deputy quartermaster general to the forces in Ireland.

4. Wendell Phillips, prominent Boston abolitionist and reformer.

5. The hero of a burlesque opera by William Barnes Rhodes first produced in 1813 in parody of "Orlando Furioso," the sixteenth-century epic poem by Ariosto.

To Mowbray Morris, March 21, 1862

My dear Morris,

I have just received yours of March 6th. I hope by next mail you will be able to give me some solution of the points raised in the letter of 16th. Feby. but meantime whilst I cannot admit I have in any degree justified you in saying I had lost heart or thrown the paper overboard I may find it impossible to do what you tell me to do—to go to the front & if I fail I shall return home. If I have not lost heart I have lost health & rather did lose it & regained it by a trip in Canada which I sought to render interesting & useful to the paper. If I had lost heart it would not have been wonderful, for never did man find himself in a more painful ungrateful position & I think it is rather hard now after I had at your request endured it so long to accuse me of yielding. In a few days I shall learn whether I can get away or not, & I will acquaint you & await instructions if I cannot manage to keep the field with the army. You must be aware how the paper is disliked by the Northern men—& that any one connected with it is regarded with ill feeling & suspicion. So it is not my fault personally if I fail— nor is it from want of effort. There are half a dozen armies in the field & no one can do more than watch one. I selected the Army of the Potomac now about to take the field as the most important & no one can say that I lost a single event or movement during my illness & absence.

      Very truly yours my dear Morris,

          W.H. Russell.

P.S.

      I think that H[ea]d Q[uarte]rs will move in about 8 or 10 days or so that in 2 mails more I shall know my fate. I have applied to

1. Genl. McClellan no answer.
2. Genl. Marcy—not satisfactory.
    Genl. McDowell (can not without Genl. McC.'s orders).
    Genl. Van Vliet (will help if he can).
    Sec[retar]y of State—no answer.
3. Secretary of War—had refused the press & does not think he can help me, but will see.
    Sumner, Ashman, innumerable Senators, private friends &c.

Since I wrote to you I rec[eive]d the enclosed which is sent as proof that I am leaving no way untried. Pray read & return it to me. I must say I dont think you were just in your note & that your conclusion was at least premature.

To Charles Sumner, March 28, 1862

                    Confidential & Private. Baltimore.

My dear Mr. Sumner,

      I would feel much obliged if you could either procure for me or tell me how to get a copy of the report of the Judiciary Com[mitt]ee on the censorship of the press, the publication of which has caused me pain & annoyance & the insinuations in which are very unjust.[1] I intended to have called upon you, but there came a number of officers down from Canada & then I had to go out with them over the camps, & other business intervened & I am now compelled to trouble you with the m[anu]s[cript]s instead of words. I need not say to you or any one who knows me in the least that I have never directly or indirectly had any interest whatever in any stock or share in the United States, but I admit that having a desire to serve Mr. Ward who had begged of me to give him any information in my power & whom I feared I had misled by the strong expression of my feeling the day before that Mason & Slidell would not be given up I sent off a telegram to him (utterly useless he since assures me for all speculative purposes) in which I used a phrase employed by him in one of his letters that week in reference to the surrender of M. & S. to intimate to him that they had been given up. "A war he said in that letter would ruin me or at best make a poor man still poorer—it would take you away from us & put an end to your history of the Great Civil War. The best news for us both would be that they were both to be handed over to you again."———I can't even get a copy of the telegram which the Censor informs me has been mislaid by the Committee. Surely it was a most injurious & unwarrantable thing in the Committee to make a reflection upon me without permitting me to say a word or permitting me to vindicate myself from the insinuation that in sending the message I was actuated by the smallest expectation of pecuniary advantage. The matter was well known enough by the time I heard it—& on going into Riggs Bank about 2 in the day I was told that M. & S. would be given up by two very good authorities having previously been informed of it by a relation of Mr. Eustis himself. I am more pained than you can imagine by having my name brought forward in this way & more particularly in connection with the Legation, but I shall not take any notice just now of the matter in public. Pray pardon this personal explanation & the request I make.

Yours most faithfully dear Mr. Sumner,

W.H. Russell.

1. See John Black Atkins, *The Life of Sir William Howard Russell C.V.O., LL.D.: The First Special Correspondent*, 2 vols. (London, 1911), 2:99–105, for a detailed account of the affair.

To Edmund [unknown], March 29, 1862

Baltimore, Eutaw House.

My dear Edmund,

I came down here with Rowan a few days ago to get a passage to F[ort] Monroe but we were refused permission & after a trip to Washington came back again & waited in hope of the new rule being relaxed but in vain. So Rowan went back to New York today & will arrive before this letter. I dont know whether your promised letter is at Washington or not but I shall look forward to it with much anxiety for I do value the criticism of a friend & I shall never be testy or uneasy under censorship which is animated by the spirit in which you would deal with my many errors. I am I confess unable to deal with the politics of a country in a state of revolution & which does not understand them itself but my letters are no doubt very hasty & watery of late because I had none of my own topics to treat of.

And now I wish in confidence to speak to you of a matter which has caused me great pain & regret & which may prove still more serious. I was of opinion up to Thursday 26th Decr. (as you may remember) that Mason & Slidell would not be given up. I wrote to you, to Duncan, to all my friends to The Times to that effect. Among them was Sam Ward. On that Thursday I received a letter from him in reference to rumours in New York & to the views of one of my letters in which he said he wd. be obliged if I could send him any information & used some such phrase as this: It would be good news for both of us to hear they were given up. I have been advised they will & have acted accordingly. War would make us all poorer than we are & it wd. also put an end to your "Great work on the American revolution." About 1 or 1.15 on Friday I rec[eive]d information with the injunction not to make it public in Washington that they would be given up which was all the more annoying to me inasmuch as it falsified my predictions in my Wednesday letter. But I set to work to write my letter for the evening messenger & was doing so when Johnson—a relative of Eustis came in, & asked if I had heard the news—they were to be given up. Mr. Corcoran, Eustis father in law had reason to know it. I went at once over to Riggs—there saw Corcoran & Riggs separately both of whom said they knew they wd. be given up—indeed Riggs told me lately he knew it positively at the time. Well I thought of Sam Ward & desiring to give the poor devil a good turn which might enable him to make a few dollars I sent off my messenger with the telegram which you have seen referred to so agreeably. I need not tell you I had not & have not any interest in any share or stock or security in this country or (I am sorry to say) out of it. I never had any concert or understanding with S.W. or any one else in reference to them or any pecuniary advantage to him or me or any living creature. But I have committed this serious mistake in not shielding both myself & the Legation from any censure by going back & saying "I have heard in the city they are to be given up & I have telegraphed to a friend since that he has reason to expect good news." The Times people don't like S.W. Lord Lyons a cautious prudent but very kind & conscientious man is much annoyed at the prospect of parliamentary attacks & God knows I have enemies enough who will make use of it to do me all the damage they can. I cant tell you how much this imprudence has grieved me. No human being thro' all my long & troubled career can ever say I violated any confidence—least of all cd. I do so for a pecuniary advantage. I am off with the expedition next week. Keep what I tell you secret unless you have heard of it elsewhere. I am perfectly free of anything but indiscretion in my desire to serve S.W. but you know well what indiscretion is called by one's enemies. Write me anything that occurs to you on the course to be pursued & ask me any questions you would like to have answered. I was going to write to the papers here but on second thoughts I resolved to keep my peace.

> Yours always dear O[ld] F[riend],
> W.H. Russell.

To Edwin M. Stanton, April 2, 1862

487 17th. St.

Sir,

But a few days ago you wrote me a pass at the house of Lord Lyons in which you desired all persons in the service of the United States to show me every courtesy & extend me every protection in their power.

Today by order I am refused permission to go as the invited guest of General McClellan with a written pass from the Chief of Staff on board one of the ships of the force under his command along with my other friends to whom General McClellan had exhibited similar courtesy.

I can not conceive Sir the object of such conduct, but you are a man of honour & a gentleman as well as a Minister of State. I am not conscious in the interval that has elapsed of any cause for the change on your part towards me. If there be one at least I should have from you in justice to myself an opportunity of knowing what it is before I leave the States for Europe which I shall do in a couple of days.

The very eminence of your position & the immensity of your powers should add strength to the appeal of one so humble as myself in any case—far more in that which is the occasion of the present communication.

> I am Sir,
> Your most obed[ien]t serv[an]t,
> W.H. Russell.

To General Randolph B. Marcy, April 2, 1862

487 17th. St. & I, Washington.

Sir,

Some days after you were good enough to inform me that General McClellan would have no objection to my accompanying the expedition under his command I received thro' the S[on] A[ltesse] R[oyale] the Duc de Chartres, a.d.c. to the General a verbal message to the same effect which was extended also to friends of mine who with myself regarded it as an invitation from the Commander in Chief of the Army of the Potomac. Subsequently I also received a general pass from you Sir, & I at once set about making my arrangements for the expedition which B[rigadier] Genl. Van Vliet was good enough to facilitate by procuring a passage for us in one of the transports. We embarked at 10.30 or 11 a.m. & were about sailing when Genl. Van Vliet was summoned to the War Office, & on his return two hours afterwards told me very kindly & courteously that Mr. Stanton had advised him not to let me proceed with my friends.

I reminded Genl. Van Vliet that I had your pass in writing & the invitation of the Commander in Chief of the Army of the Potomac as he knew to accompany the expedition. He then showed me two orders in writing signed by General Meigs & addressed to him. The first directed him not to permit anyone not in the service of the United States to enter upon any transport without the permission of the Secretary. The second said that "Colonels Neville [1] & Fletcher [2] & Captain L'Amy of the British Army having been invited by General McClellan to accompany the expedition from Alexandria they were exempted from the order of this date of the War Depart[ment]."

There was no alternative left but to leave the vessel which I had entered as your generals guest or at least as one invited. I assure you Sir I dont desire at this moment to intrude so petty a question so far as it relates to myself on your notice, but on account of the graver circumstances I deem it my duty to do so on other grounds & with real reluctance. You know Sir how scrupulous I was to obtain the leave of the General before I made any arrangements & how utterly unexpected was such interference with me. I have only to say in consolation that I have referred the detail of the circumstances to the President of the United States & that I shall also make a direct appeal to the Secretary of War against his treatment which was aggravated by its concomitant incidents. To the General I beg you will tender the expression of my sincere thanks for his intended kindness towards me & say how much I regret that I shall not have an opportunity of showing in Europe that he can lead the army he has trained so long to great & glorious combats. To you dear Sir I tender my best thanks for your unfailing courtesy.

Yours most faithfully,

W.H. Russell.

1. Lt. Col. Edward Neville, Scots Fusilier Guards.

2. Lt. Col. Henry Charles Fletcher, Scots Fusilier Guards, who accompanied the Union army in the Peninsula campaign and visited both Confederate and Union forces in the West. He was the author of the three-volume study, *History of the American War* (1864–65).

To Mowbray Morris, April 4, 1862

Washington, D.C.

My dear Morris,

The letter which goes with this will explain to you why I am forced to obey your directions in event of inability to go to the front & to return home. It is all the more provoking to me on account of the paper & of myself that such a step should be rendered necessary at a time when I had by great exertions & importunity succeeded in obtaining permission to accompany the army at such a very interesting & exciting period as the present when I was in hopes of being able to reverse Bull's Run. I am quite at a loss to account for it unless Stanton believes it to be a very popular step. The last time I saw him was at L[or]d Lyons at supper & then he wrote out a pass for me with his own hand for the special purpose of visiting Manassas. He is a coarse vigorous ill tempered dyspeptic of the most inordinate vanity & ambition & his jealousy of McClellan is almost a mania for he thinks he sees in him ye next Pres[i]d[en]t in case of success & that ye civil administ[ratio]n of ye army will be swamped by ye military. It is obvious that even if I had not your express orders to return home it would not be possible for me to remain out here with ye ban of Govt. upon me & ye orders of the Sec[retar]y of War not to admit on board their transports. He now says I hear that he will not admit foreign correspondents because he cannot *punish* them if they give aid to the enemy. Lord Lyons laughed when I told him this, & said he was not aware that such considerations had ever prevented ye Federal Govt. chastising with imprisonment subjects of Great Britain. He considers the step "the most injudicious & foolish yet committed by the Federal Govt." No General no officer would now receive me in camp or quarters throughout ye Union. I have today received an invitation from Baltimore that if I like I can get a passage with tolerable certainty to some part of Secessia, but I could not I think with honour or propriety go South immediately after so long a residence among the Northern armies & it would be prejudicial to ye paper & myself if I were to do so. Besides the difficulty of getting my letters away even if I arrived safe would be very great & they would all be very stale. Meantime I have sent over to Corvin & have begged of him if he is permitted to write to you regularly & I have asked Mr. L'Amy who will be with McClellan to send you letters as often as he can & I have further mentioned to Mr. House of the Tribune in case he goes with McDowell the probability of your taking useful letters from him. I have secured a berth in the China[1] which sails on 9th. & if I can't sell off horse waggon &c. by that time I shall leave them in charge of Mr. Anderson who will clear off for me & who expects to realize £100 or £120 at least, he may probably get £150. You cannot imagine what a change has come over ye U.S. officers since they heard of Stantons decision. Vizetelly tells me that Stanton after keeping him 2 hours on the steps of the War Office waiting for an answer to his note sent him word by an orderly that "Mr. Stanton says he has nothing to do with Mr. Vizetelly." I shall write to [you] further but as it is I fear I shall lose this mail & if so I shall see you almost as soon as my letter.

> Ever yours very truly,
> W.H. Russell.

1. Cunard's newest ship, launched on 8 October 1861 and on her maiden voyage. Built on the Clyde, the 2,638-ton *China* was the first screw steamer to be built for the Cunard's mail service.

Index